Paradise Transplanted

Paradise Transplanted

MIGRATION AND THE MAKING OF CALIFORNIA GARDENS

Pierrette Hondagneu-Sotelo

UNIVERSITY OF CALIFORNIA PRESS

University of California Press, one of the most distinguished university presses in the United States, enriches lives around the world by advancing scholarship in the humanities, social sciences, and natural sciences. Its activities are supported by the UC Press Foundation and by philanthropic contributions from individuals and institutions. For more information, visit www.ucpress.edu.

University of California Press
Oakland, California

Cataloging-in-Publication data is on file at the Library of Congress

ISBN 978-0-520-27776-2 (cloth : alk. paper)
ISBN 978-0-520-27777-9 (pbk. : alk. paper)

Manufactured in the United States of America

23 22 21 20 19 18 17 16 15 14
10 9 8 7 6 5 4 3 2 1

In keeping with a commitment to support environmentally responsible and sustainable printing practices, UC Press has printed this book on Natures Natural, a fiber that contains 30% post-consumer waste and meets the minimum requirements of ANSI/NISO z39.48-1992 (R 1997) (*Permanence of Paper*).

A garden was one of the few things in prison that one could control. To plant a seed, watch it grow, to tend it and then harvest it, offered a simple but enduring satisfaction. The sense of being the custodian of this small patch of earth offered a taste of freedom.

—Nelson Mandela, *Long Walk to Freedom* (1994)

The garden . . . is the smallest parcel of the world and then it is the totality of the world.

—Michel Foucault, "Of Other Spaces" (1986)

We've left something of ourselves here. When you've planted a garden, you've left something permanent.

—Evelyn McMahon, in Sam Bass Warner, *To Dwell Is to Garden* (1987)

Contents

Illustrations

FIGURES

COLOR PLATES *follow page 108.*

Preface and Acknowledgments

I wrote this book because I love gardens and I wanted to understand how migration and immigrants have shaped the beautiful garden landscapes of Southern California. By necessity, gardens are place based and so is this study, but the boundaries of what we can learn from this story are broader. The majority of the world's population now lives in cities and metropolitan regions and includes diverse groups of people who have migrated from different countries. How newcomers get along with old-timers is one of the key dramas now unfolding in metropolitan regions around the nation and the globe, and how we all engage with soil, plants, and water will determine the ecological viability of the planet. Gardens offer places to see these processes unfold.

Gardens are immobile, literally rooted in the earth, but they are shaped by the transnational swirl of ideas and practices, people, plants, and seeds, and in turn, gardens shape our experiences of cities and suburbs. This is perhaps nowhere as profoundly true as in Southern California, where successive migrations have defined the landscape. In this book, I reconstruct this history, and I focus on contemporary immigrants from different nations and across the spectrum of social class, examining how they are shaping metropolitan gardens. It is tempting to see gardens as little havens roped off from the public world, but I show that they are not separate from society. Gardens are embedded in complex social hierarchies and contestations over power and resources, and they simultaneously express basic human yearnings for transcendence, beauty, and belonging.

A rich array of gardens have flourished for eons in different corners of the world, but private residential gardens have predominated in Southern California, where developers and governments did not invest in the development of public parks as they did in other cities. I examine private residential gardens, but I also consider the social dynamics at the most renowned botanical garden and plant collection in the West, the Huntington, which began as the private residential estate garden of a wealthy industrialist, and I look at urban community gardens, which today substitute as backyards for marginalized immigrant laborers who live in crowded, often substandard apartments. From the wealthiest elites to some of the most disenfranchised inner-city residents and to those in between, gardens offer sources of meaning and fleeting moments of connection to the natural world.

To write this book, I tried to get as close as possible to these varied gardens in Southern California in order to capture the viewpoints, experiences, and practices of diverse people (but especially immigrants) engaged with them. Although I am a sociologist with a central interest in understanding how our positions in social groups affect our engagements with gardens, my approach has been influenced by reading in neighboring academic disciplines of history, urban planning, geography, and landscape studies. To gather data for this book, I relied on participant observation, in-depth interviews, and historical analysis, research methods that I describe more fully in chapter 1. Since this type of research is contingent on my own social location, it's important for me to share a bit about my own life and relationship to gardens.

First, I've become one of those middle-class, middle-aged women obsessed with gardens. My modest-sized backyard has been featured on a local garden tour (twice), and I once received a Golden Arrow Award for planting my front yard with drought-tolerant plants, mostly sculptural succulents and grassy plants. It's quite messy looking—it doesn't look Golden Arrow worthy—but in fact, I've worked very hard at it. Like many amateur gardeners, I'm inordinately proud of my garden—"My garden kicks ass" is the proclamation on my refrigerator magnet. But I've killed many fledgling seedlings, and I've planted so many trees and shrubs that I have now accidentally created a mass of shade in the backyard, limiting my future planting prospects. It's a humbling experience. As my friends know, I relish any opportunity to visit a garden, small or grand, and every spring my favorite form of conspicuous leisure is going on garden tours, strolling and peering in strangers' backyards. My local favorites are the Theodore Payne Foundation Native Plant Garden Tour and the Venice Garden Tour, where so many artists and architects have created wildly imaginative gardens. On these visits I'm routinely struck with garden envy (and then some guilt), but I also get ideas about what I might try next in my garden. I regularly plant, prune, and pull weeds, but I'm also grateful for the help of my sons, Miles and Sasha, who have shoveled through tough clay, carted heavy sacks of soil amendment, and transplanted stubbornly root-bound potted succulents for me. I also get regular help from immigrant gardeners who arrive weekly to blow out leaves and from my husband Mike, who will trim the bamboo. Gardens are sponges for labor, and it takes constant work to keep even a modest-sized garden.

I was raised in the San Francisco Bay Area by immigrant parents who came from different continents, my mother from the central valley of Chile, an agricultural area now developed into a mini-Napa and global exporter of fruits, and my father from the French Pyrenees. For both of them, growing up on small family farms had meant hard work, deprivation, and modest schooling. Migration routes to the city and ultimately the United States allowed them to replace the isolation and hardship of rural peasant life with creature comforts in suburban California. Neither of them ever longed to go "back to the land," and we certainly didn't know anyone who had a "country house." But on summer weekends, my father and his brothers, all of whom worked as French gardeners for upscale clients, tended their own backyard gardens and traded homegrown Pyrenees-style peppers in brown paper bags, a ritual that connected them to each other and to their collective past.

I moved with my husband to Southern California in the late 1980s, thinking, as all migrants do, that this would be a temporary pit stop. An old rivalry had taught us to detest the sprawl, smog, and supposed superficiality of So Cal, but next to the roaring Interstate 5 we tended some flowers and vegetables and got hooked on eighty-degree weather in January and life among an exotic array of citrus, hibiscus, and jacaranda trees. We also noticed that Mexican immigrant gardeners seemed to be mowing all the lawns here. Since then, we have continued to work in our garden, getting our sons Miles and Sasha to cut bamboo or turn soil whenever we can, but we too have consistently employed immigrant gardeners who arrive weekly to blow out the liquid amber, bamboo, and avocado leaves. I hate the blowers, but I appreciate the labor.

In this book, I make some critical statements about the exclusivity of private property and elite gardens, but I too participate in these privileged spaces and practices. I have worked for a private university for over twenty years, and while I have my critiques of the institution and some of the landscaping choices, I enjoy working there and regularly walking among the verdant garden spaces and the truly magnificent trees. Parts of the campus are so lush that it is called the University of Southern California's University Park Campus. Similarly, while I offer a social critique of Mission San Gabriel and the Huntington Botanical Gardens, I feel fortunate to live close enough to ride my bicycle to these historic, gorgeous gardens and to access the incredible resources at the Huntington Library.

To write chapter 4, I left these oases of privilege to conduct an urban ethnography of two community gardens in very poor neighborhoods of Los Angeles. On many early Saturday mornings I left my own garden and comfortable Craftsman home in leafy South Pasadena to drive to the inner-city community gardens, bringing my own sets of gloves, two sets of sharp clippers, and trowels in a backpack. I would pull out of my driveway feeling dragged down by visual evidence of all the weeding and trimming that I should be doing in my own front yard, but once I got to Pico Union and the community gardens, I felt palpable energy and was always happy to be there. Although my small physical size prevents me from exerting the strength it takes to carry sacks of soil, I sometimes feel indefatigable energy for gardening work, and I did my best to contribute gardening labor by clipping, sweeping, weeding, and amending soil. I also joined in the women's empowerment classes, attended meetings where I sometimes took notes and translated, and collaborated in other shared activities such as preparing meals, eating and cleaning up, and just hanging around chatting. In my back pocket I kept a tiny notepad, where I jotted notes that later formed the basis for my field notes, which I typed up that evening or the following morning. Everyone knew I was taking notes, but it is possible that at times they forgot I was there as a researcher. Less immersive techniques of interviewing, reading secondary sources, and conducting archival research, as I explain in chapter 1, provided the main sources of data for the other chapters.

I wrote this book in my home office, with windows looking out to the street, allowing my gaze to shift from the electronic screen to the octopus agave, the liquid amber trees, and the oaks and tall, skinny Mexican fan palms planted in the parkway. Gazing out the window, I regularly saw Latino immigrant gardeners scurrying in my neighbors' front yards and in my own garden to do the same work I was writing about. Once while Skyping with a colleague as we discussed our manuscripts, I paused our conversation to run out and tell the gardener to please not trim a bush. I too was enacting home owner behavior, even as I wrote this book. I also did gardening labor in my garden, fleeing to it whenever I hit snags in the writing, which was more often than I would have liked.

Many thanks are in order, as so many people generously helped me formulate this project. Early on, while beginning to think about how I might approach this study, I sought out conversations with USC colleagues in history, urban planning, geography, landscape architecture, and American studies. For this, a big thank-you to Professors Rachel Berney, Michael Dear, Greg Hise, Jane Iwamura, George Sanchez, David Sloan, and especially Jennifer Wolch, who also provided helpful feedback on some of early proposals. My stalwart friend and LA scholar Laura Pulido, from whom I have learned so much, listened to me talk about this from start to finish, sometimes in garden settings and on hiking trails in the San Gabriel Mountains.

A number of USC students assisted me with the research, including Xiaoxin Zeng, Genelle Gaudinez, and Kristen Barber. Then PhD student and now assistant professor Hernan Ramirez deserves special gratitude for helping design the interview guide and then interviewing Mexican immigrant gardeners, which was made possible by a grant I received from the USC Provost's Initiative on Immigration and Integration. As I developed the case studies, I presented the work in progress in academic settings, and I am grateful to all the people who asked probing questions and offered insightful comments on these occasions. These included presentations at the University of California–Los Angeles, Rice, the University of Pennsylvania, the University of California–Santa Barbara (three times), Pitzer College, the Centre on Migration, Policy and Society at Oxford, the Instituto de Investigaciones Sociales at the Universidad Nacional Autónoma de México in Mexico City, and the American Sociological Association meetings in Denver and San Francisco, the Pacific Sociological Association meetings in San Diego, and the British Sociological Association meetings in Warwick.

Writing a book is a lonesome process, even when plants beckon. To get through it, I developed writing partnerships with three colleagues who were also writing books, Yen Le Espiritu, Macarena Gomez-Barris, and Jessica Vasquez. On a monthly or bimonthly basis I exchanged work in progress with each of them, and we shared critical feedback and commentary, sometimes in person over leisurely meals, but other times squeezed into a busy day over Skype. The ideas presented in this book, and my life, have been enriched by these friendships and exchanges.

Once I had drafts of chapters, I also received helpful comments from Mario T. Garcia and Manuel Pastor, which helped me improve chapters 2 and 6. And although we have never met, the historian Douglas Sackman generously agreed to read drafts of two chapters and gave me the gift of seven pages of single-spaced typed comments, which vastly improved the final book and made me feel as though I belong to an old-fashioned guild that has not been thoroughly commodified. Thanks also to William Deverell for referring me to the curator Peter Blodgett at the Huntington Library, who patiently introduced me to the archival riches there. At the University of California Press, I benefited from the sensitive reviews and suggestions for revisions offered by Anastasia Loukaitous-Sideris, Sherri Grasmuck, and another anonymous reviewer. Finally, the approach and the substance of this book would be very different without the astute, analytical commentary that I received from the creative mind of Sharon Zukin, who pushed me toward clarity and away from mush. Sharon, I know this is a very Catholic construction, but I consider you the *madrina*, the godmother, of this book, and I remain grateful for your encouragement, friendship, and support.

Some of the photographs are mine, but I am grateful to be able to include photographs of Latino immigrant gardeners at work taken by photojournalist Nathan Solis, and those of the urban community gardens by the fine arts photographer Robbert Flick. I hope to forever remember the calming words of wisdom that Robbert shared when he saw me frantically and impatiently pressing the elevator button at the Fine Arts Library: "Slowly, slowly, even an egg will walk." It's an apt aphorism for writing a book, and for so many things in life. I'm grateful for the subvention funds from USC Dornsife College of Letters, Arts, and Sciences and the USC Center for the Study of Immigrant Integration, which allowed me to reproduce color photographs. Thanks to Jennifer Watts at the Huntington and Matt Gainer at USC for help in directing me to the historical archival photographs. I had no idea what I was getting into! And thank you to Naomi Schneider of UC Press, for once again having faith in an unusual book project and for shepherding it along, to Christopher Lura for assistance in the production process, and to Elisabeth Magnus for copyediting.

Nearly last but certainly not least, I am grateful to all the people who let me into their homes, gardens, and offices and showed me patience, generosity, and thoughtfulness with all the questions I posed. I realize they may not agree with my interpretations, but I hope they will recognize that I have sought to understand and report their viewpoints and experiences as truthfully as possible. Finally, my biggest gratitude and love goes to Mike Messner, who starts me off every morning with just the right amount of coffee and on a good day joins me for a drink just before dusk on a tiny patio below palms and an olive tree. Mike has supported my dedication to this project from conception to copyediting, sometimes reading drafts and always buoying my spirits and nurturing me.

In this story of migration and gardens I hope readers will appreciate that ultimately we are all newcomers moving on the land, making and unmaking homes, and in the process transforming the landscape. Some people dismiss Southern California as a dystopian, apocalyptic land of plastic and concrete built on false promises and hyperbole. Yes, some of that is true. But I choose to articulate a narrative that emphasizes the talents and radical heterogeneity that multiple migrations have spawned here, and to celebrate the beauty and potential of nature and the promise of social change that may foster a more ecological and democratic Eden on earth. I don't think it's too late.

1 Gardens of Migration

When a fire destroyed the chaparral on a hillside in LA's Griffith Park in 1971, Amir Dialameh, an Iranian immigrant who worked as a wine shop clerk, got the idea to build a garden there. He began by terracing two acres with pick and shovel and his own bodily strength, clearing burnt-up tree stumps and planting jacaranda trees for shade, as well as magnolias, pines, pepper trees, roses, geraniums, bougainvillea, ferns, and succulents. For nearly three decades, this lifelong bachelor hiked up the hill to tend the garden, working about four hours daily, scarcely taking a vacation. He paid for all of these plants on his own and installed steps and benches that he painted with colorful designs. Once word got out about the public garden, some people offered money to cover the plant costs, but he refused cash donations, reciting his rhyme "In the land of the free, plant a tree." To show his love for America, he laid out rocks to read *USA*, and when he worked in this hillside oasis he flew an American flag. This garden was his act of creation on the earth, and it became his home and his connection to humanity and the universe at large. "I created this place," he said. "It is like my family."[1]

Gardens are deceptive. They are seemingly place bound, enclosed, and immobile patches of earth with plants, yet they are products of movement and migration. In elementary school we learn that seeds scattered by wind and sea and carried across the ocean from one continent to another allow plants to sprout in new places and that bees, water, and photosynthesis allow plants to thrive. But why do gardens look the way they do? And what do gardens reveal about the people who make and inhabit them? These answers are to be found in the movement and migration of people, plants, and ideas about garden design.

In *Paradise Transplanted*, I examine Southern California gardens through a migration lens. It is my conviction that we cannot understand these gardens without acknowledging that nearly all the plants, the people and the water in Southern California have come from elsewhere. Lush tropical foliage from equatorial regions, lawns, and towering trees now dominate the landscape in this arid semidesert, and today these appear to be "naturalized," but photographs from the nineteenth and early twentieth centuries show this region as it once was: wide-ranging plains filled with scrubby chaparral and with few trees to relieve the flatness. Native landscape has been replaced by the built landscape you now see when your flight departs from LAX—a vast horizontal sprawl of buildings and a maze of streets and freeways with palm trees, shrubs, and patches of green grass growing in the crevices, some thriving in vacant lots and in between asphalt cracks, and some in gardens meticulously designed and maintained, but all of it sandwiched between sea and sun-drenched hills and desert.

The gardens of Southern California are defining elements of the region. They have been produced by the sedimentation of distinctive eras of conquest and migration, exerting an influence on who we are, how we live, and what we become. In poor urban neighborhoods and wealthy residential enclaves, gardens surround the homes and apartments where migrants, immigrants, and the fifth-generation descendants of earlier newcomers now live. These gardens can be read like tattoos or graffiti, as ways that our social and cultural expression has left marks on the landscape. In turn, these gardens shape who we are as individuals and as a society.

Gardens are diverse and laden with multiple meanings. Most basically, a garden is a plot of earth used for growing, enjoying, and displaying trees, flowers, and vegetables. Gardens can be distinguished from parks (used primarily for recreation) and agricultural farms (used primarily for food production), although there is clearly some overlap. Landscape architects Mark Francis and Randolph T. Hester define the garden as an idealization, a place, and an action, emphasizing that "by making gardens, using or admiring them, and dreaming of them, we create our own idealized order of nature and culture."[2]

In this book I underscore the sociological implications of migration and gardens, unearthing social, cultural, and economic consequences of Southern California gardens. I share what I have learned in my study of paid immigrant gardeners in suburban residential gardens; urban community gardens in some of the poorest, most densely populated neighborhoods of Los Angeles; and the most elite botanical garden in the West. To tell this story of labor, community, and status in the gardens of Southern California, I rely on over one hundred interviews, ethnographic observations, and historical analysis. I begin by framing the study with three claims, which I sketch below.

GARDENS AS MIGRATION PROJECTS

For more than two centuries, people have trekked to Southern California to fulfill dreams for a better life, and the quest for the good life here has generally included palms, orange trees, and lawn. The idea that the good life is situated in a garden is an old idea, echoing the biblical Garden of Eden and the Islamic paradise, and today, from trendy wall gardens to healthy school gardens, garden imagery continues to define our notions of ideal surroundings. As people have remade themselves in Southern California, they have transformed the gardenscape, and this interaction between migrants and the environment has produced gardens. This is a historical process encompassing the successive conquests and migrations, as I detail in chapter 2. It began with the Spanish missionaries' enslavement of Native Americans and the Anglo-American appropriation of Mexican land and continued with the widespread employment of first Japanese and now Mexican immigrant gardeners toiling in residential gardens. In the process, native landscapes have become gardens of migration.

Gardens are always produced by the interaction between plant nature and culture, and because of its conscious cultivation, every form of garden embodies both pleasure and power, but a constant defining feature of Southern California is the significance of migration. Migration culture and aspirations have shaped the gardens here since the eighteenth century. In turn, the gardens have influenced the society that has formed here.

Today, immigrants from around the globe come to Southern California, joining prior immigrants and domestic migrants who came from other parts of the country. Even when migrants have occupied subordinate social positions and have found themselves excluded from legal citizenship, subjected to racism, and relegated to bad low-wage jobs, they have actively cultivated plants and gardens. In this regard, gardens can serve as minizones of autonomy, as sites and practices of transcendence and restoration. Gardens offer compensation for lost worlds, bringing moments of pleasure, tranquillity, and beauty, and they articulate future possibilities.

These acts of migrant creation are projects of self-expression and social creativity. Building on the work of others, I have come to see gardens as a form of storytelling, as individual and community efforts to shape outdoor surroundings and plant nature in ways that we find desirable and congenial.[3] As we shape the landscape, we are crafting ourselves and projecting our ideas of how nature and culture should look. As landscape designer and historian Wade Graham reminds us, however, "The drama of self-creation isn't straightforward"; rather, it is "full of deviations, diversions, dodges, and impersonations."[4]

Sometimes we seek to transform ourselves and the garden provides a vehicle for that aspiration. Sometimes we seek a sense of freedom, or of control when our lives feel out of our own control, and the garden provides that too. From the level of individuals up to nations, gardens tell a story about the people who create them, their aspirations, yearnings, and anxieties.

We used to think of immigrants and migrants being inserted into new physical spaces and just learning to "fit in," becoming like the majority that already lived there. We called this theory *assimilation*, and sociologists, with our penchant for quirky jargon, derived many variants— straight-line assimilation, segmented assimilation, bumpy-line assimilation, and racialized assimilation, among others. Most of this focused on social institutions and groups, such as workplaces, schools, and civic spheres.

These perspectives implied that immigrants are like passive plants, when in fact they are among the most agentic, willful people on the planet.[5] They are the ones who picked up and left, who either were driven out or elected to go elsewhere and enact the drama of starting anew. The garden metaphor of the "the uprooted" and "the transplanted" might be productively reversed, as the writer Patricia Klindienst has suggested. "What would become visible," she asks, if we "focused on the immigrant as a *gardener*—a person who shapes the world rather than simply being shaped by it?"[6]

This view sees gardens as an expression of immigrant agency and creation, with immigrants using homeland seeds and plants to anchor themselves in a new place, bringing together culture and nature to materially remake a strange new environment into a familiar home. In this view, the cultivation of particular flowers, herbs, vegetables, and fruits forges critical connections to cultural memory and homeland. Bulbs and seeds, sometimes illegally smuggled across borders by friends and relatives and sometimes purchased at a local store, are planted in backyard gardens, on balconies, on windowsills, in the hidden spaces of apartment building lots, and in community gardens, providing a narrative of home continuity and familiarity that is particularly meaningful for immigrants from rural, preindustrial societies.[7]

But it would be a mistake to see this as a matter of simple ethnic continuity and reproduction. Immigrants also adopt new practices. And sometimes their garden replicas of their homeland are enthusiastically adopted by others, inverting the story of assimilation. That is what we are now seeing with the current global food fashion, as upscale restaurants and publications enthusiastically tout the joys of growing and eating *chipilin* and *papalo*, culinary herbs from southern Mexico and Central America that still remain unknown to many people in central and northern Mexico. "The Global Garden," a weekly feature by Jeff Spurrier that ran for two years in the *Los Angeles Times*, provided a multicultural tour of LA gardens and educated readers about the new edible plants that recent immigrants have brought to Southern California, including *papalo*, the pungent culinary herb popular in Puebla and Oaxaca, which has now also been featured in the upscale food magazine *Saveur*.[8] *Papalo* has now even migrated into that iconic zenith of French-California cuisine, Alice Waters's Chez Panisse restaurant kitchen garden in Berkeley, showing the power of humble immigrant culture to reshape the mainstream. To be globally omnivorous is today a sign of cosmopolitan status, and immigration and immigrant cities are vehicles for this process. Immigrant cultivation feeds and revitalizes the mainstream.

Elements of gardens have always been borrowed, copied, and deliberately inspired by other gardens, but now garden conventions and styles circulate transnationally with relative ease. These exchanges are concentrated in global, cosmopolitan metropolises that bring together people from many corners of the earth. Sometimes migrants from very urban, industrial societies who are accustomed to living in apartments without tending plants pick up new gardening ideas and practices when they come to the United States. In *The Global Silicon Valley Home*, landscape architect Shenglin Chang shows how Taiwanese engineers and their families who migrated to the Silicon Valley embraced single-detached family homes with green lawns and foliage planted around the perimeter, an aesthetic form and home preference long associated with British, Australian, and American conventions. This kind of domestic garden has now been transplanted to Taiwan, as trans-Pacific migrant commuters bring back a preference for Mission Revival–style homes with red tile roofs and carefully tended lawns that they first experienced in California. They report taking pleasure in displaying the "home's face" with a front-yard garden, although some, like many Americans, dislike the tedium of lawn care. These lawns and gardens constitute new transnational and material forms of what Peggy Levitt has referred to as "social remittances," cultural and social practices that migrants take back to their place of origin.[9]

Similar processes are under way in Beijing, Hong Kong, and Shanghai, where Southern California–style detached homes and gardens signal conspicuous consumption and "status on both sides of the Pacific."[10] In Hong Kong, a gated housing development called Palm Springs offers home buyers "the look, feel and beauty of southern California" with "palm-lined streets and picturesque scenery." These housing developments promise the California dream in Asia, and, as Laura Ruggeri compellingly suggests, they have been deliberately "imagineered" on the Southern California model, facilitated by circuits of transnational capital.[11]

Not all immigrants and transnational subjects adopt new gardening practices and forms. Elsewhere on the West Coast, affluent immigrants from Hong Kong have been criticized for refusing to adopt neo-English styles of lawn and naturalistic plantings.[12] But the point is that the material life of homes and gardens now circulates in transnational flows and that contemporary migration facilitates this process.

In my approach to understanding the role of migration in creating gardens and transforming the landscape, I underscore the influence of social inequalities. Labor migrants and refugees fleeing war, violence, and economic devastation, for example, face different scenarios in their engagements with gardens and gardening practices than do transnational entrepreneurs and engineers. While some of the privileged circulate as citizens with access to multiple passports, multiple homes, and a vast array of credentials and financial resources, others operate in a state of restricted legal and economic possibilities. It's an age of international migration that is characterized by what Steven Vertovec has dubbed "super-diversity," drawing people of different origins, legal statuses, and social classes together in metropolitan regions.[13] This too shapes gardens.

Many of the eleven million undocumented immigrants who live and work "without papers" in the United States do not own private property with expansive gardens. Yet agriculture and gardening have long served as job sectors for disenfranchised immigrant workers, especially in the western United States. Many of these same immigrant workers have operated with what Cecilia Menjivar has called "liminal legality," a gray zone of temporary visas, permits, or waiting for the possibility of regularizing status.[14] In various places around the world, agriculture and gardening jobs have employed migrants with experience working in rural, preindustrial peasant and farming societies. And that is the story throughout the West Coast region, including Southern California, where gardening became an important sector of the immigrant labor market and a route of economic incorporation, especially for Mexican and Asian immigrant men from rural backgrounds. Today, Latino immigrant men are disproportionately employed in residential maintenance gardening, but it was Japanese immigrant and Japanese American men who invented the job as we know it today. While Basque, Vietnamese, Central American, and Korean immigrant men from rural backgrounds also work in California gardening, the job is today mostly performed by men of Mexican origin.

It is also important to take account of traces, sedimentation, and vestiges of past migrations. The sedimentation of prior migrations and the vestiges of garden ideas and plants and practices that were once popular remain on the land. These now appear side by side with new plantings and practices that reflect contemporary migration. As Yen Le Espiritu has underscored, immigrant communities express yearnings for homeland not only through the physical reshaping of their surroundings but also through the imagination, so that ideas, memories, images, and practices that are disconnected from the physical space where one lives help to define home. As she reminds us, "Home is both an *imagined* and an *actual* geography."[15]

Sometimes immigrants rely on deliberately modified perceptions that allow them to see the new landscape, and their place in it, in ways that remake their original home. They are trying to maintain dignity and restore their place in the world. For example, in a study of early twentieth-century Japanese and Punjab farmworkers who were exploited in the California fields and denied citizenship, Karen Leonard found that they reinterpreted the Sacramento Valley as similar to their homeland and saw themselves as "rulers on the land . . . subverting the imposition of the racial and ethnic stereotypes that portrayed them as powerless laborers in California agriculture."[16] This too is a kind of place making and exhibits agency and imagination of the type that allows immigrants to endure challenging conditions.

Gardens, through actions and the imagination, enable migrants to create new homes, attachments, and means of livelihood that link the past with the present. Through gardening, immigrants may transcend and resist their marginalization.

PLEASURE AND POWER

Most garden writers describe gardens as sites of beauty and enchantment, enclosed havens of tranquillity fenced off from the harshness of the world. As Robert Pogue Harrison has eloquently reflected, gardens, like intoxication, art, storytelling, and religion, make human life bearable. They re-enchant the present, slow down time, provide the satisfaction of cultivation, care, and creative expression, and fill yearnings for pleasure, sustenance, and restoration.[17]

I too am convinced that gardens are life-affirming, transcendent sites, with practices that sustain us and connect us, but I think it is also important to understand how gardens are bound up with the larger society, with power, inequalities, dislocations, sickness, and even violence. People have depended on plant life to provide sources of food, magic, medicine, and comfort for eons, and now there is empirical evidence that gardens have the capacity to heal. Today some landscape designers, responding to this idea that there is a basic human desire to be around plants—sometimes called chlorophilia or biophilia—dedicate their practice to designing therapeutic healing gardens for hospitals, nursing homes, and the infirm. Research suggests that looking at a garden, or even just looking at photographs of trees and plants, reduces stress and quickens postsurgical recovery.[18] Scientists are now discovering that smelling herbal and floral fragrance releases endorphins that reduce pain and diminish stress. Even sticking our hands in soil releases serotonin. The pleasure that we take in gardens is emotionally and physically restorative.

What might gardens do for existential woes? For financial and emotional stress and the pains of injustice? For the feeling of being overwhelmed by bureaucracy and anonymous, fast-paced life in concrete cities? For feelings of displacement, the loss of family ties, and social exclusion in a foreign land? The life-affirming and restorative qualities of gardens become even more critical during periods of crisis, as Kenneth I. Helphand has shown. When war, death, and destruction loom, when entire communities have been forcibly removed from their homes and unjustly imprisoned in subhuman conditions, people have often sought relief by planting, tending, and contemplating in gardens. Relying on meticulous research, Helphand shows how soldiers deployed in World War I trench warfare, Jews locked up during the Warsaw ghetto's early period (1940–41), and Japanese Americans detained in World War II internment camps all cultivated gardens in brutal, almost unimaginable conditions, sometimes even in bomb craters, surrounded by death, destruction, and dehumanization. These gardens were not passive retreats or escapes but sites of resistance and defiance for people facing inhumane conditions. Garden making allowed these groups "a way to control something in the midst of chaos. They represented home and hope."[19] These gardens offered both sustenance and transcendence, providing food and connecting people to meaningful activity, to their pasts, and to a more optimistic future. Yen Le Espiritu has uncovered similar garden and shrine-building activities among the Vietnamese who were held in military refugee processing camps in Guam and the Philippines during the 1970s and 1980s.[20]

Not all immigrants and refugees suffer war and forced imprisonment, but as people move across regions and nations they experience hardship, uncertainty, risk, and dislocation. Gardens, especially private residential gardens and urban community gardens, enable immigrants to create new homes and forge new sources of attachment. To be a gardener is to be optimistic and future oriented, investing effort that will make the next season, the next year, and the next decade bear fruit and fragrance.

While gardens are sites of pleasure, sustenance, healing, and restoration, they can also project power and strengthen social processes of inequality and labor exploitation. Big grand gardens not only display power and domination over nature and others but are built on relations of inequality. We might look at them with awe and admiration, but we should also recognize that they embody rigid boundaries of exclusion. In fact, the construction of some gardens might require the destruction of other people's homes and livelihoods. This too is the story of Southern California gardens, which are cultivated on land that was violently taken from Native Americans.

Typically, garden grandeur conceals garden labor. Louis XIV's Versailles and Thomas Jefferson's Monticello are revered for the grand ambitions of their creators, but making these gardens required other men to move mountains. In this vein, sociologist Chandra Mukerji argues that the building of Versailles can be seen as a material practice of territorial state power: it created a garden landscape that showcased military engineering techniques in garden terracing, used basic principles of the water system of Paris to develop garden irrigation, and demonstrated the reach of French trading networks in the importation of exotic plants.[21] While Monticello is said to embody the democratic, agrarian impulses of Thomas

Jefferson and is sometimes posited as the aesthetic antithesis of the garden formality at Versailles, it was built and maintained with coerced labor, beginning as a plantation. Slaves tilled the soil for one of the most famous proponents of American democracy, as Jefferson owned over six hundred slaves in his lifetime, many of whom planted and tended his cash crops and his vast ornamental plant collections.

This pattern continues in the present. Status and distinction accrue to the owners and designers of grand gardens, but the actual gardeners who plant, tend, and maintain the gardens remain invisible. "Garden history," as Martin Hoyles remarks, "has usually been a study of ownership, design and style . . . yet the labour in making gardens is crucial."[22] The invisibility of garden labor is reproduced in garden books and magazines and is thrown into relief in Southern California, where thousands of perfectly manicured gardens are maintained by Latino immigrant gardeners. At the University of Southern California campus where I work, the garden grounds are always beautifully maintained, but every year just before graduation the flower beds are festively, miraculously plumped out overnight, with hundreds of flats of blooming annuals in crimson and gold, the Trojan colors, inserted into elaborately designed flower beds. The Latino men who do this work remain invisible because, like the gardeners at Disneyland, they are dispatched and called to duty in the wee hours before dawn, before students, professors, and visitors arrive. The gardeners are erased from the garden landscape, yet they are critical to its production.

As Douglas Mitchell suggested in *Lie of the Land*, the beauty of the California landscape obscures the human costs of labor camps and exploited migrant farmworkers who produce that agricultural landscape, and so it is with gardening labor in metropolitan Southern California.[23] When the Latino immigrant gardeners are visible and audible with the tools of their trade, the gas-powered mowers and blowers, they are subjected to vitriolic criticism. As Laura Pulido has emphasized, landscapes and spatial processes of suburbanization and decentralization in Southern California have been shaped by racial privilege.[24] The latest manifestation of this pattern features white home owners blaming Mexican gardeners for the noise they make doing the work that home owners command them to do. Privileged home gardens depend on the labor of racialized others, and today this involves a triangle of labor and cash that flows between home owners, the gardeners who own the trucks and tools, and their employee gardeners.

Gardens display power by projecting status and conspicuous consumption. Writing over one hundred years ago in *The Theory of the Leisure Class*, Thorstein Veblen outlined his theory of how standards of taste hinge on the consumption of nonproductive goods. From lavish expenditures on landscape installations, to the quotidian adoption of lawn and the proliferation of nonshade and non-fruit-bearing trees in residential gardens, and including today's pricey industry of native plants and modern landscape architectural design, public and private gardens are vehicles for conveying leisure, status, and power.

Devotion to gardening as a leisure practice is also a way of displaying cultural refinement and morality. "Conspicuous abstention from labour," Veblen wrote, "becomes the conventional mark of superior pecuniary achievement."[25] Participation in gardening clubs and garden tours, or simply gardening for pleasure and relaxation, cultivating rose bushes or heirloom tomatoes, falls in this category. Gardening and appreciation of gardens are forms of conspicuous leisure evident in private residential gardens and at botanical gardens, though less at urban community gardens. Municipal regulations that outlaw vegetable gardens on parkways or in front yards and mandate green lawns there instead codify these conventions of conspicuous leisure.

Garden making involves tension between social processes of inequality (e.g., domination, colonization, labor exploitation, and the commodification of plant nature) and the desire for and experience of enchantment. In this way, gardens are about both pleasure and power. They are sites of exclusion, dominance, and status but also restorative places that invite reflection, connection, transcendence, and sustenance, and in Southern California immigrants engage in both sides of the garden story. This is the true story of gardens here.

GARDENS SHAPE OUR LIVES

My focus on migration and gardens in this book is also driven by the belief that gardens are constitutive elements of society. They are not passive, innocent, or superfluous environments. Rather, garden sites and gardening practices help shape the social world of Southern California. Here I am inspired by the historians William Deverell and Greg Hise, whose approach to "metropolitan nature," considers "how people transform nature in particular sites and . . . how what is created in particular locales is generative for local and broader culture," and by urban scholars Jennifer Wolch and Michael Dear, who maintain that "social life structures territory. . . . and territory shapes social life."[26] This idea can be traced to Carl Sauer, the key figure in the Berkeley School of Cultural Geography, who prompted a shift from seeing landscape as just a passive recipient of human transformation. Later, geographer J. B. Jackson built on this by advancing the idea that the landscape actively influences social and economic processes, shaping the way we live and what we become.[27]

Sociologists have also called attention to the influence of landscape. As Sharon Zukin demonstrates in *Landscapes of Power*, the physical landscape in metropolitan regions is shaped by distinctive eras of social and economic regimes, reconciling market and place in a range of postindustrial situations. Migration is a central part of the story in Southern California and Los Angeles, which she reminds us, was "created by making desert and hills habitable for immigrant labor, both skilled and unskilled."[28] It required conquest and then constant reinvention, and Zukin underscores how colonized labor and the production of fantasy were key elements of this manufactured landscape.

The myth of a romantic Spanish past, as William Deverell shows in *Whitewashed Adobe*, rewrote the history of Spanish and Anglo conquest and colonization in an attempt to erase the Mexican influence in California.[29] Later, the fantasy of Southern California as the nation's racialized "white spot" and a matching agricultural and suburban garden paradise was used by boosters and developers to sell alluring visions of the place to new generations of migrants.[30] As historian Lawrence Culver argues, an antiurban ethos and focus on recreation and leisure prevailed in Southern California, supporting the development of single-family, detached homes and private backyard gardens scattered in the valleys and canyons, rather than investment in public parks such as Golden Gate Park in San Francisco or Central Park in New York City. "Instead of bringing nature into the city," he observes, "they brought the city out into nature, dispersing housing and allotting private yards rather than public parks."[31]

Much of the plant nature used to make these gardens came from other continents. Historians show that a cross-pollination across continents began with the "Columbian exchange," when Columbus's voyage of 1492 sparked an exchange of plants, animals, and diseases across the Atlantic Ocean, and this process expanded with the trans-Pacific exchange of plants and seeds.[32] These continental exchanges provided a broad array of plants and trees for the creation of fantasy gardens and landscapes. As the historian Jared Farmer underscores, California now boasts more trees than at any time since the Pleistocene era (when mammoths roamed the earth, 2.6 million to 11,700 years ago) because of the very deliberate remaking of the landscape by American settlers and migrants.[33] From the Spanish missions to orange empires, the early movie industry, and later the proliferation of California dream homes and gardens and the creation of the ultimate dreamscape, Disneyland, fantasy gardens constructed from imported plants and seeds have prevailed in Southern California.

Generations of migrants have shaped Southern California gardens, and in turn the gardens have exerted an influence on the society that formed here. For example, Mexican immigrant gardeners are today instrumental in keeping Southern California residential yards looking as perfect as they do, and in turn the regime of garden and lawn care work affects Mexican immigrant gardeners, their economic incorporation, and the life chances and opportunities for them and their families. To be sure, the outcomes are diverse. Gardening is a stratified occupation, in which some gardeners remain mired in minimum-wage jobs, while the "route owner" gardeners who own the trucks and tools earn better incomes by combining entrepreneurship and manual labor.[34] As the research of sociologist Hernan Ramircz shows, the children of the latter are achieving educational and professional success, in part due to their fathers' ability to earn better than just living wages in the occupation.[35]

Similarly, the presence of a vast army of Mexican immigrant gardeners allows many Southern Californians to escape the drudgery of outdoor domestic chores while still enjoying meticulously manicured lawns and gardens unspotted by fallen leaves or debris. The immigrant gardeners' work allows well-to-do fathers and husbands to meet the new standards of involved fatherhood and companionate marriage while still protecting home equity and property value. Of course not all home owner households include men living in heteronormative family forms, but the outcome of the immigrant gardener system is the same: the outsourcing of garden labor prompts new higher standards of lawn care, with repercussions for protecting wealth, leisure, and social relationships. Middle-class people who have recently moved here from the Midwest often express surprise at the tidiness of Southern California lawns. There is scarcely a leaf on the ground, and it is the widespread normalization of Mexican immigrant gardening service that allows for that unnatural tidiness.

WHY HAS SOCIOLOGY IGNORED GARDENS?

Walk into any remaining brick-and-mortar bookstore, and you are likely to see shelves bulging with books about gardens. Hundreds of gardening books are published every year, especially in the United States and the United Kingdom, suggesting just how important gardens are to people. I have read many of them, and I find the popular books fall into three types. First, there are the "how to" guides, offering detailed directives on preparing soil, when to prune, and so on. Another segment consists of the heavy coffee table books with glossy photographs of garden perfection, usually portraying gardens of historical importance or big estates (these tend to be pricey). Then there are garden memoirs, which divulge confessional, personalized accounts of gardening joys and challenges.

The libraries, I discovered, are bulging with scholarly books on gardens written by philosophers, landscape architects, literature scholars, urban planners, environmentalists, art historians, and cultural geographers. A good deal of the scholarly literature is confined to discussions of what we might call "the grand gardens," which is the term I loosely use to refer to Italian renaissance gardens, Islamic gardens, and the gardens of kings, emperors, and industrialists. "The great innovators" of landscape design (e.g., Gertrude Jekyll, Frederick Law Olmsted, André Le Nôtre) also fill many serious books. Yet the mundane practice of keeping a small kitchen garden or an ornamental residential garden, and what that means to participants and the society at large, with a few excellent exceptions in

England, Australia, and the United States, has received little scholarly attention and sociological analysis.[36] A growing literature critically analyzes the causes and consequences of the American lawn obsession.[37] More recent publications also focus on urban community gardens and the revival of urban farms, which were reinvigorated with the onset of the global financial crisis of 2008.[38]

For the most part, sociologists have ignored gardens. I believe this is because sociology grew as a distinctively urban discipline, one dedicated to studying groups and institutions in cities and attuned to the significance of social problems and social inequalities. Gardens are identified with nature— although they are intersections of culture and nature—so they are perceived to be divorced from society and urban processes. In addition, they have been overlooked as irrelevant, frivolous, and possibly feminine, another cause for disregard. As the geographer Matthew Gandy has noted, "The idea of a radical separation between nature and cities is a powerful current running through Western environmental thought."[39] Nature is thought to be somewhere "out there," in rural areas far away from cities and society.[40] In fact, elements of nature surround us constantly, and gardens provide places where we may have the closest daily contact with plant nature. In this regard, the writer Michael Pollan suggests that a garden "may be as useful to us today as the idea of wilderness has been in the past."[41]

Another reason that sociology has ignored gardens as sites of inquiry is that the discipline is not generally concerned with the quest for pleasure unless it involves deviance and transgression. This is particularly true of the sociology of migration, which has focused on assimilation, development policies, labor exploitation, economic incorporation, and social mobility. Sociology assumes the negative: that sites of pleasure cannot reveal relations of power and inequality. Rural sociology and environmental sociology are subfields revolving around plant nature, but studies here have not pursued investigations of gardens and society.

Yet the connection between people, plants, and places is an ancient one, and I find inspiration in the declaration by the prolific British naturalist writer Richard Mabey that the meanings we assign to gardens and "our vernacular relationships with nature should be taken every bit as seriously" as other arenas of social life.[42] In this book, I rely on ideas from geography, history, sociology, and landscape architecture to animate my study, and I am also inspired by historian Douglas Sackman's claim that "the making of a garden is a cultural and historical project." Garden landscapes, he reminds us, are "infused with market forces and bound up in a web of economic, political, and ecological exchanges" spanning the globe.[43] Looking at these connections, and at who makes and maintains the gardens, how they are used, and what they mean to people in Southern California, can reveal the tensions and dynamics of our contemporary society. Sociology's earliest inquiries involved understanding the transition from rural, preindustrial, feudal societies to urban industrial capitalism, and the challenges of these transitions are still relevant today as we consider global migration and diverse global metropolitan areas such as Southern California. Studying gardens can give us a fresh way of visiting classic themes of sociological interest.

Paradise Transplanted emphasizes that gardens are diverse and in flux and that they always embody pleasure and power. For this reason, I deliberately chose to study very different types of gardens that would allow me to reveal the untold stories of gardens and migration. Two of the garden sites I examine in this book illustrate just how populist, on the one hand, and how elitist, on the other hand, Southern California gardens can be. In inner-city neighborhoods of Los Angeles where people live below the poverty line, I studied how urban community gardens offer opportunities for poor, often undocumented Mexican and Central American immigrants to create restorative ties and feelings of home. At the top end of the class spectrum, I analyzed a museum-like garden, the new Chinese Suzhou-style scholar's garden at the Huntington, which displays a form of premodern elite refinement and depends on financial contributions of wealthy Taiwanese and Chinese donors. The residential gardens of Southern California provide the third contemporary case. While backyard gardens are generally seen as places of leisure and relaxation, these gardens require constant labor, and I shift the study focus here to the immigrant garden labor system.

Through my analysis of diverse types of gardens, I aim to show how immigrants, migration, and the transnational circulation of ideas and practices have shaped gardens in Southern California and how in turn the gardens exert an influence on contemporary society at large, sometimes with echoes beyond this region.

THE PLACE AND THE STUDY

Southern California is today a sprawling metropolis that includes a diverse population of twenty-two million people living in a nearly contiguously built area that extends from the US-Mexico border to Santa Barbara, bordered by the Pacific Ocean to the west and the desert to the east. Over 60 percent of Californians live here, with the majority (about twelve million people) packed into the Los Angeles region.[44] It's a multiethnic, multiracial place, with immigrant communities from around the globe. Students in the Los Angeles Unified School District speak more than ninety languages at home. Forty-eight percent of LA's population claim Latin American origins. Today Mexican immigrants are by far the largest immigrant group in Los Angeles, California, and the nation, but immigrants from China, Korea, Vietnam, the Philippines, Central America, Iran, Russia, and many other places have also made their home here in Southern California.

An unmistakable suburban style prevails here, and decades ago the writer Dorothy Parker supposedly called Los Angeles "72 suburbs in search of a city." Today, Los Angeles County alone consists of eighty-eight municipalities, and now many of these suburbs have become or are becoming what the geographer Wei Li has called immigrant "ethnoburbs."[45] Suburban white flight characterized Los Angeles in the mid-twentieth century, but new immigrants have been setting down new roots in the Southern California suburbs and towns for many years now, and increasingly this is a nationwide pattern, with many new immigrants forgoing the inner city to settle in the suburbs.[46] Property is costly here, with the residential enclaves along the coast including some of the most expensive properties in the world, while more affordable detached homes with garden yards are to be found further inland. Prices fluctuate, but the median value of an owner-occupied home in Los Angeles County is nearly half a million dollars.[47]

"Anything grows here," you hear people say, and it's mostly true. The region has been molded and sold as a garden paradise on earth, and plants and people from around the globe mingle here in a mild climate that is often called "Mediterranean" but that contains diverse microclimates and geologic formations offering year-round growing possibilities. As the

British architectural critic Reyner Banham observed in his classic book, "Some of the world's most spectacular gardens are in Los Angeles, where the southern palm will literally grow next to northern conifers, and it was the promise of an ecological miracle that was the area's first really saleable product—the 'land of perpetual spring.'"[48]

The idea that Southern California is an Edenic "island on the land" is still celebrated, but critics such as Mike Davis have countered that it is in fact an "evil paradise" on the brink of ecological disaster, with apocalyptic earthquakes, droughts and floods, and explosive social and racial rebellions responding to deep chasms of inequalities, unfettered capitalism, and environmentally destructive development.[49] The way a lot of gardening is done here—with chemical pesticides and herbicides, scarce imported water, and exploited immigrant labor—is no doubt contributing to a flawed paradise, but the Edenic trope remains dominant. In fact, it is the way most people experience gardens. Close up, at the micro level, encounters with gardens and plants usually bring pleasure and feelings of calmness.

This is a vast region to cover, and I attempt to understand contemporary intersections of migration and Southern California gardens using three empirical case studies, each focusing on a different theme: labor, community, and status. I chose this focus for the sake of practicality and to show the range of sociological processes in garden making (by contrast, I could have focused solely on gardening labor in all three sites). Because I seek to reveal the social meanings people assign to gardens, their engagements with plants, and the social relations and processes supporting them, the methods I use are in-depth interviews and ethnographic observations.

I conducted the empirical field research sequentially, starting in 2007 when a grant allowed me to hire the research assistance of Hernan Ramirez, then a PhD student and now an assistant professor of sociology. Together we designed an interview guide that asked Mexican immigrant maintenance gardeners primarily open-ended questions about occupational experiences, such as job entry, duties, income, wages and expenses, relations with residential clients and coworkers, and dangers encountered on the job. Hernan, the son of a Mexican gardener and himself experienced in working on his father's jobs, contacted potential interviewees, starting with a small circle and snowballing out to others, ultimately interviewing forty-seven men. Hernan's familiarity with the social milieu of *jardinería* opened

doors to trust, and he conducted the interviews with sensitivity, thorough-
ness, and rigor, always probing at just the right moments. We read through
these transcripts and coded the data into themes for analysis, a fairly standard procedure that I followed for the other case studies too. Several years
later, I conducted fifteen audio-recorded interviews with home owners and
landscape designers, asking them about their own garden practices and
maintenance, including questions about their relations with the Mexican
immigrant gardeners who work for them.

The next stage of research centered on the social dynamics that brought
about the Liu Fang Yuan, the first phase of a Chinese Suzhou-style scholar's garden built with $26 million in donations, much of it from Chinese
and Taiwanese philanthropists, and introduced in 2008 at the Huntington
Library, Art Collections and Botanical Gardens in San Marino. I was
interested in the process of how this distinctively non-European garden
was introduced into the Huntington, the aspirations and intentions for it,
and the ways in which both Chinese American and non-Chinese visitors
experienced and perceived the garden, and I designed an ambitious
research plan to interview the professional staff, donors, docents (guides
in the garden), and first-time visitors to the garden. I conducted rich,
informative interviews with some of the highest-ranking professional staff
at the Huntington, but I was unable to interview donors and visitors in the
garden. This is an old, familiar problem of gaining access to elites and to
powerful institutions, and I detail some of these difficulties in "studying
up" elsewhere.[50] Analysis of text, therefore, became important. Ultimately
I depended on my analysis of Huntington brochures, the promotional
DVDs intended to cull new donations, and news reports about the garden,
supplemented by six audiotaped interviews with key figures involved in
the fund-raising, planning, and building of the new Chinese garden and
three interviews with Chinese American local residents. My observations
at the garden and the related lecture series round out the analysis. Since I
do not read Chinese, I relied on the assistance of Xiaoxin Zeng, a graduate
student in sociology, who translated Mandarin materials that appeared in
local Chinese newspapers.

To understand immigrant life in urban community gardens, I immersed
myself in social life at the "Franklin" and "Dolores Huerta" community gardens—those are pseudonyms—located in the densely populated Latino

immigrant neighborhoods of Pico Union and MacArthur Park/Westlake, just west of downtown Los Angeles. Here I was assisted by Jose Miguel Ruiz, who had grown up in Pico Union and had recently returned after college. We began in the summer of 2010 by going to the gardens at different times of day, on different days of the week, and after we met some people there we fell into a rhythm of participating in the monthly Saturday morning *limpiezas*, the collective cleanups that are required of the plot holders, where we pruned, raked, swept, pulled weeds, chopped plant debris for compost, and carted sacks of soil and compost. It wasn't all hard work, for we regularly feasted on sumptuous meals with homemade salsas, tacos, *pupusas*, and quesadillas cooked in the gardens on small propane stoves or charcoal fires. We both graduated from the "Women's Empowerment" class that was taught on Saturday mornings at the Franklin garden by a Guatemalan social worker, and we attended the monthly garden community meetings, run by a paid organizer of Green Spaces (a pseudonym for the nonprofit organization that administers one of the gardens), where I was often asked to take minutes and read the meeting rules in Spanish and English. There were more meetings too, but we also spent many hours at these gardens sitting on benches, in conversation and joking. Binders full of typed field notes from these encounters, audio-recorded interviews with twenty-five of the community garden plot holders (Jose Miguel conducted five of these), and five additional interviews that I conducted with community leaders provide the data.

I have never paid interview respondents in cash (as some social science researchers do), but to show my appreciation at the community gardens I gave people plants and bags of groceries containing nutritious novelty items such as nuts, dark chocolates, stalks of brussels sprouts, and a festive plant. Several years ago I wrote a book about Latina domestic workers in Los Angeles that has now been translated into Spanish and been published in Mexico, and when I gave copies of this book to community garden members others asked for copies of their own. Women, and some of the men, were moved by this book. For me, this was not only a gift but a way of showing I had a commitment to telling their stories and a gentle reminder that I would be writing about them too.

At the community gardens, I was both physically and emotionally situated as a participant, gossiping, joking, eating, and sharing conversation.

While I identify as Latina and speak Spanish, my comfortable professional class life insulates me from the daily hardships insiders in this community face. Yet I too was grappling with some of the same family issues, and over time I felt myself drawn to social life at these urban community gardens. As researchers, we are taught to leave the field once we have reached data saturation, but I stayed longer than I needed to, mostly for my own needs. An ongoing methodological concern in participant observation ethnography is the extent to which the researcher's presence transforms the social scene. It is impossible for me to really know how my presence changed social interactions, but I do feel as though I was transformed by my experiences with these urban community gardeners. Observations and a half-dozen research interviews with change makers and other innovators inform the discussion of visions of the future that I present in the final chapter.

This book is also based on my extensive reading and analysis of secondary historical works and my review of primary archival documents at the Huntington Library. Although I am a sociologist, I firmly believe that we cannot understand contemporary society without taking historical context into account, and for a project such as this one, where I aim to show how what came before shapes the present and future, history is crucial. In chapter 2 I construct a 240-year historical chronology of migration and garden making in Southern California. The chapter's focus is on residential gardens, the dominant form that unfolded in this region, where developers and cities invested meagerly in public parks, but there is some overlap with citrus agriculture, which provided much of the wealth and many of the labor camps from which many regional residential gardens emerged. In addition, I used secondary sources to research the history of labor in US residential gardens (included in chapter 3), the history of urban community gardens both in the region and nationally (included in chapter 4), and the development of modern botanical gardens in Europe and the United States (included in chapter 5).

OVERVIEW OF THE BOOK

Each chapter in this book examines Southern California gardens of migration and the impact of gardens on the way we live. Chapter 2 reviews the diverse migrations that have made Southern California, from the Spanish colonial conquest to the present, emphasizing how the sedimentation of past migrations shapes how gardens look and how gardening is done here today. Since the eighteenth century, garden making in Southern California has included violence, exclusion, and exploitation in the quest for a new and improved Eden. Multiple migrations are now sedimented on the land, visible in the trees and gardens that remain.

Chapter 3 focuses on the work it takes to keep up the private garden paradises of middle-class and upper-class home gardens. Southern California's gorgeous residential gardens require constant labor, and in this chapter I focus on home owners and the Mexican immigrant gardeners they employ. Everyone is guided by different dreams and aspirations in these gardens, and exchanges of labor and money shape the private residential gardens. Suburban gardens are places of leisure and beauty, but for the Latino immigrant gardeners they serve as the twenty-first-century factory floor, offering the hope of a better life and the mundane site of hard work. Residential maintenance gardening is a racialized and gendered occupational niche, the masculine parallel to paid domestic work.

Gardens are natural sites to congregate and converse and relax with others. In the urban community gardens of Los Angeles, some of the poorest, most marginalized newcomer immigrants gather to grow homeland vegetables and share community ties and build new places of belonging. Chapter 4 focuses on life in these urban gardens, where undocumented immigrants who are excluded from other spaces of Los Angeles collectively transform discarded urban patches of ground into oases of freedom, belonging, and homeland connection. On previously abandoned lots, they are producing bountiful vegetables and herb patches, vibrant community connection, and places of great beauty. As they tend to their gardens, they are tending to themselves, practicing care of self, family, community, and the land.

Modern botanic gardens developed in Europe to show off the spoils of empire, conquest, and colonization and to harness the power of scientific knowledge, and in the American West wealthy industrialists sought to convey their own personal grandeur by collecting diverse plants and displaying majestic beauty that echoed the Roman Empire and European aristocratic life. These were fundamentally gardens of status and distinction.

Figure 1. In Southern California postcards such as this one, culture was portrayed as a benign and innocent presence surrounded by plant nature. This item is reproduced by permission of The Huntington Library, San Marino, California.

Chapter 5 considers these historical legacies and examines the process through which the Huntington Botanical Garden built a representation of a Chinese Suzhou-style scholar's garden. This is a type of garden that first emerged in fifteenth-century China, when scholar-officials designed elite residential garden compounds for scholarly reflection. I suggest that the process surrounding the replication of this type of garden at the Huntington reflects the increasing power, status, and wealth of a segment of the Chinese American and Chinese and Taiwanese immigrants in Southern California, the rise of China as a global power, and the acknowledgment by a dominant cultural institution that it can no longer continue to ignore and exclude significant members of the region or the possible philanthropic contributions they bring.

Chapter 6 considers new interventions and possibilities for Southern California gardens of the future. In this book I offer a place-based study of gardens, but it is my hope that the discussion will also resonate with what is unfolding elsewhere. Certainly other metropolitan regions are also grappling with the challenges of meeting environmental sustainability while respecting diverse cultural sustainability and promoting social justice.

I have spent time trying to decipher and understand the social world of gardens and migration in Southern California because I believe gardens offer a portal to understanding our social and existential conditions and because global migration is fundamental to this region and to the era in which we live. Gardens here in Southern California are more than simply enclosures of roots and foliage. Gardens are conscious acts of transplanting, created and sustained by continual migration. They are vehicles for our engagement with the natural landscape and also expressions of the forces of exclusion and domination. At their best, gardens are aspirations for transcendence, beauty, and alternative social worlds.

2 Ellis Island on the Land

Los Angeles is a residence city of marvelous beauty. On every
hand it requires but a few steps from business activity to
carry one into the bowery repose of the tropical gardens
which every citizen seems to take so much pride in keeping
up about his home, whether it be one of those neat little cottages or one of the more imposing and more costly structures. Such gardens! Sunny Italy can boast of no greater variety of fruits. . . . Flowers never fail a day in the year, and such
wealth of roses, calla lilies, geraniums, heliotropes, century
plants, all varieties of cactus, tulips and hundreds of others,
which, in the Eastern States, are only seen in the hot houses
all year, affording highest earthly pleasure and satisfaction to
one and all who even pass by along the shady sidewalks.

The Land of Sunshine, Fruits and Flowers (1893)

In the late nineteenth century, Southern California was sold as a garden
tonic to cure the ailments of Anglo Protestant midwesterners and easterners. "The Land of Sunshine" promised a paradisiacal Shangri-La full of
exotic flowers, fruits, and foliage, a new Eden free of the foreigners and
undesirable immigrants who were just then crowding into Chicago, New
York, and Boston. Already it offered a veritable smorgasbord of exotic
plants transplanted from Asia, Australia, South Africa, and Latin America,
boasting palm trees, rubber trees, pampas grass, date palms, Italian
cypress, and of course, citrus trees heavy with oranges. Roses were so
plentiful in winter that Pasadena patricians decided to make a rose parade.

Figure 2. At the turn of the century, Southern Californians loved to pose in front of Victorian houses covered in roses. These images helped real estate developers lure Anglo midwestern and eastern migrants to Los Angeles. Here, two women pose with a dog, who is sitting on a horse, in front of the residence of S. B. Lewis, on West Adams Boulevard, Los Angeles, around 1898. Courtesy of University of Southern California, on behalf of the USC Special Collections.

True, it was an arid land requiring the importation of water and coercive systems of labor, including migrant laborers from Asia and Mexico, but the newly arrived Anglos remained breathless about making the deserts and hills bloom. Even the land formations promised relief from the dreary boredom of the midwestern prairie. A 1893 promotional pamphlet guaranteed it in capital letters: there would be "NO MONOTONY" here because "outside the Mojave and Colorado deserts there is not one dull, monotonous plain."[1] Boosters, real estate developers, and railroad industrialists lured newcomer migrants to Southern California with the promise that a good life could be lived here in a fragrant, sunny garden.

In Northern California the Gold Rush had drawn the newcomers, but here it was a garden rush. From the beginning, they reached for transnational imagery of faraway places to define Southern California landscapes. They compared the region to "Palestine in natural features" and described its climate as "milder in winter than Rome."[2] Because they could grow guava, palms, and bananas, they flirted with describing it as tropical, as when a 1874 promotional treatise heralded a "semi-tropical" California. That model, however, was quickly discarded as evoking associations too wild for white Anglo-Americanization. The newcomers settled on adopting a Mediterranean motif, "an Italy without the Italians," as Carey McWilliams put it, planting English-style lawns and midwestern flower gardens with palm and cypress trees.[3] In the late nineteenth and early twentieth centuries, the World's Fairs facilitated the transnational circulation of garden ideas, popularizing a Japanese-style garden aesthetic that remains influential today and promoting the idea that Southern California was a paradise for purchase, one big flowering and fruiting garden ready for splicing up into subdivisions.

The history of garden making in Southern California is the story of conquest and colonization, but also migrant desire, fantasy, and the quest for Edenic tranquillity and well-being. The gardens were built through successive migrations and conquests of Spaniards over Indians, and Anglos over Mexicans, and the exploitation of racialized labor. This began with the Spanish Franciscans enslaving Indians in the late 1700s to work in the mission vineyards, orchards, and gardens, and it continues today, with the beautiful residential gardens of the early twenty-first century relying on the constant work and sweat of Mexican immigrant gardeners. In between, Chinese, Japanese, Mexican, Filipino, and Italian immigrant men worked in the fields, the orchards, and the ornamental gardens filled with plants brought from around the world.

In each era, different garden landscapes and labor regimes emerged, with the dominant groups putting subordinate men to work, demonstrating their power and imposing their own ideas about garden beauty. Historian Douglas Sackman suggests that we can look at Southern California history "as a succession of landscapes, each bearing the inscription of a dominant economic actor and activity, and each written over by the next as if the land itself were a palimpsest."[4] A palimpsest is a manu-

Figure 3. The oldest known photo of the Los Angeles Plaza, circa 1865. Expansive terrain, including vineyards and orchards, appears in the background. This item is reproduced by permission of The Huntington Library, San Marino, California.

script where the writing has been written over, with traces of the earlier text remaining visible, and so it is with Southern California gardens. Traces of earlier eras of migration and the transnational circulation of ideas, people, plants, and seeds remain sedimented on the land. You see this in many neighborhoods here, with hulking hundred-year-old Chilean wine palms or mature Australian eucalyptus next to newly unfurled lawns and shrubs that just yesterday popped out of canisters purchased at Home Depot.

Southern California is today famous around the globe, identified in photos and film images by citrus trees and by palm trees silhouetted against sunset skies. These plants are now naturalized fixtures of the landscape, but they too are products of migration. Unlike settlers who arrived in, say, Michigan's Upper Peninsula, migrants to Southern California quickly discovered that just about anything could grow here in the alluvial soil and temperate climate—if fed sufficient water.

The Victorians loved palm trees, and when they came to late nineteenth-century California they planted lots of them. Palms were the plant trophies

Figure 4. By the late nineteenth century, land that had been used for vineyards, grazing, and citrus orchards was subdivided and sold. Workers transported and transplanted enormous palm trees, such as this one, which was moved from the Wolfskill Orchard to the Southern Pacific Railroad Depot in 1889. Its move punctuated the arrival of more newcomers to Los Angeles. Courtesy of University of Southern California, on behalf of the USC Special Collections.

of empire, the bounty from imperial conquests of Asia, South America, and Africa. In England and Europe and on the East Coast of the United States, palm trees could grow only indoors or in hothouse enclosures. Here in Southern California, they would majestically line elegant boulevards and driveways of regal estates, and eventually big palms would stand sentinel on small, modest residential properties too. In the image above, workers are shown transplanting a tall palm tree to the new Southern Pacific Railroad Depot (the Arcade Station). Maybe this Washington fan palm helped assuage any doubts the newcomers had about finding a tropical Eden at the end of the line. In the late nineteenth century and in the decades that followed, railroad and real estate developers transformed the landscape from a cornucopia of vineyards and orchards into tract lots with gardens.

Only one palm tree, the California fan palm (*Washingtonia filifera*), is actually native to Southern California. While more than two hundred palm species from tropical forests thrive in collections here, only about ten species of palms are commonly planted in the region.[5] Today developers of new shopping malls and office parks invest thousands of dollars to plunk down mature palm trees (a big one may retail for $8,000). These are the ultimate status trees, producing neither shade nor fruit, and in the early twentieth century Southern Californians planted them like mad. In 1931, LA's forestry division planted over twenty-five thousand palm trees in one year.[6] Palms are thirsty trees to establish, and here they rely on imported water from distant sources, supporting the illusion that it is all one big oasis here.

The tree that produces the prized Washington navel orange originated in Asia and came to the region via China, Europe, Brazil, and Washington, D.C. Local legend has it that three young saplings were sent in the 1870s to Mr. Luther Tibbet and Mrs. Elizabeth Tibbet in Riverside, a couple who had come here from Maine. These trees germinated the seeds of a citrus industry that would define the economy of Southern California in the late nineteenth and early twentieth centuries.[7] Plants from around the world poured into Southern California during that period, and one expert estimates that 98 percent of the plants in Southern California are now nonnative.[8] Even LA's official civic flower, the exotic bird of paradise (*Strelitzia reginae*), is not a native but hails from South Africa. Over time, these migrant plants have become naturalized fixtures on the land.

The migration of people, plants, and seeds has produced Southern California gardens, revealing tensions between power and pleasure, nature and culture, and competing ideas of beauty. Garden making here is the story of the search for power and profit, reliance on the ethnic succession and exploitation of a revolving door of immigrant workers and the display of status through the cultivation of nonproductive plants collected from around the world. But Southern California gardens are also the sites of pleasure and the quest for beauty, tranquillity, and transcendence, reflecting the homemaking yearnings of migrant newcomers, and it is not only elites who have expressed these strong life-affirming impulses. To understand the making of Southern California gardens I adopt a migration lens that acknowledges the fundamental tensions between nature and culture and between power and pleasure.

THE NATIVE GARDEN

Before the Spaniards arrived, was Southern California a chaparral-covered desert or a cultivated horticultural paradise? The conventional thinking has reified the binary of hunter gatherers and agriculturalists and held that California Indians functioned as the former and that Europeans were needed to introduce agricultural civilization and progress. Revisionist environmental history now offers rich evidence of indigenous land management in California, which included tending the land by practicing a wide range of horticultural techniques, including deliberate, purposeful burning, pruning, and harvesting of plants. Selective fire and harvesting techniques allowed native people to simultaneously live off the land and provide stewardship. These practices would allow the subsequent European migrant settlers to thrive off the land. As the ethnoecologist M. Kat Anderson puts it, the Indians "maintained, enhanced and in part created a fertility that was eventually to be exploited by European and Asian farmers, ranchers, and entrepreneurs, who imagined themselves to have built civilization out of an unpeopled wilderness."[9] The first Europeans who arrived in California did not find a "pristine, virtually uninhabited wilderness but rather a carefully tended 'garden' that was the result of thousands of years of selective harvesting, tilling, burning, pruning, sowing, weeding and transplanting."[10] The vast landscape south of the Tehachapi Mountains contained native sycamores, pines, oaks, and willow trees, as well as toyons, sage, and wild vines.

To create a new European settlement here and elsewhere on the North American continent, Indians were decimated, conquered, rounded up and enslaved in the missions, or forced to migrate to other places. These violent processes laid the foundation for the erasure and devaluation of Native American horticulture and for the importation of new types of European horticulture.[11] Through these processes, as the environmental historian William Cronon notes, European newcomers were inventing the idea of American lands as "uninhabited wilderness."[12]

Native plant landscapes were supplanted with flower gardens, vineyards, and citrus groves. In Leslie Marmon Silko's novel *Gardens in the Dunes*, an Indian girl in the Riverside area crawls, hides, and plays among "immigrant shrubbery," peonies, roses, and dianthus brought from other continents.[13] Violently kidnapped from her tribal family, she escapes from an Indian boarding school and is adopted by white parents, and among the plants (the new father is a botanist) and later on other continents she seeks a new kind of home. As Silko's novel underscores, the migrations of conquest transformed nature and landscape. With the shift from Indian to European migration and dominance on the land, a new ecological invasion of plants took place, starting with the Columbian exchange and the Spanish missions and continuing with Mexican and Anglo-American migrations.[14]

Gardens of migration are layered on conquered Native American land, but it is also possible to see Native Americans through a migration lens. Native Americans—appropriately called the First People in Canada and parts of the United States—were here first, but they were also migratory. Like the Native Hawaiians who came from Polynesia, the First People in Southern California came from elsewhere too, but these migrations occurred thousand of years ago.[15] The groups included the Chumash, the Gabrieleño, the Luiseño-Cahuila, and the Yuma. More recently in the twentieth century, coercive migration and relocation policies forced Native Americans from Oklahoma and other states to California. Consequently, California is today the state with the largest Native American population in the nation.

Native Americans are immigrants too, calling into question the essentializing binary of migrant versus native. Newcomer Native Americans displaced from their homelands in Guatemala and Southern Mexico now live in Southern California. Many migrated here as a consequence of U.S.-sponsored military genocide, and some of them are now speaking Zapotec and ancient Mayan as they plant Mesoamerican indigenous vegetables and herbs in the middle of inner-city Los Angeles, sowing seeds from distant homelands and sometimes using the Mayan calendar as a guide for the most propitious planting time.

SPANISH MISSIONS AND RANCHO GARDENS

The Spanish Franciscan padres were *not* the first farmers of California, but they are usually credited as such, and Mission San Gabriel Arcángel— where six thousand Indians are buried in a mass grave—was the jewel when it came to plants and horticulture, serving as the center of agriculture in the California mission system. To visit Mission San Gabriel today is a haunting experience, for this beautiful place was once the scene of coerced baptisms, burials, floggings, and forced labor, including horticultural work. Visitors today see the church, a small museum, and sites of eighteenth-century labor next to a lovely walled garden inspired by Moorish and Spanish traditions, with citrus, olive trees, and hedges and rows of cypress. It is a place meant to inspire spiritual contemplation and reflection, but it was here that the Spanish missionaries created California's system of coerced Indian labor. They first forced the Indians to prepare the parched land for cultivation by building hydraulic irrigation systems to bring water from the mountains, then put them to work growing an array of non-native productive plants and flowers, pressing olive oil and wine, tending livestock and tanning hides, and making soap and candles by standing over boiling cauldrons of tallow set in deep outdoor furnace pits. These were sites of brutal intensive labor. Today, we savor Mission figs, Mission olives, and Mission grapes, but we can easily forget the legacy that ushered in these foods.

The land around the San Gabriel Mission had nearby water sources, so this made the site a good choice for the Spaniards. A historical account from the late nineteenth century states that "the site now occupied by the San Gabriel Mission buildings and adjacent village was a complete forest of oaks, with considerable underwood," and that a hollow near the mission "was almost impassable from the dense undergrowth of brambles, nettles, palmacristi, wild-rose and wild-vines."[16] The mission was established in 1771; the first oranges were planted here in the 1820s, and the first grape vine, La Madre Viña, grew into vineyards that would span two hundred acres by 1834.

The Old Mother Grapevine is now a neatly manicured circular shrine surrounded by a big lawn, adjacent to a senior recreation center. When I visited on a summer weekday, two young Chinese men (maybe college stu-

Figure 5. La Madre Viña commemorates the first grapevine planted at the San Gabriel Mission. Photo by author.

dents?) were clipping the vine and nearby hedges. Clusters of grapes hung from the vines. I asked when the grapes would ripen and who would be eating them, but they could not tell me, saying they had been volunteering only a short while. At first I thought it odd to find Chinese volunteers speaking Mandarin while working in the mission garden, but given the Chinese immigration to the San Gabriel Valley since the 1970s, it makes perfect sense.

The plants here made multiple migrations. The Spanish Franciscans brought fruit trees from Mexico, which had come directly from Europe after having been imported there from expeditions to Asia and from Persian and Moorish connections. These included orange, lemon, grapefruit, pomegranate, walnut, almond, plum, quince, and apricot trees, as well as raspberries, strawberries, grape vines, and apple, pear, peach, and fig trees. The Franciscans also brought corn, *chiles*, and beans from Mesoamerica. All of these migrant plants were thriving here more than a

Figure 6. Succulents, cactus, flowers, and trees grow inside the San Gabriel Mission walls today. Photo by author.

century before California became part of the United States. And the Spanish missionaries incorporated plants that were native to the Americas, using nopal or prickly pears as fence borders at the missions—these are now decorative features of the ornamental walled garden at the San Gabriel Mission—and growing wheat, hemp, and more. By the time the Mexican government shut down the missions and confiscated Mission San Gabriel, an intensive network of canals and dams irrigated six thousand acres with 163,578 vines growing in four vineyards and 2,333 fruit trees; it provided water sufficient for nearly thirteen thousand head of cattle and an Indian population of "1,323 souls."

The mission gardens were places of human suffering and of stunning garden beauty and bounty. When Anglo navigators and explorers came across Southern California missions, in Ventura, Santa Barbara, San Fernando, and San Gabriel, they marveled at the bountiful agricultural, floral, and fruit displays that they saw growing here. Here's how one Anglo visitor to the mission in Ventura in 1793 described what he saw: "The garden of Buena Ventura far exceeded anything I had before met with in this region, both in respect of the quality, quantity, and variety of its excellent productions. . . . not one species having yet been sown, or planted, that had not flourished, and yielded its fruit in abundance, and of excellent quality. These have principally consisted of apples, pears, plums, figs, oranges, grapes, peaches, and pomegranates, together with the plantain, banana, cocoa nut, sugar cane, indigo and a great variety of the necessary and useful kitchen herbs."[17] Other visitors recorded seeing a profusion of flowers, including hollyhocks, oleander, sweet pea, calla lilies, nasturtiums, roses, marigolds, and the native Matilija poppy. Palm trees and pepper trees grew in every mission garden in Southern California and still define essential graceful elements of the "Mission-style" garden.

Three ingredients allowed for the creation of these lush, productive groves and gardens: imported plants, coerced indigenous labor, and rechanneled water. In turn, the missions provided the material culture and practice that would inspire a new romantic template for the West. Propagated first by Helen Hunt Jackson's *Ramona*, an 1884 novel that grew into a massive booster pageant and myth, and later by promoters of all sorts, "Mission style" remains an alluringly romantic style for the region, but it is more popularly known for Stickley furniture and the built environment of white stucco buildings with red tile roofs and patios than for the profusion of plants, the olive, fig, and pepper trees. And when the plants are invoked, it's typically with attribution to the Spaniards, not to the Indians who did the work of digging canals and cultivating the orchards. The mission gardens were whitewashed, just as the adobe buildings and civic festivals were, with attribution to the Spanish rather than to the Indians who labored in them.[18]

Under pressure from secular interests, Mexico secularized the missions beginning in 1835, and this began the era of land grants and ranchos. At Mission San Gabriel, the Indians were ordered to destroy the vineyards, but they refused to do so. One historical account suggests that this was because they liked drinking *aguardiente* alcohol, but quite possibly the Indians refused to burn the vines because they felt connection and responsibility to preserve the plants they had worked so hard to cultivate. By 1858 there were about a million bearing grape vines in Los Angeles County.[19]

Figure 7. Rancho garden, near Antelope Valley, with flowers, shrubs, and trees. Courtesy of University of Southern California, on behalf of the USC Special Collections.

More than fifty land grants were issued in Southern California between 1822 and 1848, and the ranchos relied on a pastoral landscape and economy, the tending of sheep and cattle. Ranchos typically included patios with cutting gardens that provided flowers for home altars, and herbal gardens including mint, lavender, rue, and rosemary. They featured graceful pepper trees, "Castilian roses," and datura (angel's trumpet). The ranchos had modest gardens, but the plants came from Mexico, Europe, and the Andes. Fragrant jasmine, having been introduced to Moorish gardens in Spain from Persia and India, also flowered in the ranchos in the era of the transition of empire.[20] While plant cuttings from the missions made their way into ornamental gardens, newly imported plants from nurseries in the Midwest, the East Coast, and Australia gradually entered the scene. This transitional era was marked by the intermarriage of many elite Californio women with Anglo-American men, but the historical record on what this meant for patio gardens remains scant. In the second half of the nineteenth century, ornamental residential gardens flourished more profusely in Northern California, where wealth and water were concentrated.

In 1848, after the Mexican-American War and conquest ended with California becoming part of the United States, rancho land holdings were reappropriated, stolen, subdivided, and ultimately sold in the 1880s real estate boom. This was a violent period from the 1850s through the 1870s targeting Mexicans, several of whom were lynched in front of the San Gabriel Mission.[21] The San Gabriel Mission, which, though founded to "Christianize and civilize" Indians, had begun with their enslavement, rape, beatings, and coerced labor in the fields, continued as a place for hangings in the late 1880s, leading scholar Laura Pulido to call it the "most intense site of racialized violence in Southern California."[22] Throughout Southern California, Mexicans and Chinese were hanged from trees, and as historian Jared Farmer has shown, many towns in California commemorated such vigilante violence by naming "hangman's trees," inscribing an anti-Edenic narrative of violence on the land and prompting us to reflect on the veneration of plant nature in these acts.[23]

"IRRIGATE, CULTIVATE AND EXAGGERATE": THE GOLDEN AGE OF ORANGES AND GARDENS

Fueled by citrus, the 1880s inaugurated an economic boom and the golden age of gardening in Southern California. Orange groves carpeted Ventura, Los Angeles, San Gabriel, San Bernardino, Riverside, and Orange counties. In 1870, there were only thirty thousand orange trees growing here, but twenty years later over one million trees were producing oranges for sale.[24] The population grew quickly too, with LA's population increasing from 50,000 in 1890 to 1.2 million by 1930. The majority were Anglo-American migrants from the Midwest and East, but by 1930 over one-third of LA's residents were Asian and Mexican immigrants.[25] This was a new racially bifurcated society, with mainly Asian and Mexican immigrants working in the Anglo-American-owned citrus fields, on truck farms, in home gardens, and in the elaborate gardens of the elites.

The railroad companies, also in the real estate business and ready to profit, were key players in selling Southern California. They promoted the image of a garden paradise with a mild climate and fertile soil. The Southern Pacific Railroad company and the California State Chamber of Commerce produced pamphlets, brochures, and tourist magazines such as *Sunset Limited* (which became *Sunset* magazine), *Land of Sunshine*, and *The Inside Track*, alliteratively promising that Southern California was "emphatically the land of fruits and flowers, always fresh and fascinating," and tantalizingly describing the citrus fields here as "one integrated landscape of cities, orchards and mountains where residents lived in harmony with their environment."[26] New irrigation with canals bringing water from the San Gabriel Mountains and underground aquifers allowed places like Riverside and Ontario to transform from dusty dry towns to lush oases with expansive citrus groves. Eager to sell land here, the railroad companies promoted the health benefits of the mild climate and the oranges and flowers. With dramatically lower train ticket prices in 1887, after the Santa Fe railroad line was completed, a frenzied real estate market took off, with over sixty new towns laid out over the former ranchos during the next two years.

In these newly irrigated towns, on the avenues and in private gardens, the California dream of home and garden, and orange juice on demand—Frederick Jackson Turner reportedly drank it three times a day in his Oak Knoll residence in Pasadena—materialized. Wilmington, Ontario, Los Angeles, Riverside, Redlands, and Upland developed beautiful lush gardens and tree-lined streets. Carey McWilliams reported that during this era "irrigate, cultivate and exaggerate" became the new motto in Southern California, and the vegetation inspired the boosters to create Paul Bunyan–like tall tales embellished with descriptions of perennial sunshine and spectacular flowers and vegetables.

> In particular the products of the soil, its Brobdingnagian vegetables, loomed larger than life in tourist reports. One reads of tomato vines nineteen feet high; of cabbage plants that grew twenty feet in the air; of strawberries so big that they could only be consumed by three large bites; of cucumbers seven feet long; of horseshoe geraniums "as big as small trees" growing in hedges six feet high; of a Gold of Ophir rosebush in Pasadena with 200,000 blossoms; of a grapevine in Santa Barbara that, in 1896, bore twelve tons of

grapes; of squash that weighed three hundred pounds; of daisies that grew on bushes as large as quince trees and lilies fourteen feet high.[27]

From the 1870s until the Great Depression, Southern Californians became obsessed with gardening. Elsewhere, people loved gardening too, but cold climates put a damper on what they could grow. Here, exotic plants from around the globe would grow year round. As Douglas Sackman writes, "Gardening became a source of livelihood and pride. Southern Californians grew fruit trees, and they grew ornamental trees. . . . Each bustling enclave—Pasadena and Ontario, Pomona and Anaheim—vied for the title of garden spot of earth."[28] Sackman underscores that gardening, in this context, had implications far beyond civic beautification and displays of status. It was an ideological, economic, environmental, and technological project. It required land grabs and the establishment of new property lines. Moreover, the grand gardens of the elites, like the new real estate developments, required the control and channeling of vast industrial quantities of water. This was made increasingly possible in 1913 with the completion of the Los Angeles Aqueduct, engineered by William Mulholland, which brought water from the Owens Valley on the east side of the Sierras. To ensure the expansion of Southern California industry and gardens, supplies of water from hundreds of miles away had to be imported.

Both citrus fields and flower gardens fueled the economy, and there were quick profits to be made. The British architectural historian Reyner Banham would later describe the land grabs of Southern California development as unfolding on "the plains of pure Id." As he put it, "These central flatlands are where the crudest urban lusts and most fundamental aspirations are created, manipulated and, with luck, satisfied . . . where the craftiest techniques of sale were worked out, and where the most psychotic forms of territorial possession . . . dirty-up the pretty dream of urban homesteading out of which most of Los Angeles has been built."[29]

The orange was seen as a harbinger of civilization, legitimizing the Anglo-American conquest, and migration—of the landowners, the workers, and many of the plants—became the foundation of both the citrus groves and the gardens. The puffed-up rhetoric deployed by the boosters was stunning for its arrogance and breathless quality. The 1889 publication

Figure 8. Since poor and working people of Los Angeles did not have money for taking photographs of their homes and gardens, few visual records are available. But this modest wood house in what is now downtown Los Angeles reveals a front yard garden with flowers and what appear to be a fruit tree and a cypress tree, circa 1890. Courtesy of University of Southern California, on behalf of the USC Special Collections.

The California Fruits and How to Grow Them boasted that citrus fruit cultivation was "one of the highest of the agricultural arts" and heralded "the quality of our agricultural citizenship." The California Fruit Growers Convention put it even more boldly, with the title of the pamphlet *Hand in Hand Go Horticulture and Civilization.* As Sackman explains, "The dominant narrative made it clear that Anglo-Saxon immigrants had work to do in California: that of reinventing Eden." This required selling land to Anglo migrants and putting the others, Indians, Mexicans, and Asian immigrants, to work in the citrus fields.[30]

This garden rush required creative marketing. Postcards, such as the one shown below, conveyed Edenic imagery of oranges, flowers, and palm trees to midwesterners and easterners. Beautifully designed orange crate labels showing idyllic garden landscape scenes advertised fruit and

Figure 9. Postcards and orange crate labels that showed orange groves and palm trees glimmering in the sun below snow-capped mountains helped broadcast to the rest of the nation the idea that Southern California offered therapeutic landscapes with fruit and year-round sunshine. This item is reproduced by permission of The Huntington Library, San Marino, California.

Southern California itself, but industrialists and boosters innovated other methods too. To sell the new garden paradise to midwesterners, they packed up railroad cars full of Southern California fruits and flowers for a traveling sales tour. For the World's Columbian Exposition in Chicago 1893, seventy-three railroad cars full of fruits and flowers were sent for display from Southern California, and these were shaped into spectacles such as a thirty-five-foot tower of fruits. For this event, the boosters also transplanted palm trees, tropical ornamental plants, and lawn to Chicago. Such garden and fruit tours, together with *Land of Sunshine* and *Sunset* magazine articles showing mansions with rose gardens and orange groves beneath the snow-covered San Gabriel Mountains, lured Anglo Americans to Southern California.[31] California governor Perkins, speaking excitedly to a horticultural fair in Los Angeles, even invented a new verb, *to emparadise*, as he praised the newcomers for populating the region with plants from around the globe.[32]

This was a profitable, productive Eden. Not all the citrus ranchers and orchard owners started off wealthy, but the labor exploitation of thousands of Native Americans, Mexicans, Asian immigrants, and white migrants helped them become wealthy. In Claremont, California, citrus rancher Lee Pitzer—the namesake of the progressive liberal arts college—built his orange empire with the labor of Sikh immigrant workers who were paid $25 to $50 per acre to prepare the land for cultivation. As historian Matt Garcia has shown, they hauled away boulders and later built canals, homes, and dormitories.[33]

From Riverside throughout the San Gabriel Valley, the prized seedless Washington navel orange, which required ample year-round labor, spawned a series of segregated settlements, *colonias*, and towns, an "instant townscape." Carey McWilliams reported that Riverside, Pasadena, and Redlands were the first cities in California to adopt ordinances regulating the size and arrangements of trees on public streets, resulting in beautifully laid-out "city-towns."[34] Booster literature from the 1890s described the scene this way: "There are few more beautiful cities than Riverside. Miles of beautiful avenues and streets, tree-lined, flower-bordered and sprinkled daily, so as to make driving a comfort and a pleasure.... There is not anywhere a sign of a fence, but green, carefully trimmed hedges, and rows of trees which embrace the eucalyptus, fan palms, Grevilleo, Robusta and Monterey Cypress."[35] Further south in Orange County and the coastal ranges, ranchers grew Valencia juice oranges, and since these required less year-round labor, rural and more sparsely populated settlements prevailed.[36]

Meanwhile, the newly rich citrus barons and elites who migrated here for the pleasant climate lived in estate homes with grand gardens. They were newcomers to the region too, striving to build new lives and investing ample fortunes in their residential estate gardens. Until the turn of the century, before the first landscape architects graduated from US programs, Southern California's grand gardens were designed largely by horticulturalists and nurserymen from England, Scotland, France, Belgium, and Germany.[37] These men brought garden ideas from their European horticultural backgrounds, but already there was an openness to California plants and to exotics (non-native plants) reaped from empire and expeditions. At the Wattles Estate garden in Hollywood, shown below, Alexander

Figure 10. Business elites favored Italianate garden styles with Italian cypress trees, palms, neatly trimmed hedges, topiaries, and terraces, but these gardens also included a potpourri of global influences. This photograph from 1926 shows the Wattles Estate garden, which was commissioned in 1907 by a businessman from Omaha who began "wintering" in Southern California. The Wattles Estate garden in Hollywood boasted a Japanese garden, an Italian rose garden, a palm court, and exotic plants from around the globe. Since 1975 part of the Wattles Estate has been the site of the Wattles Farm Community Garden. Courtesy of University of Southern California, on behalf of the USC Special Collections.

Urquhart served as head gardener from 1910 to 1930 and incorporated garden plants and ideas from Japan and Mexico into a garden of terraces and expansive lawns.

Many of the business elites liked Italianate garden style, but there were also influential outliers and eccentrics. In 1885, Charles Fletcher Lummis, a Harvard-educated East Coast newspaper writer, arrived in Los Angeles after walking 3,507 miles from Cincinnati. He would become one of the greatest champions of southwestern "Mission style," guided by romantic

Figure 11. This painting, by an unknown artist, hangs at the Charles Fletcher Lummis house and shows the rustic style of Arts and Crafts architecture and gardens that Lummis innovated and promoted. Photo by Michael Messner.

ideals of early California and the look of adobe California mission architecture. He promoted a uniquely imaginative California version of the Arts and Crafts style at his home, "El Alisal" (Place of the Sycamores), which one can still visit along the Arroyo Seco area and the 110 freeway that runs along Highland Park, between downtown Los Angeles and Pasadena. The house features local river boulders and rocks, a bricolage of missionlike arches and a bell tower, faux adobe walls, and thick, hand-hewed wooden doors that Lummis reportedly built and claimed should last one thousand years. Today, the garden is planted with succulents, cactus, and native plants set among dirt pathways and river rock boulders, but back in the day Lummis grew eucalyptus trees, roses, and a wide variety of chili peppers (another emblem of his Southwest taste), introducing a distinctive departure from the East Coast and midwestern styles. Other aficionados of anti-industrial craftsmanship built adobe houses planted with cactus, while wooden Craftsman bungalows surrounded by lawns, oaks, and shrubs became a popular vernacular.

The upper class, however, wanted European refinement, not rustic gardens. They favored aspects of Italian renaissance gardens, with axial designs, fountains, and parterres, and the warm climate allowed them to incorporate into this frame a potpourri of exotic ornamental plants that would not grow outdoors in Europe or back east. They enjoyed living and entertaining outdoors here, appreciating the views of well-tended gardens with rose bushes and palm trees from the comfort of vine-draped porches, with maybe some orange groves and snowcapped mountains in the distance.

These Gilded Age estate gardens reflected the United States' ascendant position in reconfigured arrangements of global power. Historian Vera Norwood suggests that they signaled the growing dominance of North America and local elites' adeptness in recreating European-style landscapes.[38] And specifically for elite women of the era, "this public display of American imperialism was balanced by the private meaning of their gardens as landscapes defining traditional womanhood."[39]

The residential garden became a vehicle for the expression of refined womanhood. On the East Coast, the wives of industrialists were hiring architects to design their homes and gardens on the basis of styles they had seen in Europe, and when done, they hired photographers to capture these people-less images on film.[40] This practice extended to the West Coast, with magazines such as *Architectural Digest,* and *California Southland* featuring photos of elaborate California residential gardens. Photographer Frances Benjamin Johnson first came to California to photograph the gardens of Phoebe Hearst in 1903, and in 1917 she returned to capture colored photos of estates in San Diego, Pasadena, Montecito, and Santa Barbara, which she later showed to national audiences. Perhaps predictably, they gave mixed reviews. Some critics thought there was too much color in these California gardens.[41]

Nineteenth-century power elites were striving to show their cultural refinement, status, and moral superiority through the appreciation of nature. While today "the appreciation of nature" commonly makes us think of Thoreau and Ralph Waldo Emerson retreating to the forest for reflection and solitude, the historian Rochelle L. Johnson reminds us that during this time gardening became a popular way to display such appreciation and thereby to show class distinction and gentility.[42] In the gardens of elites and the upper middle class, refinement would be attained by following the dictates of new horticultural designers and writers such as Andrew Jackson Downing. Gardening became an aspirational activity, so that "discerning reading and informed gardening were the pursuits of a person with good taste."[43] Neither pulp fiction nor harvesting a homely carrot would do, so by the 1890s the San Gabriel Valley featured numerous elaborate garden estates planted with exotic ornamentals. Garden clubs followed soon thereafter. New and improved hybrid plants pioneered by plant breeder Luther Burbank (1849–1926) in Santa Rosa, California, also found welcoming homes in Southern California gardens.

Millionaire migrants from the East Coast and the Midwest built palatial estate homes and gardens on Orange Grove Boulevard in Pasadena, which became known as "Millionaire's Row." Nineteenth-century American industrialists such as Adolph Busch (beer), William Wrigley Jr. (chewing gum), and David Gamble (son of Proctor & Gamble) settled here surrounded by gardens full of cycads, palms, succulents, citrus, and roses. As one observer of the day put it, "Nowhere else in the world had such a class of settlers been seen. Emigrants coming in palace-cars instead of 'prairie-schooners,' and building fine houses instead of log shanties, and planting flowers and lawn grass before they planted potatoes or corn."[44]

Collections of rare and exotic trees and big expanses of lawn telegraphed upper-class distinction in Southern California. These grand gardens included citrus and many nonproductive, non-fruit-bearing trees, brought from around the globe. The well-to-do showed off their status and affluence, and they took pleasure and sought healthy living in their private paradises. As Victoria Padilla's often-quoted observation put it, "In the eighties and nineties a man's status was symbolized by the sweep of the lawn that separated his house from the street and the number of specimen trees and palms that grew thereon. For such plantings conifers were often used, and the garden that did not have an araucaria, a deodar, a hedge of Monterey cypress, several oaks, and a pine or two was a poor place indeed."[45] Palm trees became popular in the late nineteenth century, and by the 1890s a plant specialist had counted thirty different types of palms in Santa Barbara, as well as other exotic trees from Asia, South

Africa, and the Mediterranean.[46] Australian eucalyptus were grown as windbreakers and also for ornamental purposes, as were acacia trees.

The estate gardens that concentrated in the sunshine below snow-capped mountains in Pasadena and the San Gabriel Valley towns drew breathless admiration. One excited newcomer in the 1890s wrote rhapsodically of Pasadena, "I am fascinated and enthralled by your sun-kissed, rose-embowered semi-tropical summerland of Hellenic sky and hills of Hymettus." Charles F. Holder, the journalist, businessman, and naturalist credited with starting the Tournament of Roses Parade for the elite Valley Hunt Club, wrote, "Nature seems always at her best, and the products of nearly every zone meet here. The banana and the pine, the palm and the apple grow in the same dooryard."[47] A 1915 *Sunset* magazine article summarized San Gabriel Valley estate gardens this way: from "Pasadena eastward for sixty miles the foothills of the orange belt are being transformed by the landscape gardeners of the financial elite."[48]

The Anglo-American elites were new migrants to the region, and they were reinventing themselves and the regional garden landscape. Palm trees, especially the slow-growing varieties such as the Chilean wine palm, conveyed aristocratic bearing and seemed to import a sense of imperial heft, providing an immediately manufactured history in a land where Europeans had not been settled for long. "Palm Drives" and "Palm Avenues" also conveyed a sense of regal distinction along boulevards and the long, winding driveways leading to private estates.

Throughout Southern California, but especially in the San Gabriel foothills near Pasadena, industrialists created parklike botanical gardens, assisted by European horticulturalists, nurserymen, and garden designers.[49] Abbott Kinney, under the sway of the Italian motif, developed Venice Beach as a residential and resort community, and he indulged in amateur botany and expressed his enthusiasm for citrus and eucalyptus trees on his 530-acre estate, "Kinneola," near Claremont and Sierra Madre. On the grounds of what now serves as the Los Angeles Arboretum and Botanic Garden in Arcadia, Elias J. "Lucky" Baldwin developed the Rancho Santa Anita into a wild fantasy garden, with palms, gingkoes from China, and Australian tea trees.

Of the two most celebrated public gardens of the era, only the Huntington remains. The other belonged to Adolphus Busch, and from 1906 until

Figure 12. "Palm Drives" and "Palm Avenues" became familiar sights in California. Courtesy of University of Southern California, on behalf of the USC Special Collections.

1928 it was a major tourist attraction of Southern California, serving as a marketing vehicle for Anheuser-Busch beer and delighting visitors with meandering pathways, sheep grazing on meadows, and a fairyland dell with Grimm's fairytale gnomes imported from Germany.[50] Looking at the photos with gnomes and figurines of forest animals, I am struck by how much Busch Gardens departed from the serious European estate gardens, already presaging the search for fantasy and fun in Southern California.

The display of power and the quest for pleasure came together most imperially at the Huntington estate, a vast European-style garden that

TERRACES, UPPER GARDEN

Figure 13. One of the most popular attractions in early twentieth-century Southern California was Busch Gardens, where visitors strolled along serpentine pathways among sunken gardens of terraced lawn planted with palms and pine trees. Courtesy of University of Southern California, on behalf of the USC Special Collections.

began when Henry E. Huntington, an industrialist of real estate, electricity, and water and the owner of the Pacific Electric Railway, purchased a 600-acre citrus and avocado ranch in San Marino in 1903. He built a Beaux Arts mansion for his second wife, Arabella Huntington (who happened to be his uncle's widow and was reportedly the wealthiest woman in the nation). Some believe that Henry Huntington built the garden to entice Arabella away from her homes in Paris and New York City, transforming a rough working ranch out west into a garden of gentility and graciousness. Beginning in 1905, Huntington commanded his German-born, Austrian-trained horticulturalist and "superintendent" of the estate, William Hertrich, to oversee the ranch, and he directed him to design and install a grand ornamental garden of collected exotics and Italian baroque

Figure 14. Upper-class residential gardens of Southern California in the early twentieth century often featured fountains, palms, and cycads (sago palms) around mansions inspired by those of European aristocracy, as this photo of the garden by the loggia of the Huntington Beaux Arts mansion shows. This item is reproduced by permission of The Huntington Library, San Marino, California.

fountains, a garden that would look as though it had been there since eternity. Hertrich had his hands full.

The task required ingenuity, the hard labor of many men, and William Hertrich's international expeditions to Mexico, Guatemala, Europe, Samoa, New Zealand, the Caribbean, and Europe in search of exotic rare plants, seeds, and bulbs. Hertrich designed the grounds with sweeping vistas, allées, fountains, and big lawns and organized the garden into distinctive areas, including clusters of giant bamboo, a rose garden, a lily pond, a palm garden, and a desert garden that now features more than ten thousand varieties of cacti and succulents. Hertrich reports in his memoir that he "transplanted desirable trees from wherever they could be found; some of them stood thirty to fifty feet high and weighed from ten to twenty tons apiece."[51] Using horse-drawn wagons, he brought mature palm trees from Los Angeles, Santa Barbara, and San Diego. He even brought two charred palms from the estate of Henry's uncle, Collis P. Huntington, that had caught fire in San Francisco's 1906 earthquake and fire (the palms recuperated and thrived in San Marino).

Huntington had the ambition and the means to command a grand-scale garden. When he became enamored of Japanese-style gardens, he purchased the entirety of a local commercial Japanese teahouse and garden on the corner of Fair Oaks and California Avenues in Pasadena, and he ordered Hertrich and his crew to transport and reassemble it on the estate. They completed the project in three months. The garden included a bright red drum bridge and a display including "a Japanese house complete with a Japanese family in residence who were expected to appear in kimono attire for guests."[52] World's Fairs routinely displayed these sorts of Orientalist colonial fantasies at the turn of the century, and Huntington could well afford to do the same at his private estate.

In Southern California, the making of these estate gardens rested on migration and a racialized and stratified system of design and labor. The Anglo-American elites employed European horticulturalists and garden designers to design the grand estate gardens and import their exotic ornamental plants, as well as Mexican and Asian immigrants to move the soil and tend the gardens. Many of the same Chinese, Japanese, Filipino, and Mexican migrant workers who tended the orange groves found employment in the estate gardens, but this labor force shifted over time. After the Chinese Exclusion Act of 1882, estate owners turned to Japanese and Mexican gardeners. Charles Saunders, a prolific garden writer, commented in 1926 that "if the average Californian's taste for excluding Asiatics extended to the plants of Asia as well as to people, the gardens of the state would be poorer by many a charming tree and shrub whose presence with us we owe to that wise old continent across the Pacific."[53]

Still other transnational influences arrived from Japan to Southern California gardens via the World's Fairs. Huntington was not unusual in wanting his own Japanese garden, for westerners became fascinated with Japanese aesthetics during the late nineteenth century. Japanese gardens, bonsai, and the art of flower arranging were directly promoted by the

Figure 15. The Japanese garden may be the most popular garden at the Huntington, and the moon bridge, commissioned by Huntington and built by Japanese craftsman Toichiro Kawai, remains a favored focal point. The Japanese-style garden has been open to the public since 1928. This item is reproduced by permission of The Huntington Library, San Marino, California.

Japanese nation-state through the vehicle of the World's Fairs of the late nineteenth and early twentieth centuries. In today's age of globalization and instant high-tech communication and travel, it's difficult for us to grasp the critical role of World's Fairs in disseminating ideas and styles. These gatherings were held nearly every two years between 1855 and 1914, and powerful nations literally assembled and displayed visual spectacles of their political, economic, and cultural power and status for viewers. These were shows of national cultural capital.

The first Japanese garden and teahouse built in the United States was created for the 1876 Philadelphia Centennial International Exhibition. Next, the Chicago Fair of 1893 featured a "Japan Building" and Imperial Japanese garden, purportedly inspiring Frank Lloyd Wright to incorporate lessons from Japanese architecture into his designs.[54] The Japanese government also sent garden installations to the 1894 California Midwinter International Exposition to San Francisco; since then, it has remained as the Japanese teahouse in Golden Gate Park, and copies of it appeared in Pasadena, San Diego, and elsewhere.[55] These installations grew bigger over time, and at the St. Louis Louisiana Purchase Exposition of 1903–4, Japan's exhibits covered nearly seven acres.[56] Scholar Carol Ann Christ argues that Japan expertly mastered modern forms of display and used them to raise their international status as an imperial power over China, consolidating a "colonizer's stance" in Asia.[57] Meanwhile, Anglo-Americans and designers on the East Coast and the West Coast, including Southern California, eagerly embraced the beauty, exoticism, and simplicity of Japanese garden styles. The Japanese influence also showed up in the simplicity and the low, broad proportions of Southern California's Craftsman homes.

GARDENS BEYOND THE ELITE ENCLAVES

How did the "golden age of gardening" affect nonelites of the region during this period, from the late nineteenth century through the 1920s? Developers and planners had designed Los Angeles to be "the nation's white spot," and racial segregation defined distinctive neighborhoods. Photos show white middle-class communities where simple farm houses and Craftsman bungalows had porches laden with potted plants, foundation plantings of hydrangeas and begonias in the shade and roses and geraniums in the sunny areas, and lawn in front. After the San Diego Panama California Exposition of 1915, which featured Spanish Colonial-style buildings (in what is today Balboa Park), many local real estate developers of the 1920s built stucco, pseudo-Spanish-style buildings.[58]

Anglo newcomers from the Midwest and the East were inspired by the possibilities of the mild climate to plant flamboyant, colorful ornamentals that smacked of the tropics. As Victoria Padilla recounted, "Many newcomers to Southern California, excited at finding themselves living in a land of no snow and but little frost, liked to believe that they were actually dwelling in the tropics and grasped at everything that would make their gardens suggestive of the more torrid zones. Geraniums, cannas, poinsettias, bougainvilleas, bananas—all those plants which are tenderly nurtured under protection in the East—were grown in abundance. Color became rampant, purple vied with crimson, magenta with orange, pink with scarlet, all a part of a southern California garden."[59]

These gardens sound lovely, but they probably would have failed as Veblenesque indicators of distinction. Garden elites and critics disdained their riotous jumble of color. Padilla, writing after World War II, asserted that in the 1920s "the average gardener had little real understanding of planting as practiced in a subtropical climate and little or no conception of the proper arrangement or selection of ornamentals." While she approved of the judicious expertise of the European horticulturalists who supervised the grand estate gardens in Santa Barbara and Pasadena, she deplored "many of the little homes that lined the streets," which "often displayed glaring inconsistencies and incongruities of plantings," and she concluded that "the sins of these amateur gardeners blotted many a landscape for years to come."[60] Even Carey McWilliams, who wrote trenchantly about the plight of migrant farmworkers and Japanese American internment, could not resist registering his disapproval, condemning "the petticoated palm tree" as "an abomination, a blot on the landscape, hideous beyond description." He also hated seeing bougainvilleas next to red geraniums. Writing in the early twentieth century, he wrote: "Even to this day, the landscaping of the region is incongruous, confused, and shows everywhere the absence of a developed tradition within the region." The garden photographer Frances Benjamin Johnston also piled on the criticism, claiming that amateur gardeners in San Diego seemed to "scorn the subtleties of color harmonies and contrasts" and to neglect "the important factors of continuous blooms, or of carefully considered design in their garden plans."[61]

Cultural critics may have deplored the way white working-class suburban gardens combined ornamental and productive plants (a garden style

Figure 16. In the 1920s, Southern California real estate developers built stucco, Spanish-style homes, and many dwellers planted colorful ornamental gardens with bougainvillea and palm trees. Here, workers transport a mature palm tree to one of these developments in 1926. Courtesy of University of Southern California, on behalf of the USC Special Collections.

that is once again popular in the early twenty-first century). South Gate, established in the 1920s, seven miles south of downtown Los Angeles, featured single-detached homes and gardens, but as historian Becky Nicolaides has shown, these backyards were initially valued for the utilitarian production of food for home consumption, sale, and barter. Until the postwar era, many Southern California residents, like Americans elsewhere in the country, regularly mixed work and leisure in their home gardens as they grew vegetables and fruit trees and tended rabbits, chickens, ducks, and geese, producing food both for family consumption and for sale. A report from a University of Southern California sociology dissertation gives us an idea of how residents actively used their yards in the working-class suburb of Bell Gardens during the 1930s: "Children play in the streets, on lawns, and in dusty dooryards. Women dig industrously [*sic*], sit in a spot of shade, or perhaps wash clothes in the open. Men work in gardens, on houses, or on automobiles. On a sunny afternoon, people are to be seen everywhere."[62] People were gardening, but this was part of their livelihood, and in the process they were creating not a private paradise but a public culture on driveways, in yards, and on sidewalks. Residential gardens here took on public dimensions.

Another gardening development of this era was the construction of "small farm homes" of the 1920s. According to Rachel A. Surls, these were homesteads built on one-half- to three-acre lots in the San Fernando and San Gabriel Valleys, vigorously promoted by the LA Chamber of Commerce and marketed primarily to white midwesterners. The agricultural writer Edward James Wickson published *The California Vegetables in Gardens and Fields* in 1913, advocating the growing of small and medium-sized vegetable and flower gardens as the route to health, virtue, and self-reliance.[63] By 1930, there were five thousand of these small farms producing flowers, food, and chickens, and together with the citrus industry this allowed LA County to reign as the top-producing agricultural county in the nation until the 1950s.[64] Alien Land Laws ensured that these small farms stayed out of the hands of Asian immigrants, while Mexican workers lived in segregated *colonias* near the orange groves where they worked.[65]

It wasn't all one fragrant flower garden, but even poor, working-class, foreign-born immigrants and racial ethnic minorities had gardens of their own. Racial segregation—what historian Matt Garcia referred to as "a Southern California brand of Jim Crowism"—characterized Southern California neighborhoods in the early twentieth century.[66] The Mexican citrus workers of the San Gabriel Valley settled in *colonias*, segregated worker settlements outside the city, and used their garden spaces for both productive vegetables and ornamental gardens. A reporter writing in 1920 in the *Los Angeles Examiner* on the Mexican *colonia* in La Verne citrus housing observed that in Mexican *colonias* "little gardens of hollyhock and phlox brighten the place and the swarthy women and children swarming about the cottages plainly rest there in love of home."[67] A senior thesis at Pomona College in 1932 reported on the varied quality of homes where Mexicans lived but concluded that "all of the houses, whether of the rich or poor, are brightened by the gay flowers so dear to the heart of the

Mexican woman."[68] And a Protestant reformer of the 1920s described "deplorable housing conditions" where Mexicans lived in El Monte but also noted that some included "humble dwellings of four and five rooms" with "clean yards, neat homes, and flowers everywhere."[69]

In the early twentieth century, Mexicans became home owners and tended their own gardens. According to historian Douglas Monroy, real estate companies subdivided tracts and sold homes to Mexicans for about $600 during World War I, and these tracts became "garden spots," where Mexican residents "understood themselves to be reestablishing Mexican communities in the new land."[70] When the economist Paul Taylor visited the citrus belt *colonias* in the 1920s, he was startled to find how many Mexicans in the *colonias* of Azusa, Claremont, Covina, El Monte, La Verne, Pasadena, La Puente, and Upland had homes of their own, many with gardens.[71] Before World War I, Mexicans also rented crowded, substandard housing near downtown Los Angeles, and a 1913 report of the house courts where Mexicans lived on Hollenbeck Street describes these dwellings having "minute gardens, seeds having been supplied through the Commission by a benevolent lady."[72] Evictions disrupted social life at the house courts and forced these Mexican families into "leaving the cherished gardens behind," but the LA Housing Commission assisted Mexican families with renting or purchasing small plots, where they resumed growing vegetables and flowers.[73] With the Mexican Revolution, Mexican families of diverse social classes, including teachers, lawyers, doctors, and entertainers with upper-class lifestyles and values, migrated and resettled in Southern California, so it is likely that they brought different gardening conventions.[74]

GARDENING LABOR

Familiarity working with plants allowed workers and racialized immigrants to create spaces of autonomy and economic livelihood outside the citrus fields. Chinese, Russian, Japanese, and Italian immigrants developed "truck gardens," often using family labor to grow vegetables on small plots, and then either sold vegetables in downtown Los Angeles at the city market created in 1909 or transported vegetables in trucks to their consumers in outlying areas. Chinese truck farmers sold produce directly to citrus workers in the San Gabriel Valley and to railroad workers.[75] Some moved into gardening and landscaping too, and Mexican men found work as groundskeepers and gardeners at the Claremont colleges and residential gardens of the rich in the 1920s.[76]

It was Japanese immigrants and Japanese Americans, however, who invented the occupation of residential maintenance gardening. They also developed plant and flower nurseries, cultivating carnations and chrysanthemums for sale as cut flowers, as well as plants for sale to local residents looking to spruce up their yards. For them, the nurseries and gardens became a suburban source of ethnic entrepreneurship and eventually the means of upward social mobility. While many Chinese men went into laundry service, setting up shops in Chinatowns, the Chinese did not go into domestic gardening work. Both Chinese and Japanese immigrant men had performed outsourced domestic household chores, and both groups worked as truck farmers, so this raises the question, Why did the Chinese not go into gardening? It is possible that the Japanese were viewed as more aesthetically desirable and less offensive than the Chinese, who were associated in late nineteenth-century xenophobic campaigns with the Yellow Peril, immorality, prostitution, and opium dens.

While the World's Fairs whetted Anglo-American aesthetic appetites for Japanese gardens, bonsai, and the art of flower arranging, China and Chinese aesthetics remained closed off to the world. Moreover, in California, Chinese cultivation was seen as inferior and filthy. Many Anglos believed that Chinese cultivation of vegetables, which reputedly involved human feces and urine, was filthy and repugnant. An 1886 editorial in the Auburn *Stars and Stripes* newspaper declared: "Ever since the establishment of Chinese gardens, the residents of this place, and more especially those living in certain localities peculiarly exposed to the miasmata arising from the gardens, have been subject to endemic and epidemic diseases, and the rate of mortality, particularly among children, has been absolutely fearful to contemplate. . . . The evil consists mainly in the Chinese mode of cultivation, which is filthy and disgusting in the extreme."[77] With their backgrounds in household domestic service, agriculture, and truck farming, Chinese immigrant men in this era may have tried to work in domestic gardening, but their attempts would have been thwarted by Anglo hostility and exclusion as well as by Japanese competitive protection of their gardening occupational sector.[78]

Although the Issei (first-generation Japanese immigrant) gardeners had been tending to their employers' yards as early as the 1890s, it was in the 1920s that the maintenance gardening occupation began developing rapidly among Japanese Americans in Los Angeles. Los Angeles by then had an expanding number of suburban neighborhoods with detached homes and garden-filled yards, and affluent white home owners began hiring Japanese gardeners to do maintenance upkeep. Japanese gardeners worked in various yards, developing a route of paying customers. Anglo-American fear, hatred, and anxiety about the growing economic power of the Japanese had by then resulted in legislation that pushed the Japanese from land ownership and into the laboring class. Rather than the traditional "push pull" model of international migration, this dynamic involved California Anglo-Americans pushing the Japanese foreign-born out of independent land ownership and into wage labor. This was a racially defined restrictionist movement. The California Alien Land Law, which was passed in 1913, denied aliens ineligible for citizenship the right to own land in the state of California, but historians agree that the law targeted primarily the Japanese. The intent of the law, and of its subsequent amendment in 1920, was to drive the Japanese out of agriculture and truck farming, eliminating their competition with white farmers.

Farming experience in Japan and California, racist legislation, and the ability to leverage images associated with Japanese horticultural aesthetics and artistic talent facilitated the entry of Japanese immigrant men into the gardening occupation in Southern California, while a context of racial discrimination and hostility prevented them from finding opportunities for advancement in the wider economy. As they were dispossessed of their land, they moved to the cities and suburbs, including into boardinghouses in LA's early Japanese ethnic enclaves, where they started their own suburban maintenance gardening businesses.[79] Racism and exclusion pushed them toward domestic gardening.

By the 1930s, maintenance gardening was institutionalized as a Japanese American man's job not only in Southern California but all along the West Coast, including Oregon and Washington. Gendered and ethnic hiring networks and small crews consisting of brothers, uncles, and cousins prevailed, and Mexican immigrant men followed in their footsteps.

THE FORCED MIGRATION OF WATER

As population and development in Southern California grew, so did water needs. The story of how water came to Southern California is complex and dramatic, and the politics, economics, and technology of Southern California water could easily fill an entire book series. Here, I emphasize three points.

First, Southern California water is imported from elsewhere, flowing hundreds of miles from Northern California and the Colorado River before it ever reaches a sprinkler of a suburban lawn here. The water system remains the most massive metropolitan hydraulic system the world has ever seen, and all of the lush Southern California gardens and bountiful agriculture depend on water that migrates hundreds of miles from the north to this dry region. Some of this water travels four-hundred-plus miles and then flows uphill, climbing the Tehachapi Mountains, the site of two active earthquake fault lines.

Second, thirsty gardens absorb a good deal of this imported water. And because of the prominence of single-unit homes with front and back yards, as much as 70 percent of residential household water use here occurs outdoors, watering lawns, filling swimming pools, and quenching the thirst of exotic plants that were imported from tropical rain forests.

Finally, water is a commodity, and in Southern California the Metropolitan Water District (MWD) controls, distributes, and sells water over a huge swath of land, from Ventura County to the US-Mexico border.[80] The MWD formed in 1927 to provide water for the Southern California region, and today it encompasses twenty-six cities and water districts, providing drinking water to nineteen million people in six Southern California counties. Developers, the water utility companies, agribusiness, business owners, and residents have all colluded in this project to shape nature so that water demands in this semiarid environment of Southern California are largely fed by imported sources. Water is also engineered to flow uphill—toward money, as the saying goes—and bought and sold.

As Maria Kaika has put it, water is a "materially produced commodity" that is "neither purely natural, nor purely a human product."[81] Expanding population and the lawn-dominated suburban gardens of the late twentieth century have consistently raised water requirements in Southern California.

POSTWAR SUBURBAN GARDENS

In the affluent postwar years, Southern California pioneered the expansion of suburban homes with pools, patios, and ornamental gardens designed for nuclear family leisure, a process facilitated by government measures such as the Federal Housing Administration and the GI Bill.[82] Thousands of domestic migrants had poured into Southern California, drawn by aerospace and manufacturing jobs and a good life symbolized by backyard barbecues and sons mowing big lawns. The California dream of living in a detached home with pool, patio, and garden became a new template of aspiration, one achieved through white flight and racial covenants.[83] New "ranch-style" homes and gardens popularized in the 1950s, inspired by earlier designs from Southern California architect Cliff May, had big plateglass windows that brought in light and a view of the residential gardens, and many featured backyard patios that would serve as outdoor living and dining rooms.[84]

Leisure gardens became a big business. With the shift from productive to ornamental residential gardens, new products and businesses proliferated, including plant nurseries, chemical fertilizers and herbicides, and lawn mower shops. Suburban residential gardens now prompted more mass consumption as home owners bought landscaping plants to fill their front and back yards. In 1949, California surpassed New York in nursery sales, and since then California has remained the national leader in nursery sales.[85] New chemical products appeared and promised glossy garden results. DDT was first used during World War II to control malaria and typhus, but by the 1940s and 1950s it was also widely used as an insecticide on American lawns. Later in the 1970s Monsanto would introduce Roundup and genetically altered plants that would withstand the chemicals designed to kill weeds and insects.[86]

Locally, government and industry devised new plants to populate the expanding residential suburban gardens of Southern California. Between 1957 and 1991, legislation authorized the Plant Introduction Program at the Los Angeles County Arboretum and at three other regional public botanical gardens expressly for the purpose of breeding and propagating new plants for the rapidly developing suburban residential gardens of Southern California. The program produced trees that would not be too tall for small yards, small shrubs with long-lasting floral display, and attractive glossy and evergreen leaves (not the paler green-gray leaves of the less thirsty plants, which characterize the Mediterranean plants popular today). Plants with blue flowers, such as *Agapanthus* 'Ellamae' (a.k.a. lily of the Nile) and blue hibiscus, became fashionable, and by the 1970s and 1980s smog-tolerant and fire-resistant plants were being developed. All of these were purely ornamental plants designed to adorn suburban gardens; not one was a food plant.[87] New hybrids for suburban gardens proliferated, and according to landscape scholar Christopher Grampp by the 1980s California nurseries regularly offered "more than 3,000 species of plants, many genetically engineered to yield showy flowers and strong scent, long stems, uniformly straight trunks, rapid growth, extended germination periods, insect and disease resistance, and hardiness."[88]

These efforts allowed for the mass marketing of exotic plants that had once graced only the grand estate gardens of Southern California. Now these plants—many of them originally imported from other continents— were reengineered and shrunk to suit the smaller lots, adorning modest-sized suburban tract homes with a wide variety of colorful foundation plantings too. As tract homes expanded, so did plant nurseries filled with colorful annuals, shrubs, gardening tools, chemical fertilizers and pesticides, and packaged potting soil.[89] Magazines such as *Better Homes and Gardens* and *Sunset* celebrated 1950s-style middle-class women's domesticity, joining the cult of true womanhood with gardening. Flower shows, garden clubs, magazines and flower arrangement classes taught women how to get it just right.

Domesticity extended from the kitchen into the backyard. "Where should the house stop and the garden begin?" This was the title of a 1952 *Sunset* magazine article.[90] The ranch-style home with a residential garden and patio designed for outdoor living took inspiration from the Spanish patio and yet seems to have been an autochthonous project, one devised, produced, and disseminated from Southern California. For the growing suburban middle class in Southern California, outdoor living in the patio and garden became an important leisure ideal.

Beyond serving as a setting for wholesome nuclear family activities, middle-class suburban home gardens incorporated new styles and symbols that American GIs brought home with them from tours of duty in the South Pacific, such as the transnational "tiki" or pseudo-Polynesian style. In his business, garden designer Wade Graham reports excavating Southern California backyards, finding remnants of "tiki"-style gardens full of pseudo-Polynesian statues, bars constructed out of lava rocks, and overgrown tropical plants, such as giant bird of paradise and monsteras. Graham makes a case for the liberating, sensual qualities of these suburban backyard gardens: "Tiki represented everything that the GIs and every other average postwar American craved after years of Depression and war but weren't allowed by the pedantic, puritanical modernist priests and purists who controlled the design PR machinery. It was fundamentally and loudly 'about' taboo things, and it wasn't subtle: it prominently featured images of bare-breasted women—often of dark complexion— dancing in the firelight, in primitive tableaux made of premodern materials such as bamboo and volcanic rock, and cocktails—lots of cocktails."[91]

Who wouldn't like to enjoy cocktails in a sensual tropical fantasy garden? But I think we can also recognize the tiki garden as a colonial masculinist fantasy. As Margaret Salazar-Porzio has shown in her analysis of the development of Shelter Island in San Diego, these Polynesian-inflected built environments served as material manifestations of US empire and military might in the Pacific, as symbolic trophies of American imperialism that the GIs brought back after World War II.[92] Similarly, the private tiki backyard gardens celebrated male adult leisure, forming the accessible outdoor suburban stand-in for something like the den or the Playboy club, echoing the comfort of global triumph and postwar affluence, and replacing the toolshed or the greasy car engine with a new fun outdoor gathering space of prosperous male domesticity.

Finally, another striking feature of the tiki gardens is the extent to which many of these appear to have been homemade. This is quite a contrast to the upper-middle-class outsourcing of gardening that prevails today, underscoring the postwar practice of self-reliance and a thrifty approach to residential garden making. Members of the newly comfortable middle class were doing the labor of making and maintaining their own gardens, not hiring landscape designers, architects, and low-wage immigrant gardeners.

The grand estate gardens of Southern California had declined in the 1930s, but the smaller suburban tract homes and residential gardens that developed in the mid- and late twentieth century were rigorously planted with water-absorbing lawns, raising regional water requirements. This thirst was partially addressed by the further development of the coerced migration of water with the Colorado River Aqueduct in 1941. Urban and environmental studies professor Robert Gottlieb reports that by the 1960s more than eighty cities had sprung up in Los Angeles County, enabled by annexation to the MWD, and discussions for importing still more water were imbued with many unrealistic assumptions and proposals, including one to bring water from the Pacific Northwest and British Columbia. "Even the fanciful concept of towing icebergs from Alaska to Southern California appeared from time to time," he writes.[93] While Los Angeles County had remained the highest-earning agricultural county in the nation in the 1940s and 1950s, by the 1960s the open landscapes with citrus orchards, walnut groves, and small truck farms had been replaced by tract housing developments. Green lawns and residential gardens became the new big water guzzlers.

BLACK MIGRANTS

Black migrants from the South came to Los Angeles in search of jobs, in hopes of leaving behind southern-style Jim Crow segregation, and in part, guided by home and garden dreams too. More than half of the early Spanish pueblo settlers had African multiracial roots, but significant numbers of African American migrants from the South came first in the 1880s and 1890s, when they found jobs mostly in services, with the women concentrated in domestic work and the men working as barbers, railroad porters, waiters, and janitors. By 1930, 87 percent of black women and 40 percent of black men worked in domestic service, but historical records suggest that most African Americans here did not work in agriculture or as residential gardeners.[94] This was perhaps because of the close association of these occupations with the plantation. Furthermore, since Asian, Mexican, and white migrant workers were already working in the fields here, those groups had a ready-made route to residential gardening jobs. And given the racial hostility and discrimination against African Americans, it is also possible that many white home owners were reluctant to employ black men as residential gardeners.

Yet homes and gardens of their own were a draw for black newcomers to Southern California. In a 1913 article, "Colored California," W. E. B. DuBois, the most prominent scholar writing about race in that era, described the black residents he met in early twentieth-century Los Angeles as "without doubt the most beautifully housed group of colored people in the United States."[95] Segregation policies shaped Southern California, but by 1910, 40 percent of African Americans who lived here were home owners (this at a time when only 2.4 percent of blacks in New York City and 8 percent in Chicago were home owners), leading DuBois to proclaim Los Angeles as a housing mecca for blacks.[96] The vast expanse of Los Angeles kept the price of property affordable, and the relatively small size of the black population may have minimized white racial hostility to black home ownership, although racially restricted housing covenants prevailed.

Later during World War II, thousands of black migrants from Arkansas, Louisiana, Oklahoma, Texas, and Mississippi came to Los Angeles for wartime jobs, settling in Little Tokyo, along Central Avenue, and in South Central Los Angeles. They found employment first in wartime munitions plants and then in postwar car, tire, and steel plants and in aerospace firms, such as Hughes Aircraft in Culver City and McDonnell Douglas in Santa Monica. According to historian Josh Sides, the majority of these black migrants came from metropolitan areas, not farms.[97] It's hard to know the extent to which rural traditions of tending crops and kitchen gardens were prevalent among the majority. An African American community gardening advocate that I interviewed suggested that kitchen gardens of black home owners in Los Angeles remained hidden in backyards for reasons of racial safety, as a part of a legacy of slavery, but I was not able to corroborate this. Regardless of the metropolitan origins of black migrants who came to LA in the mid-twentieth century, African Americans are today growing southern homeland foods such as collard greens and okra in community gardens in Watts and Altadena. Most black home owners in Los Angeles have lawn, shrubs, and trees in their gardens.

Deindustrialization and economic restructuring in the 1970s and 1980s would erode the manufacturing base of jobs, leading to African American class bifurcation. By 2000, 43 percent of LA's working-age African Americans were unemployed, living in poverty and underclass urban neighborhoods, while African American professionals and business owners were settled in beautifully landscaped residential communities such as Baldwin Hills and Ladera Heights, sometimes in homes with lush gardens tended by Mexican immigrant gardeners.

NEW IMMIGRANT INFLUENCES

Since the 1980s, three migration patterns have shaped gardens in Southern California. The first is growing socioeconomic inequality, characteristic of many global cities during this period, which has redefined the social and environmental landscape between the haves and the have-nots in Southern California. By 2000, the Los Angeles region was among the most economically segregated regions in the country.[98] This is not necessarily a chasm between newcomers and fifth-generation Angelenos. Vast disparities of socioeconomic status characterize contemporary immigrant communities in Southern California, with many Taiwanese, South Asian, and Iranian newcomers enjoying high levels of education, professional status, and financial capital, while Mexican, Guatemalan, and Salvadoran immigrants are at the bottom echelons in all of these indicators, and Koreans, Armenians, and some Chinese immigrants fall somewhere in between. Social class does not entirely dictate garden-making resources, but it does circumscribe access to property, plants, labor, and time for garden making and enjoyment. Today, Mexican immigrant men fill positions as residential maintenance gardeners, while wealthy Taiwanese and Chinese immigrants have been included in shaping and financing displays of Chinese garden culture at the region's premier botanical garden.

The second pattern is increasing racial and ethnic diversity in many of the Southern California residential suburbs that were predominantly white in the 1950s and 1960s, a trend that reflects both the migration of affluent and middle-class Asian immigrants and the growing number of upwardly mobile second- and later-generation Mexican Americans.[99] To some extent this has happened in Orange County, Ventura County, the San Fernando Valley, and elsewhere in Southern California, but it has been particularly notable in the San Gabriel Valley, where the first suburban Chinatown formed in Monterey Park between 1960 and 1990, as Chinese immigrants bought suburban homes and white home owners fled.[100] The entire west San Gabriel Valley, a suburban landscape that encompasses many municipalities, is now racially diverse, with residents of European, Asian, and Mexican descent, leading geographer Wei Li to call it an "ethnoburb," while another scholar classifies it as a "majority-Asian American and Latina/o space."[101] The San Fernando Valley, once predominantly white, now includes many suburban areas with Mexican, Central American, Armenian, and African American communities too.

Third, because Mexican immigration in recent decades far outstripped the volume of any other international migration stream, Southern California has seen a return to Mexican roots, and significant numbers of Central American immigrants are shaping the region as well. While demographers agree that new immigration to Southern California has declined since the 1980s and 1990s, there are many lasting impacts on the landscape. Residential cities that were once predominantly white Anglo-American, such as Anaheim, South Gate, and Downey, are now Latino, and neighborhoods that were until recently African American, like Inglewood and Compton, also now have a majority of Latino residents, predominantly Mexicans. LA's urban core is predominantly Latino, and as growing numbers of Latinos have become home owners they have moved to suburbs too.[102] Some Mexican immigrant home owners have begun growing corn in their front yards in East Los Angeles, but their residential gardens are far more diverse than this, usually containing lawns and roses.

"It is a sort of island on the land," Helen Hunt Jackson purportedly said about Southern California, but now it is an island of plants and people from around the globe.

In Southern California, perhaps even more than anywhere else, gardens are palimpsests, cultivated in layers by the diverse migrations of plants, people, and water. Garden making here shows power and conquests that have included violence, coerced labor, chicanery, waves of ethnic succession, exploitation, and exclusion. But gardens here has also been about the quest for the promised land of milk and honey, a "reinvented Eden" full of flowers, fragrance, and fruit. Through our daily practice, we are still collectively writing the story of Southern California gardens, laying down new layers over past sedimentations. It remains an unfinished story. Yet a contemporary visitor to Southern California can hardly miss seeing how residential gardening here now relies on environmentally unsustainable practices and on the labor of mostly Mexican immigrant men, the topic of the next chapter.

3 The Gardeners of Eden

It's noisy in the suburbs. From eight o'clock in the morning until dusk (8:30 p.m. in the summer), blowers and mowers are buzzing continuously. Only constant immigrant labor and the most efficient gas-powered machinery can keep private home gardens looking the way they do now in Southern California, which is to say mostly like perfect patches of paradise. Private residential gardening is now outsourced to Latino immigrant men who tend to plant life and debris outdoors, while Latina nannies and housekeepers tend to human life and its detritus indoors.

Ramon Espinoza is one in this vast army of immigrant gardeners. Six days a week he starts early, rising at 5:30 a.m. in his cozy family home in Inglewood, near LAX. He picks up his two employees in Los Angeles, and the three of them cram into the cab of *la Toyotita*, a tiny truck overloaded with mowers, blowers, hoes, rakes, and shovels. When traffic is flowing, they career down the 405 to the San Fernando Valley. At one house after another, they scurry out, his younger workers (who are also kin) doing the heavier work, unloading machinery, mowing, edging, and trimming. Fifty-four year-old Ramon first walks through the yard, checking out what needs to be cut and cleaned up, armed with clippers hanging from a leather tool belt so that he can prune stray branches or deadhead dry

Figure 17. In the 1950s, postwar prosperity allowed many middle-class families to purchase homes in new tract developments. Fathers and sons performed suburban masculine domesticity by mowing lawns. Photo by Fred A. Raab.

blossoms. Next, he trudges along with one of the much-maligned blowers to ensure that not one leaf or twig is left on the patio, the driveway, or the sidewalk. "The clients don't want to see any of that. They need to see everything clean," he confirms. "That's why they are paying me." By the end of the day, Ramon and his crew will have slogged through a dozen residential gardens, both front and back yards, including larger properties in the posh Westside enclaves like Pacific Palisades and Bel Air. This is the new California dream-escape, and from modest bungalow to sprawling estate, it's always immaculately mowed and manicured.

In the classic postwar California dream, father and son mowed the front lawn together. The iconic photo above shows a young boy pushing a mower over a pristinely trimmed green lawn and, in the background, the dad with the edger and the neighbor's sleek trophy car. It's full of straight lines and triangles, suggesting both the antiseptic triumph of newly conquered nature and the glories of suburban comfort. To leave no doubt that this is domestic masculinity in motion—and that the suburb is the final

Figure 18. Today, most lawns in Southern California are mowed by Latino immigrant gardeners. Photo by Nathan Solis.

frontier—the boy carries a rifle and wears a Davy Crockett coonskin cap and a fringed jacket. The boy is my husband today, and this photo graced the book jacket of his memoir, *King of the Wild Suburb.*

On television shows like *Leave It to Beaver,* boys and men just like him pushed simple reel mowers on placid lawns surrounded by white picket fences. I still remember the old-fashioned, mechanical sound it makes because my father pushed one on Saturday afternoons too and finished with an edger, cutting big ugly gaping holes in the grass growing around the sprinkler heads. He also mowed other people's lawns and tended their begonias when he worked as a gardener in Atherton and Woodside. That's where Silicon Valley's high-tech billionaires live today, but in the 1950s and 1960s those mansions and sprawling ranch-style homes were filled with the families of San Francisco's financial elites. Until the 1970s, paid gardeners on the West Coast tended rich people's residential gardens, and most of the gardeners were Japanese American. Middle-class families then relied on fathers and sons to mow the lawns, but today that is a rare sight in the middle-class neighborhoods of California. Unpaid male family labor is now replaced by Latino immigrant gardeners like Ramon and his crew. These *jardineros* work six days a week, often with their own family members. Fathers and sons are still mowing the lawn, but these are now Mexican men and their sons tending other people's private gardens.

As the suburbs expanded in late nineteenth-century America, the man mowing the lawn and the lady as manager of the home and garden defined new gender ideals that reached their apogee in the postwar era, as the GI Bill swelled the ranks of suburban home owners. Today, this gendered template of women tending to life in the domestic interiors and men tending to the domestic exteriors still lingers, but now it is increasingly Latino immigrant women and men doing this work for others. Latina nannies, housecleaners, and caregivers work indoors, while Latino immigrant gardeners tend to the plant life and the dirty work of mowing lawns and removing fallen leaves outdoors.

Domesticas and *jardineros* are gendered mirror images, dual vestiges of nineteenth- and twentieth-century ideals that take shape in new racial, immigrant, and class formations. Unlike many brown and black men, Latino immigrant gardeners can freely circulate in white middle-class and upscale neighborhoods and stride through private gates into other people's backyards. Their tool-laden trucks and mowers and blowers serve as their passports. When I interviewed and surveyed nannies and housecleaners in Los Angeles for my book *Domestica*, I learned that many of them crave and occasionally form close personal relations with the children and families where they work.[1] By contrast, the gardeners do not perform intimate care work. They remain outsiders, physically outside the house, and socially outside the mainstream, dismissed and disparaged as unskilled purveyors of noise-blasting "mow, blow, and go" gardening services. Their work supports the conspicuous consumption of domesticated nature and the nonproductive lawn, helping to maintain high property values in Southern California and reminding us of the saliency of many of the insights from Thorstein Veblen's 1899 classic book *The Theory of the Leisure Class*.

In this chapter I show how the immigrant gardener labor system involves a triangle of dreams that connect home owners, route-owner gardeners (who own the trucks and the tools), and the *ayudantes* (helpers, the paid employees of the head gardeners). The home owners want residential dreamscapes, impeccably maintained home lawns and gardens, and the Latino gardeners seek living wages and economic solvency. Sometimes the gardeners hire relatives or bring family members to the job on weekends and school vacations, and they do so because they are trying to get ahead. Everyone is chasing a different dream, and gardens, money, and labor connect them in an expansive web that stretches across the big properties and smaller suburban tracts of Southern California. Relying on audio-recorded interviews with Latino immigrant gardeners, home owners, and a handful of landscape designers, this chapter reveals how paid residential gardening is organized, how it shapes the gardens and ultimately all of us who live here. Ethnic succession and gender succession characterize these changes in residential gardening labor. Everyone has come to Southern California in search of the good life, and residential gardens and gardening are pathways to those California dreams. Latino immigrant men perform the hard labor, and other groups reap the benefits.

WHY ARE SO MANY CALIFORNIANS HIRING GARDENERS NOW?

People in the West are supposed to be independent and self-reliant, and Californians love the outdoors. You would think Californians would be rushing out to embrace nearby nature in their front and back yards, toning their abs as they mow and eagerly sinking their hands in the soil to claim authentic, organic, ecological virtue. To understand why that is not happening (or is occurring in very selective ways), we need to pan out to a broader macrostructural focus. Crucial social transformations have now set the stage for many Californians to hire Latino immigrant gardeners.

First, the US economy and society are characterized by more inequality than half a century ago. While not everyone shared in the prosperity of the postwar years, the United States experienced increased income equality from the 1950s to the 1970s, when the GI Bill, government supports for education and housing, and a strong manufacturing base fueled an expanding middle class. Since the 1970s, deindustrialization, globalization, and the replacement of government solutions and protections with market dynamics have led to job polarization throughout the United States. By the 1990s, Los Angeles had emerged with the dubious distinction of having higher inequality than most other US cities.[2] In metropolitan areas such as

Los Angeles, a managerial and professional class emerged that is now fully accustomed to purchasing a myriad of services that their families once did themselves. A Latino immigrant laboring class now does that work of washing cars, cleaning homes, caring for kids and the elderly, and staffing all types of restaurants. In this new gilded age, gardening is one more expression of outsourced domestic work.

Second, the cultural meanings and social uses of residential yards have changed over time too. The front yard is for public viewing, and the back-yard has become a privatized space of leisure—although, paradoxically, there is now less time for leisure. Middle-class home gardens, observes the landscape architect Christopher Grampp, have morphed from utilitarian productive spaces to "outdoor family rooms," places for unwinding and entertaining.[3] With its propitious climate, Southern California pioneered this trend in the 1950s, but I would argue that economic uncertainty and the stress of public work life have exacerbated the need for cocooning in these private leisure gardens. People seek leisure, outdoor beauty, and the protection of property value, not labor, in their home gardens, so there are new expectations of garden perfection. This has led to a dual trend: the veneration of leisure gardening and the popularization of DIY or do-it-yourself alongside the hiring of Latino gardeners to do the heavier, regular maintenance and the less immediately gratifying garden chores.

A third factor that explains the hiring of gardeners and landscape serv-ices has to do with property values. Guided by real estate lust, middle-class and affluent Americans have been pouring more money into their home gardens and yards, but this has fluctuated wildly from the early mil-lennial real estate boom years and the bust of the Great Recession. The National Gardening Association (NGA), an organization that conducts market research for industry, reports that the amount Americans spend on lawn and landscape services ballooned from $25 billion in 2001 to $45 billion in 2006 and then declined to $30 billion in 2009.[4] This includes money spent on weekly garden and lawn maintenance services, as well as on landscape design services and installation. The big market crash that began in 2007, the real estate bust, and contraction in new construction account for the decline. In Southern California before the Great Recession, real estate prices had soared, and professional landscape designers, con-tractors, and some gardeners had benefited from these price spikes.

"Flippers," real estate investors looking to make quick profits, purchased run-down properties and hired landscapers and gardeners to spruce up the yards. Many home owners spent more freely too, confident that there would be financial returns. A young landscape designer told me that when she had first started, "people were wanting to put a lot of money into their landscape to really build up their home prices, but that's not the case now." Shaking her head, and lamenting her diminished earnings, she said, "It's definitely a different mind-set now." Still, home prices here remain among the highest in the nation, with the median home value of owner-occupied homes in LA County remaining at a half million dollars throughout the financial crisis, when diminishing incomes and joblessness brought hardship to many.[5] As we will see in more depth, Latino gardeners also feel the squeeze.

A fourth factor in explaining the growth of paid gardening labor in recent decades is women's continued entrance into full-time employment, coupled with the emergence of new meanings of involved motherhood and fatherhood and new demands for high-performance children. These elevated standards of child rearing and achievement have also changed home gardens. Families with children at home report that they are all strapped for time, and Americans are working longer days and weeks. In her classic book *The Overworked American*, economist Juliet Schor showed that during the 1970s and 1980s work hours increased across American industries and across low-, middle-, and high-income categories, prompting a new generation of Americans to work for a full month more than their immediate predecessors had. A more recent study of dual-earner families raising children in Los Angeles concludes that outdoor leisure has become "a fading commodity for families pulled in many directions."[6] Who has time for gardening?

We are all familiar with the multitasking, time-squeezed mothers and the "second shift" of housework that employed women do, but also notable in recent decades are rising standards of involved fatherhood and new expectations for middle-class youth to achieve in school and in extracurricular activities. Fathers are now expected to become actively engaged dads, changing diapers, overseeing bath time and homework, and volunteering as coaches in youth sport leagues. Many men enjoy these fatherhood activities, but as sociologist Majella Kilkey and her colleagues in the

United Kingdom suggest, men with demanding professional jobs now also struggle to combine paid work with family life. In London this has led to the hiring of Polish immigrant handymen to do the things that the dads used to do around the home, and in Southern California Latino immigrant gardening labor substitutes.[7] Professional-class men in London and Los Angeles attempt to balance work and fatherhood by relying on the domestic masculine labor of immigrant men.

The children in middle-class and upper-middle-class families have also been given a new set of marching orders. Doing household chores or going out to mow the lawn has been replaced with the command to succeed in the increasingly competitive spheres of school, sports, and artistic enrichment activities. As Annette Lareau has demonstrated in *Unequal Childhoods: Class, Race, and Family Life*, middle-class children now undergo "concerted cultivation" for achievement by parents who supervise complicated schedules of extracurricular activities, lessons, and tutoring. With the rise of children's extracurricular activities and compulsory youth sports, fueled by adult volunteerism, many middle-class kids and their parents are now out at the soccer or baseball field on Saturday, not at home mowing the lawn. In *It's All for the Kids*, sociologist Michael Messner delves into this world of adult volunteerism and cites a 2008 study that found two-thirds of American youth play in at least one organized sport. The percentages are even higher among suburban affluent families.[8] A landscape designer that I interviewed confirmed that in this context mowing the lawn had been absorbed by other activities, so that now her design installations took that into account. "Many people," she said, "recognize that they're working and they have a lot of other family commitments, and they're not going to be spending much of their weekend in their garden, if any at all." When busy clients started requesting organic vegetable gardens, she accommodated their time squeeze constraints by installing kitchen gardens requiring almost no labor. "I'll do a kumquat tree, some rosemary, and then I'll put in maybe some sage, oregano and some thyme," she explained, "and you can pretty much leave them except for your miscellaneous trimming now and then."

Parents who like to garden find that juggling the demands of children and work prohibits them from spending time in the garden. Dr. Elaine Woo is one of these people. She is cheerfully harried and seemingly unflappable as she manages her private practice and a household shared with her husband, a software engineer, and their two children. When we talked, she laughingly recalled that as a teen she had "loved gardening so much" that she had aspired to become a farmer. Her Chinese immigrant parents sensibly counseled her to finish high school, and today she is a busy doctor. Before she departs for the office, she must launch the kids *and* check her e-mail, reports on patients' lab work, phone messages, and website inquiries—all before 9:00 a.m. Sometimes she sees patients in the evening, but she is also working at raising her two kids, ages nine and fourteen, living in the here and now with them, and grooming the children for their best possible future. She beamed with parental pride when she told me that her teenage daughter Sandy got good grades and had already scored in the 100 percentile on standardized tests. If Sandy continues with her competitive gymnastics, she may win coveted admission to an Ivy League college or perhaps a scholarship. Dr. Woo still loves gardening and nature, and she and her husband have painstakingly planted dozens of trees and shrubs on their expansive hillside property. Many of these have died, and our walk through her yard turned into a tour of plant and tree morbidity. Dr. Woo frets over the wilting Japanese maple tree, which she knows needs transplanting, and the now overgrown bamboo that she planted to prevent hillside erosion is threatening to take over the world. For water conservation purposes she would really like to take out that remaining patch of lawn, but between work and the kids, there is no time for her to get out there and do these garden chores. Her own gardening will have to wait until the kids are grown; meanwhile, she says, the gardeners can do most of it.

THE IMMIGRANT GARDENER LABOR SYSTEM

Japanese immigrant men began tending suburban gardens for the well-to-do in the 1890s, when residential developments were growing in Southern California. By the 1930s, maintenance gardening was firmly established as a Japanese man's job niche, not only in Southern California but also in Northern California, Oregon, and Washington. These Japanese immigrant men came from rural origins, and in California they had initially worked as agricultural laborers and as flower and vegetable "truck farmers," innovating small businesses where they and their family members also did manual labor with plants.[9] Pushed out of land ownership by racist legislation (e.g., the California Alien Land Law of 1913, later revised in 1920 and 1923), these Japanese men basically invented suburban maintenance gardening as we know it today, initially using bikes, carts, and wheelbarrows and later sedans and pickup trucks to transport their tools and go to gardening jobs in different home yards, developing a route of paying customers. As residential gardeners, they capitalized on the horticultural skills they had learned in the agricultural fields in Japan and California, and also the cachet of Japanese horticultural aesthetics, which was bolstered by Japanese-style gardens and bonsai that had been displayed at the World's Fairs in St. Louis, San Francisco, and Chicago. Discrimination against Japanese people, however, continued, and consequently many Nisei (second-generation) sons, even after achieving education, stayed in gardening. After the brutality of World War II removal and internment, many Japanese men resumed their gardening routes, and still more Japanese men joined their ranks as the postwar housing boom provided plentiful jobs in residential gardens.[10] One Nisei who spent his childhood helping his Japanese father tend residential gardens in Beverly Hills and Brentwood in the 1960s writes that "back then, Los Angeles was teeming with Japanese American gardeners. . . . Half of my Japanese American friends were sons and daughters of gardeners, and the other half, the grandsons and granddaughters of gardeners."[11]

Japanese gardeners began hiring Mexican workers as far back as the 1930s, but this became more common in the 1960s and 1970s.[12] Mexican immigrant men initially learned the trade from their Japanese employers, and when the Japanese men retired out of the job the Mexican men, most of them from rural backgrounds where they had cultivated corn, beans, and livestock, took over the gardening business. By 1970 there were already more Mexican than Japanese men working in Southern California gardening, and this trend exploded in the 1980s and 1990s, the boom years of Mexican immigration. By 2000 the numbers of Japanese men in gardening had dwindled. As the older Japanese gardeners retired, their sons and grandsons found new occupational doors open to them, and Latino immigrant men, most of them from the central western states of

Mexico, took over and developed the gardening business. The straw hat replaced the pith helmet, and a round of ethnic succession had occurred. The Japanese gardeners exited residential gardening with the satisfaction of having launched their families' upward social mobility and assimilation, as this Japanese gardener's poem suggests:

From my lawn mower
I can make child and grandchild
grow into doctors
—*Mochizuki Goro*[13]

Today it's a crowded market and difficult to start your own gardening business, but the Mexican immigrant gardeners who started in the 1970s and 1980s benefited from the wide-open opportunities of that era. Jorge Ramirez is typical of this generation. "When I came here in 1972, my brother was already working with a Japanese guy, so I went to work with him too," he explained. He was a wage worker for four years, but when he married in 1976 his Japanese employer "passed a few houses" to him and he began working on his own. "He gave me machinery," Jorge explained, "but he told me I needed to buy my own truck." Jorge sighed and shook his head, reminiscing how gasoline had cost 36 cents a gallon back then, while it now hovered around $4.50 a gallon. But since the 1970s he too has raised his prices, a move enabled in part by his hard work and experience and that of his crew, but also by his obtaining two important pieces of paper: legal status and his landscaping contractor's license. With the state contractor's license, Jorge may now legally install complicated sprinkler systems and expensive hardscape driveways, paths, and patios. That's where the real money is, and keeping a couple of workers doing gardening maintenance floats the whole business and keeps the referrals for big contracts flowing.

Ramon Espinoza, who has now logged a couple of decades tending Southern California gardens, snapped his fingers as he animatedly described how quickly the gardening business grew in the 1970s and 1980s. "*Rapidísimo! Pa'rriba! Pa'rriba! Pa'rriba!*" (Rapidly! Up! Up! Up!). His own father had migrated in 1975, working first for a Japanese gardener and then on his own. Ramon joined his father in 1982, and within six months he had hired a worker and acquired, he said, his own truck and a route worth $5,000 (meaning enough jobs to gross $5,000 a month). "Today," he acknowledged, "it's harder to get started, and there's a lot of competition." Another longtime *jardinero* plainly asserted, "We never imagined that one day we *Mexicanos* would dominate the gardening manpower here."

The immigrant gardener system is stratified and consists of the self-employed gardeners, who own the trucks and tools and collect the fees, and their wage-earning employees. The self-employed gardeners are both entrepreneurs and workers.[14] They share many of the same concerns as small businessmen, but most of them are also doing the manual labor of driving trucks and working in different gardens every day. Not all gardeners succeed in becoming self-employed, and interviews with forty-seven Mexican gardeners suggest that making the transition from work as a gardening employee to self-employment and management of one's own route of clients has become increasingly difficult in today's competitive market.

CULTIVATING PRIVATE PARADISES

The gardeners of Eden work in other people's private paradises. As paid gardeners, they need to respond to what their clients want in their residential gardens. What is that exactly? Residential garden conventions and styles here have been shaped by over a hundred years of American suburbanization, by migrations of people and plants, and by new social and cultural trends. Home owners "inherit" the legacy of past plantings, often literally the trees, lawn, and hedges of the prior home owner, or they move into new places that copy convention, and they may remove and add new plants. The gardeners must respond to all of these needs. Residential garden vernacular in Southern California now encompasses a potpourri of styles and plantings, but the thirsty lawn, with a variety of ornamental shrubs planted around the foundation of the house, still prevails. Who started this, and how does it affect garden labor?

It is a style attributed to the lasting legacy of Andrew Jackson Downing (1815–52), the first American landscape designer. Although he was mostly self-taught and received no formal education beyond age sixteen, he married into money and fashioned himself into a mail-order plant nursery entrepreneur, a horticulturalist, an author, and America's first celebrity garden designer. While he incorporated British picturesque "natural" garden styles, Downing started the practice of setting the suburban house on a green lawn, a pattern familiar to anyone who has ever seen an American suburb. Historians and landscape professionals agree with landscape architect Christopher Grampp that in the United States, "Downing has had more effect on the home grounds, especially the front yard, than any other single designer."[15]

Downing loved the lawn. In 1846 he wrote that without a well-tended lawn, "no place, however great its architectural beauties, its charms of scenery, or its collections of flowers and shrubs can be said to deserve consideration in point of landscape gardening." A well-manicured lawn, he promised, would give even "humble cottage grounds . . . a universal passport to admiration."[16] Almost as if giving Veblen fodder for developing his theory of conspicuous consumption, he denounced the productive turf used by English jockeys and American farmers in favor of the nonproductive display of neatly mowed grass, "softened and refined by the frequent touches of the patient mower."[17]

Andrew Jackson Downing also shaped our ideas about garden labor. He wrote many books, but his 1841 book, *A Treatise on the Theory and Practice of Landscape Gardening, Adapted to North America; with a View to the Improvement of Country Residences,* is recognized as his most influential. In it he offered guidelines for establishing a residential garden in good taste, detailing gendered prescriptions for domestic garden labor. The man of the house, he wrote, should tend the vegetables, fruit trees, and lawn and maintain the walkways "with perhaps the assistance of a common gardener, or labouring man, for a day or two, at certain seasons of the year." Meanwhile, the woman of the house should cultivate flowers. Downing spelled out just how women should do this: "three times a week, an hour or two, in the cool mornings and evenings of summer, in the pleasing task of planting, tying to neat stakes, picking off decayed flowers, and removing weeds from the borders."[18] A nice home and garden, Downing assured his readers, would lead to moral virtue and express patriarchal power. He applauded the small, modest homes and gardens of growing suburbs in the United States and, according to urban historian and architect Dolores Hayden, strove to connect male lawn maintenance with male pride of home ownership. Both Downing and the new firms selling lawn mowers and grass seed sought to elevate the masculine mystique of lawn by associating mowing with men's power and ownership of property. "After the lawn mower was patented in 1869," Hayden writes, "some manufacturers promoted it as a romantic device for courtship or equated the ownership of a modest lawn mower with the proprietorship of a vast estate—a sales pitch quite in the spirit of Downing's original *Treatise*."[19] Lawn mower companies cleverly invented a new market by associating manliness with lawn care.

The masculinization of lawn and the feminization of flowers received more support from other influential writers of this era. Catharine Beecher Stowe (1800–1878) published *Treatise on Domestic Economy for Use of Young Ladies at Home and at School* in 1842 and with her sister Harriet Beecher Stowe, the abolitionist author of *Uncle Tom's Cabin*, coauthored *The American Woman's Home*, published in 1869. That book featured an illustration showing an elite, upper-class woman gardening while her servant holds a parasol, echoing images and directives also dispensed by British author Jane Loudon in *Gardening for Ladies*, an instructional gardening manual purchased by many Americans in the 1840s.[20] More than Downing or Loudon, Catharine Beecher Stowe instructed American women in the most efficient practices for homemaking, mothering, and gardening, all for spiritual purposes. Women not only would establish their virtue through nurturance and care of children and husband but would serve as *managers of the home*. As we'll see below, the legacy of this ideal today is seen in the gendered patterns in which many Southern California home owners communicate with gardeners: the Latino immigrant gardeners report that when home owners communicate a request it is nearly always the women, not the men, who do so. Women's domestic managerial responsibilities extend to the garden, even when they are managing the paid gardeners who do the masculine garden work of mowing, pruning, and debris clearing that their husbands used to do for free.

Today Mexican immigrant gardeners must learn how to tend all kinds of ornamental plants from Asia, Africa, and Latin America. Besides lawns, home gardens in Southern California regularly feature perimeter plantings of thirsty hydrangeas and camellias (originally from southern and eastern Asia), colorful impatiens (widely hybridized, but with African origins), bougainvillea vines, trumpet vines, and jacaranda trees (South America), citrus (Southeast Asia), and boxwood hedges (from Europe). In recent years with growing awareness of water scarcity, Mediterranean groupings of olive trees, rosemary, and lavender have become popular, as have drought-tolerant Australian and New Zealand plants such as phormium and kangaroo paws. Sculptural succulents, cacti, and euphorbia (with origins in Mexico, South Africa, and the Southwest) and scrubby native plants (with origins in California!) have also enjoyed newfound popularity. An extensive infrastructure of plant nurseries emerged to meet the demand for decorative plants in the postwar suburban boom. Today, home improvement stores have captured a big swath of the business of selling these plants to home owners. The result? Many prosaic Southern California residential yards are now packed to the gills with exotic plants from around the world, and Latino gardeners must learn to tend all of them. The majority of these men have horticultural experience from Mexican ranchos, but on the job as suburban gardeners they acquire new skills and knowledge about a vast array of plants.

While idealized backyard spaces for sanctuary and entertainment were set in the postwar years, the ante has been upped in recent decades. A range of shelter magazines, from *Sunset* to *Better Homes and Gardens*, the advent of HGTV (that's the Home and Garden TV channel, which began in the mid-1990s), and popular garden books whet domestic garden yearnings with glossy photographs and with copy showcasing "spectacular backyard wonderlands" and "garden masterpieces." These feature not only perfectly blossoming flowers in eye-popping color palettes and lush greenery but also outdoor rooms and kitchens with built-in barbecues, sinks, pizza ovens, refrigerators, and extensive countertops. The "staycation home and garden," resembling a personal resort with pool, spa, and fire pit, is also popular, often telegraphed by the ubiquitous palm trees and perhaps a pergola laced with fragrant climbing jasmine vine, or Dionysian grapes hanging from an arbor. These are fantasy dream-escapes, and just as fashion models and celebrities are routinely airbrushed and digitally enhanced, so too are these images. The colors pop and everything always looks unattainably perfect. These photos give people ideas about how to transform a blank slate of soil into a particular kind of garden paradise.

Pools, fountains, and lawns absorb lots of water in Southern California home gardens, and when I asked landscape designers what clients are currently requesting they reported that although there is growing concern about wasting water people are still reluctant to get rid of their lawns. Clients say they want drought-tolerant, low-maintenance plants, but they can rarely bring themselves to totally get rid of the lawn. One landscape designer recalled a client who had wavered. "He was really excited about the idea of not having a lawn, but he couldn't bring himself to do it. He was like, you know, 'I want to, but here in Southern California, you drive down the street and everybody has some grass.' And we are taught and conditioned that this is beautiful, that this is what a nice garden is. It has a lawn, it has plants around it." Some residents have ripped out the lawn, motivated in part by rising water rates, environmental concerns, and rebates from municipal water districts. For most home owners, however, the lawn is still the order of the day here in Southern California, and that is the decisive factor shaping the work of the *jardineros*.

All of the home owners that I interviewed had retained or planted at least a patch of lawn on their properties. Some people claimed they were fiercely against lawns but said they kept them for real estate resale value, reminding us that the home garden is not only a site of leisure and tranquillity but also an investment, typically the largest equity most Americans own. Succulents and native plants have grown in popularity here, but most people still like a lush green look in their gardens. As one landscape design contractor put it, "I think people like the idea of saving water, but they don't like how it looks. . . . Just because something is drought tolerant doesn't mean they look good in a drought."

Latino immigrant gardeners may be consulted for advice on plants and trees, but they are not the key decision makers on what these residential gardens will include. This is determined variously by home owners who "inherit" the previous home owners' plantings when they move to a new place, by home owner residents' decisions about what to add or rip out, and by design ideas from the landscape professionals they might consult. A closer look at a handful of home owners and their gardens gives us an idea of the diversity of residential gardens where Latino gardeners work today and also shows how home owners use their yards and the different amounts of labor they do in their gardens.

Polly and Don Axelrod live in a secluded hillside home with a red-tile roof, built in contemporary Spanish style. Their front yard features a wide, well-tended lawn and a front courtyard with a circular three-tiered fountain and a colorful collection of decorative plants, including bluegrass, spiky purple cordyline, phormium, pampas grass, palms, and magenta-hued bougainvillea. Inside, from the combined kitchen/dining/family rooms, a big plateglass window looks out to the backyard entertainment space, which shares some of the same plant palette as the front courtyard, as well as jaw-dropping views of mountains, valleys, faraway high-rise buildings, and the coast. There's also a swimming pool, a barbecue with both gas and charcoal grills built into gently curving countertops, a fire pit with built-in seating and spiky plants behind it, a teak dining table that seats ten, a covered brick patio with lounge chairs and vines growing up the pergola, lawn, and a lush secret side garden. The other side of the pool features a bar and six stools set against a small grove of nonfruiting loquat and olive trees. There's a profusion of plants, yet it's all very neat and tidy, almost antiseptic. There's lot of water splashing too, as no less than five fountains grace the front and back gardens, not including the six fish fixtures spouting water into the pool. As I approached the house, I could hear the steady hum of machinery—not blowers or gas-powered mowers but the electrical equipment powering the many fountains.

In Los Angeles, San Diego, and Santa Barbara, many homes and yards of the affluent are set in remotely located foothills, such as the one where the Axelrods live, in settings that allow for maximum residential privacy. As British architectural historian Reyner Banham observed in his classic book on LA, "That is what foothill ecology is really all about: narrow, tortuous residential roads serving precipitous house-plots that often back up directly on unimproved wilderness." At these homes and yards, "an air of deeply buried privacy" prevails. Irrigation and the work of paid gardeners allow all kinds of lush horticultural fantasy to flourish here in the canyons and hills, but as Banham noted, a key feature is "dense-growing small-leaved shrubs that can be used to make thickets of instant privacy essential to the fat life of the delectable mountains."[21] These gardens appear natural, but they require small armies of constant labor and regular irrigation.

The Axelrods constantly hire many people to come work in their garden. They bought the house a dozen years ago, and since then they have paid five different landscape designers and contractors to install most of the plantings and entertainment features. Don Axelrod works in insurance, and Polly, at age sixty, is a recently retired nurse. There are no children at home, and the couple use their home and garden to entertain friends and Polly's nieces, who bring their children over for swim parties. How do they keep the garden looking so perfect? Polly explained to me that she calls a landscape design contractor four times a year to do "a tune-up," and she really likes this person, a white woman with good aesthetic sensibility who is knowledgeable about plants, and with whom she feels an easy rapport. After they discuss "what's working and what's not working," the designer brings her own crew of Latino workers to change the plantings. Meanwhile, the Axelrods also pay another crew of Latino gardeners to do the weekly garden maintenance for a fee of $170 a month, and a pool cleaner comes regularly too. Polly and Don do minimal "hands-on" gardening on this eleven-thousand-square-foot parcel of land. Polly loves flowers but she's never really liked getting her hands dirty, she confided, so she tends two potted plants, including a pretty pot of perennially blooming impatiens that is set in front of the big plateglass window, adorned with big pumpkins and flanked by two angel statues. Don cleans out the water fountains twice a year.

Other home owners who live among similarly lush landscapes take a more "hands-on" approach to gardening but still rely on the labor of Latino immigrant gardeners. Dr. Ignacio Aleman and his wife Clara live with their four kids, who are now in their teens and twenties, down in the valley, in a sprawling San Fernando Valley ranch-style home on a sixteen-thousand-square-foot lot. Clara works as a teacher and tends the vegetable garden, which boasted bountiful tomatoes, *chiles*, and zucchini when I saw it at the end of summer, but the kids do no garden work (unless asked to help move a heavy item), and the garden is really Dr. Aleman's baby. Like many of the gardeners, he is a Mexican immigrant, having moved to South Central LA with his family as a young child. He is part of the 1.5 generation, raised and educated here, and now part of the affluent sector of the Latino middle class. His early fascination with plants and nature led him to science, school success, and ultimately a thriving medical career, but now the stress of his long commute and his work at a university hospital and a clinic that serves indigent Latino patients has led him back to the garden. And what a garden it is. There's the standard big front and back lawn, but a lush profusion of plants and decorative features makes it a personalized standout. This is the work, not of landscape designers, but of Dr. Aleman, who has imagined and installed most of it. He designed and built the koi pond himself. When a mature English walnut tree died, he cut burls from the trunk and used these to mount staghorn ferns on the patio wall. Using the principles of physics and seasonal changes of the sun's movement, he designed and single-handedly built a large covered dining pavilion, adjacent to the cacti and succulent garden. He has nurtured dozens of bonsai trees, now displayed on a shelf that he built along the back fence. To prevent delicate potted palms that line the pool from getting fried in the sun, he placed colorful umbrellas from the ninety-nine-cent store in each pot. Dr. Aleman reminds me of Leonardo da Vinci, blending talents in art and science, with an added dose of the DIY ingenuity that comes from growing up poor.

We sit on cushioned rattan chairs on the back covered patio during the interview, surrounded by a cozy jungle of plants, with Mozart and Bach concertos playing on the outdoor speakers and water splashing from a three-tier fountain (identical to the one in the Axelrods' courtyard). It's lush here but not too tidy—there are pots with struggling plants waiting to bloom and a few discarded plastic containers. A few feet away, inside the glass sliding door, teens are watching soccer on a big-screen TV, but the garden patio seems tranquil and far away. "I sit here as much as I can," he says. "I don't have much of a chance on weekdays, but as much as possible on weekends." This is his retreat, where he reads, prepares lectures on his laptop, and drinks coffee on early mornings, and the family also entertains here, under a ceiling fan, lights, and two heat lamps. The patio is enclosed by a shade cover that offers respite from the sun but still allows enough light for a profusion of shade-loving orchids, bromeliads, lobelia, fuschias, moss, and Australian tree ferns to thrive, and true to form, Dr. Aleman custom-engineered the patio cover to allow for air and light circulation and installed it with help from his brother, a welder. He also put in a water-rain system for the ferns.

The Alemans' home garden has many of the same entertainment features found at the Axelrods' (pool, spa, covered dining patio, lawn, and many ornamental plants), but Dr. Aleman has designed and built it himself and does a lot of the hands-on gardening, which he finds a relaxing and rewarding respite from his job. The same crew of Latino gardeners that the Alemans have employed for twenty-five years arrive weekly to do what he refers to as "the macro work" of mowing and cleaning up for a fee of $190 a month, and once a year he hires the same gardeners to do tree pruning, but Dr. Aleman does daily vigilance of walking through the big backyard daily before work to inspect the plants, checking for new growth, dead blossoms, insects, and so on. On Thursday, the day before the gardeners come, he trims back foliage and often strews a pile of clippings on the ground for the gardeners to clean up.

Latino gardeners in Southern California also work in much smaller residential gardens located in working-class neighborhoods, including East Los Angeles, where I interviewed Doreen Nishimoto, a fortyish teacher who lives alone in the modest home where she grew up. This lot is much smaller, just under four thousand square feet, and it still retains many of the plants that her parents, a Japanese gardener and a homemaker, put in years ago. They include a four-foot-tall hedge around the front lawn, where three mature plumeria trees bloom, and bushes planted around the foundation of the stucco house. The backyard is a tangle of overgrown fruit trees and vines, including a Japanese persimmon, a plum tree, a kumquat, a yuzu (a particular kind of Asian citrus), Japanese wisteria, a profusion of potted cacti and orchids, and several gigantic staghorn ferns that have taken on a life of their own. Doreen tells me that at one point the collection of potted cymbidium orchids numbered eighty, but because of lack of care—these periodically need to be divided and repotted—"only about fifty" now remain. There's lots of overgrown plant life here, as well as the remnants of past life—her childhood playhouse, still with the sign "Doreen's Playhouse," her dad's old Datsun pickup and his gardening tools, and the rusty poles of an old clothesline. Rather than the dream-escape of leisure, this place recalls a productive utilitarian backyard that has been gently disregarded for years and is currently used for neither recreation nor production.

Doreen Nishimoto remembers how beautiful the garden was when her parents were alive: "It was very pretty, and everything was well maintained when they were here." But it is too much for her to take care of on her own. Although she valiantly tried to trim the front hedge with her father's old hedge clippers, it came out crooked, and so she asked the Latino gardeners, who had already been mowing the lawn for over fifteen years, to do it too. "It's nice because I don't have to think about it," she says. The gardeners now mow, trim, and maintain the front and back yard for a monthly fee of $40. She feels she should do more herself, like divide and repot those remaining fifty cymbidium orchids, but she is exhausted from her job teaching second graders and overwhelmed with maintenance and repairs on this older home. Back in the day, her Japanese American father worked as a gardener tending residential gardens in the Hollywood Hills, and her mother tended to flowers and a vegetable patch at their home while her dad mowed the lawn. Today, a crew of Mexican immigrant gardeners work in nearly all of the yards on her street in the City Terrace area of East LA. She marvels at the change from the days of her childhood in the 1970s. "At that time," she recalls, "we didn't have gardeners in the neighborhood. Everybody just took care of their own." Now "Nobody wants to work on the yard," she says, shaking her head and chuckling. "Nobody had a gardener before in this neighborhood, 'cause we're the working-class neighborhood. We *were* the gardeners." The ethnic succession from Japanese to Latino gardeners is complete, and the gardeners' sites of work have expanded beyond all-white suburbs to ethnoburbs and even the Mexican capital of the United States, East LA.

NEGOTIATIONS: HOME OWNERS AND GARDENERS

When home owners hire a Latino gardener, there is no need to place an ad or consult advertisement flyers or business cards that gardeners sometimes leave on the front steps. Instead, they ask their neighbors or simply approach gardeners who are already working next door or down the street. A gardener's work reputation hinges on garden appearance. "The best advertisement," one gardener declared, "is a house where the client is not afraid to spend." He recalled just such a house that had served as his best referral, causing joggers and residents in cars to stop and admire the front yard garden and inquire about hiring him. At the outset, home owners and gardeners verbally negotiate a price that typically covers a weekly garden maintenance service for a monthly fee. Fees set at that moment may remain frozen for years, sometimes decades, the gardeners say. This is exactly what I discovered in my research with Latina nannies and house-cleaners working in Los Angeles.

Once hired, many home owners have very little communication with the gardeners.[22] Gardeners, who work on-site only once a week (maybe twice for a big estate house) and who may rarely even *see* the home owners simply don't enter the domestic emotional sphere the way nannies and interior domestic workers do.[23] They are caring for plants and property, not children and elderly. They work outside, not inside. It's generally a less charged transaction, one devoid of the employer-employee relationship encountered in other workplaces. Home owners who hire gardeners do not have expectations that they will establish chummy relationships, and some do not learn their gardeners' last names. Lesser requirements will do. One home owner writes that this suffices for her: "What I do know about him is this: he is Central American; he has crooked teeth; he laughs a lot. He shows up when is supposed to, which is why I have not fired him, as I did his predecessor."[24]

Interviews with both Latino immigrant gardeners and a variety of home owners suggest that communication is sparse. Some home owners report that they don't know the names and phone numbers of their gardeners. Polly Axelrod knew the name of the route-owner gardener to whom she wrote the monthly check, but he was now infrequently on-site to do the work himself. He sent his crew, and Polly confessed, "Honestly, I don't know their names." When I asked what she most disliked about her garden, she didn't hesitate—it was communicating directives to the gardeners. "When things need to be trimmed, like over there . . . and I'm not able to tell the gardener to get it done, 'cause his hours have changed, I find that very frustrating," she said. "I know it needs to be cleaned up and I want it done. And it's hard for me to call him and ask him to do it, 'cause I'm not sure if he knows what I'm saying."

Latino immigrant gardeners have varying levels of English fluency, and things can get lost in translation. All of the route-owner gardeners have learned enough English to negotiate their jobs and navigate their businesses, but their crew generally have fewer years living in the United States and less English fluency. Language barriers arise, but home owners like Polly, who do not speak Spanish, have devised a solution: "When I get really desperate," she said, "I have my housekeeper call him and tell him what to do." More typically, a domestic worker will emerge from the house to place a request. The Latino gardeners have mixed feelings and responses when Latina domestic workers come out of the house with these commands. Some men feel the women are loading them up with extra work without extra pay, and other gardeners do not respect these women as legitimate authority figures capable of giving them directives. Others accept the situation, stating that at upscale homes it is part of the job requirement to get along with the domestic workers, who serve as the eyes, ears, and voices of the home owners. "They are the ones directing the houses," reasoned one gardener, "because the *señores* aren't there." Best to stay on good terms with them.

Continuing the nineteenth-century tradition of women as *household managers*, it is typically women who communicate with the gardeners. Like visiting anthropologists, the Latino gardeners readily note this gendered pattern: as one gardener observed, "It's rare that the *señor* comes out. Here, the woman is in charge of that." In some homes, where the men are more dedicated and focused on the garden than their spouses, they may take a more active role, perhaps calling to request repairs on a broken sprinkler or a special tree trimming. However, these men seem to be exceptions. More common is Barbara Klein's pattern. Her husband, a busy CEO who traveled frequently, was far more involved and personally invested in the garden than she was. He had overseen the hiring and planting of a new oak tree after a storm pulled one down, and he had consulted with a landscape design contractor for the newly refurbished pool area with a covered dining pavilion. Yet the task of communicating her husband's questions and requests to the gardeners fell to her. "I tend to manage the household stuff," she explained, "but you know he's got more at stake somehow in the yard, and more opinions, and more demands." Sometimes, she continued, " it doesn't make sense for me to be the intermediary, and I just say, 'You've gotta call Jorge and talk that over with him.' . . . If it's just delivering a message, like 'Please get to the hedges as soon as you can,' I would do that." In this instance, language translation was no barrier. The Kleins had lived abroad and both spoke fluent Spanish, yet their Latino gardener spoke accent-less English so they communicated with him in English. She didn't know if he had been born in the United

States or had been one of the 1.5 generation who migrated as a young child—again pointing to the depersonalized relations in gardening—but she did know that it was odd to have a Latino gardener who spoke English without an accent. "It's kind of a surprise to have a native English-speaking person mowing your lawn," she remarked, underscoring the widespread normalcy of immigrant labor in maintenance gardening.

Money remains a driving factor in these negotiations. Home owners may love their gardeners' work, but even satisfaction with impeccable gardening service does not prevent them from switching to less costly gardeners. This became especially pronounced during the recession. Deandra Lane, a twice-divorced mother of two and a realtor, had employed two different gardeners over the years, first José and now Reynaldo. José did the gardening when she lived with her first husband, and after she divorced and remarried, José did substantial landscape installations and weekly maintenance at the new property. Between the two-paycheck household and a booming real estate market, money flowed freely, and they spruced up the backyard with a gazebo and extensive plantings that José selected and installed. After the second divorce, she and her children downsized to a bungalow on a smaller-sized parcel (six thousand square feet). José initially did the gardening here too. She felt comfortable communicating with José, and she had nothing but superlatives to describe the quality of his work. "José is a real gardener, an artist really," she said. She liked him, and he was willing to do whatever extra task she requested without charging extra. Over fifteen years, she had even gotten to know José's children, whom he sometimes brought to work.

Deandra was now a single parent supporting her two children, and money was tight. The real estate business was still down, and she needed to cut back on spending. Paying $100 a month to José was more than she could afford, so she asked if he would agree to come twice a month, for a fee of $50. He said no because this would "mess up his schedule," so she tried to care for the lawn on her own. This did not last long. A gardener working at a neighbor's yard saw her and asked if she need his services. She hired Reynaldo on the spot, and he agreed to come only twice a month for an affordable monthly fee of $50. She didn't like talking to him, and compared to an artist like José the new gardener was "more a mow, blow, and go guy," she said. But that was no problem. Deandra tended to the easy-care succulents, and when it was time for the annual pruning on the tall camphor trees in the backyard she called José. She respected and trusted the quality of his work, and she felt a level of comfort and familiarity in her communication with him. For her, the new arrangement was a money saver.

For the gardeners, the lack of a formal contract or personal contact with the clients is not a problem. They are eager get on with their work, and none of them expressed the need for more chitchat with the clients. "They don't talk to you very often," Maurilio, a husky man with thick bronzed fingers, agreed. "You get there and you know what work you need to do. They just speak to you at the beginning or maybe just to let you know it's time to prune the roses, clean up the azaleas after the blooms dried." Some of the gardeners do resent excessive phone calls to their home, as some clients will call at odd hours and Sundays to request urgent help with broken sprinklers or to complain about something. The gardeners would like to enjoy one day off a week, Sunday, to relax with their families, but they know that failure to respond may result in being fired. It's a competitive market, and they cannot afford to risk losing good clients, so they need to drive out and tend to these urgent requests. Pedro Gomez, one of the most entrepreneurial and financially successful gardeners, owned four trucks and employed eleven full-time employees, whom he supervised through cell phones. Yet even he emphasized the importance of personally making emergency house calls to clients. "If there's an emergency, you have to go," he said. "I don't care if the house is small or large, pays a lot or a little. I have to keep my clients, I have to offer the same level of service to *all of them*." The cutthroat competitive market, where other gardeners were lurking and ready to work for less money, made him respond with this round-the-clock service. Other gardeners concurred, and they pieced together different strategies for maximizing their gardening earnings.

The real problem for the gardeners of Eden is customers who want to pay less and other gardeners who are willing to work for less. Wildly inflationary prices for gasoline, a recession and a real estate collapse that have left even middle-class professionals feeling strapped for cash, and a context where home owners can easily replace their current gardeners with a less costly crew working in the neighborhood have put the economic squeeze on gardeners. Most home owners want to continue paying the same, and some, as we have seen, are financially strapped and strive to pay less.[25] Below, I examine different strategies the gardeners use as they seek to survive and thrive in *jardinería*.

SURVIVING THE SQUEEZE

The gardeners say that hard work and *ganas*, putting out effort and taking initiative, is indispensable. "You can't be afraid of hard work—I mean, really get the shirt wet," said one gardener, aptly capturing what the job requires in Southern California. "If you work and you put in a little more *ganas* [effort]," another gardener echoed, "you'll come out a little better."

There is no substitute for hard work, but to build a thriving gardening business the gardeners need to do extra jobs for extra pay. This includes pruning trees and tall hedges in winter, planting trees in fall or colorful annuals like petunias or tulip bulbs in spring, cutting brush on hillsides, installing hardscape, or removing debris. That is where the real money is. As one gardener explained, "My profit comes with planting plants, but gardening"—by which he meant the weekly maintenance route of different residential gardens—"pays so-so." Another said that once he got a new client, he tried to do all of the extra jobs: "Once I get a house, I don't want anyone else to get in there, just me. I know how to install sprinklers, everything." Gardeners typically do a markup on plants and materials they might be installing, charging say $45 for a flat of annuals or ground cover that might cost $30. Combined with labor, a big planting might bring in $400 to $800.

Most of the gardeners know that a California landscape contractor's license is necessary for installing irrigation and hardscape, but only a few of them have it. A gardener who lived in Santa Barbara had built a thriving business in "extras" in part through his affiliation with a successful landscape designer, who recommended him for big jobs in the coastal estate homes of Santa Barbara and Montecito, where Oprah keeps a seaside vacation home. These proved much more lucrative than the regular route. During the week, he regularly employed three men to do the weekly gardening maintenance, but for the extra jobs, which didn't necessarily

Figure 19. Gardeners' trucks are typical sights all over Southern California and are typically packed tightly with tools. Photo by Nathan Solis.

involve plant care, he hired more workers. He had just bid $12,000 for a job tearing down fifty old rotting trees, and he currently had his crew digging trenches for the installation of underground cables for a home security camera system. Other gardeners were more cautious and did not risk installing irrigation or hardscape without the landscape contractor's license.

With the recession, many customers cut back on the big "extra" landscape improvement jobs, so this affected the gardeners' earnings. Gardeners with many years of experience learn to read the global economic trends by the extras their customers are requesting in the gardens. "When the US economy is good, you figure it out because the clients say, 'Do it! Right away! Here's the check!' And when the economy is bad, *de volada*, right away you know because the clients say, 'Listen, just leave it! No, don't move it!'" said one gardener. "With the ones that work in investments, it's notorious, you get it right away. *Ay cabrón!* A recession."

Other strategies for surviving and thriving include self-exploitation ("sweating the shirt") and exploiting the labor of the hired hands, the *ayudantes*, who are often kin or from the same town in Mexico. Some gardeners bring their sons, and occasionally wives and daughters, to the jobs on weekends. The paid *ayudantes* work hard and during summer put in long

Figure 20. Some gardeners move into the related business of tree trimming and landscape clearing. Competition is fierce, so they place cards advertising their services on doorsteps in affluent neighborhoods. Photo by author.

days, and their average pay hovers near minimum wage, amounting to about $400 to $450 a week. Tree trimmers or those with driver's licenses, who can legally drive the trucks, earn more.

TROUBLESOME TRANSACTIONS

Home owners may switch gardeners, and gardeners with thriving routes may quit troublesome clients who make unreasonable demands or who refuse to pay. What angers the home owners enough to fire the gardener? Typically they grow angry when the gardener fails to take initiative on something they wanted done, or when the gardener takes initiative on something they did not want cut. Since communication between both parties is sparse, this comes down to a game of mind reading.

Polly Axelrod had grown increasingly frustrated with the current gardener and his crew. "If he sees weeds, he doesn't necessarily pull them. I keep debating whether to get another one and I just haven't done it," she sighed. "I want someone who is a little more proactive." When I asked what exactly they did, she said: "Pretty much mow, blow, and go. And they water everything. I tell them that I want everything watered, and I want them to hose everything off. And they do trim some stuff." Trimming dead blossoms, especially in this heavily planted garden, and hand-watering this profusion of thirsty plants required far more labor than the phrase "mow and blow" suggested. The gardeners had recently neglected to trim the kangaroo paws in the courtyard for three weeks, and she was displeased. "It kinda takes them that long to do something," she said, pursing her lips in disapproval. Polly had other complaints too, ones often voiced about gardeners: "I don't like to see things shaved off straight. I want it to grow a little more naturally, and keep it trimmed up. . . . They just take their Weedwacker and make it straight, and I don't like that." The gardeners had also broken decorative angel statues on the poolside patio, probably, we surmised, as they carried heavy machinery through to another area of the garden. As I see it, many of these problems arise because of the structure of the job and the fee scale.

Home owners feel they are paying for a service that they are not receiving, and meanwhile the gardeners are paid by the job. They need to work fast. In many cases, they are not paid enough to spend hours at one property doing the meticulous hand clipping that allows bushes to fall in soft naturalistic tufts. As one gardener said, "In all these upper-class neighborhoods, they want five-star service but they want to pay three. Or two."

Time is of the essence, so the gardeners have Taylorized the job, breaking it down into a series of discrete repetitive tasks that are performed in one yard after another.[26] They drive up to a house and unload the machinery; as already noted, some of these canyon and foothill homes are very remotely located, so this takes time. Typically one gardener mows and edges the lawns and trims bushes in straight lines with gas-powered hedge clippers, while another may use hand clippers and a blower to clean up the debris. They must work at a steady pace. To avoid excessive time and gasoline expenditures, they cluster the day's jobs in one area, as it is a time saver if they can sequentially do several houses on one street. Standardized fees result in the standardization of gardening work. Gardening services are simultaneously democratized, but devalued as cheap "mow and blow."

Some upper-income home owners will pay more for customized services. Ralph and Julie Hutchins lived in a uniquely beautiful home filled with antiques and a fantastic art and plant collection. They had fired their last gardener when he cut a large sweep of lavender "to the height of a tea cup," causing the beneficial bees to go away and erasing a prominent focal point from where they sat and entertained on the patio. They now paid another gardener, Juan, $450 a month to come twice a week, and he meticulously pruned their substantial plant collection that covers six distinctive "garden rooms" in the particular way they wanted. It all looked extraordinary. Not many people, however, are willing or capable of paying $450 a month for gardening services. Consequently, the straight lines reign. A landscape designer-installer who had interacted with many home owners offered some insights on these dissatisfactions: "I always say people love to hate their gardeners," she said. "But I think people aren't always communicating exactly with their gardeners. . . . I hear the complaint, 'Out of all the things he could have done, there's weeds here, why did he cut this branch?!' I've heard this thousands of times."

The gardeners are perfectly willing to hear these criticisms and to prune and trim as requested, but they need to be compensated for their time and efforts. They take a lot of pride in a job well done, and those with thriving routes find that they can be more selective about their clients. Sometimes these gardeners may even quit a problematic client. Victor Jimenez, who had been working in Southern California gardens for several decades, recalled customers who had been abusive but said he no longer tolerated that. "I'm well situated now," he said. "I don't need to be humiliated. I like to be punctual, I like to get there on time, I like to arrive clean, I like to arrive with good tools so that my work can shine. If someone doesn't appreciate my work, let them tell me." But even he agreed that "sometimes the clients expect more than what they are willing to pay for." He recalled a customer who had scolded his workers when they stopped to eat lunch, sitting by the side of the garage, during a full day of pruning. This violated his sense of dignity, and he quit that job. By contrast, he said, "I appreciate the trust that other clients have in me, because not all people are predisposed to see one of us as a *human being*. They see us as the ugly men of the house, the ugliest that arrive, that's us and the servant. We're the employees that are messed with the most there." Blatant disrespect and dehumanizing treatment from clients were cause for quitting, but clients' frank talk about pruning or even routine late payments were tolerated.

Dealing with capricious residential clients is part of the job, and this factor also explains why the large landscaping companies have mostly shunned residential gardening: it is too much hassle. The nation's largest landscaping services company, ValleyCrest Landscape, was founded right here in the San Fernando Valley and now encompasses more than one hundred locations around the world with ten thousand employees. It has realized business success—over $1 billion in annual revenue—not by servicing private residential gardens but by maintaining the gardens and lawns at theme parks, shopping malls, golf courses, and museums.[27]

CULTIVATING THE CALIFORNIA DREAM

The regime of affordable Latino immigrant gardening labor generates the landscape that we see today in Southern California residential neighborhoods. Walk down any street in middle-class and affluent neighborhoods here and you may marvel, as I do, at the perfect patches of mowed lawn with scarcely a fallen leaf in sight, and a cornucopia of blooming flowers and bushes. In the showy front yards and the private backyard dream-escapes, the California dream materializes weekly on the ground, thanks to the roving crews of hardworking gardeners. In this section, I examine how the immigrant gardener system shapes residential gardens, and the subjective aspirations and regrets expressed by both the home owners and the gardeners.

The suburban home set back on a lawn and surrounded by foundation plantings remains in place, but now with Latino immigrant gardeners doing the work there are higher standards of garden perfection. A land-scape designer called it a "tight" aesthetic of "perfection." She compared it to Tennessee, where her relatives lived. "Over there, it's a looser aesthetic. I think because so many people [there] are caring for their own gardens, they don't have an expectation of perfection. Whereas if you pay some-body, there's an expectation for it to be perfect all the time." Another home owner attested to wide differences even across the state. "I do notice when I go to the Bay Area, there's leaves everywhere." It is this immigrant labor that allows for LA's glossy aesthetic, a Hollywood set design "look" that extends to the gardens.

How does this affect the home owners, the residents who enjoy these perfect gardens? It allows some of them to enjoy and appreciate the gar-dens free of doing the labor, yet they may also be estranged from the plant nature there. They may not even notice a dry, withering tree in a corner of their lot unless the gardener brings it to their attention. With the regime of immigrant gardening labor, many of the gardens do not require home owners' attention. "The yard is self-perpetuating. I don't have to do any-thing," said one interviewee. Another declared, "I want them to take care of everything," and still another said appreciatively, "The gardeners main-tain it for me. It's nice, 'cause I don't have to think about it." This was not true for all of the home owner interviewees, but it may be the new normal. And there are gendered outcomes of this.

Gardening, like motherhood, is associated with virtue, integrity, and morality, and it is something women are supposed to want to do. For this reason, many of the women that I interviewed felt that they "should" like the goodness of gardening. It's widely seen as a womanly and desirably relaxing activity, part of adorning the home. It's featured on magazines, and elite women have formed clubs and associations around gardening beautification since the nineteenth century. With the regime of Latino gardeners doing the work, new narrations of self arise expressing deep wistfulness and yearnings, particularly for women. Doreen Nishimoto remembered how relaxing it was when she grew herbs. "I should grow my own vegetables, but now," she said, "it's just something else I need to get done." She flirted with the idea of growing herbs and vegetables again but doubted she could stick with it. "It's just a lot of work and I don't know if I'll take care of all that stuff." In fact, she lamented that she could not find time to sit on her front porch. Others listed gardening as something they might do in the near future, after the kids were grown, or after a vacation.

Women conveyed yearnings to grow flowers, plant life that holds the most expressive association of femininity. One woman's gardening activity was watering the potted blooming violets on the porch, and Polly Axelrod forthrightly admitted that although she never liked getting her hands dirty she enjoyed buying pots of blooming flowers, especially orchids, which she displayed indoors. Outdoors, she restricted her hands-on labor to two potted plants. "I do the pots, that planter," she said, pointing to the impatiens. "It's kind of narrowed down to not as much maintenance for us." Another woman vowed, "When the kids are out of elementary, I'm going to start spending more time out there." Women voiced these wistful aspirations of "I should" in the same breath that they listed the other activities in their lives that consumed so much time and energy, such as work, children, and caring for elderly parents. Barbara Klein was reflexive and confessional in explaining her detachment from gardening.

> I've gone through periods of thinking I wanted to like to garden, trying to like to garden, going to gardening workshops, reading a lot about gardening, trying and trying to garden, failing a lot, having it not be really satisfying, and then I finally reached a realization, maybe right before my kids were born, that I don't like to garden, so I don't have to garden. And that was kind of a relief at the time. . . . I know all these people who are just rhapsodic about it! What is the deal, why can't I feel that way about gardening? I thought, oh if you just like kind of let go of your schedule, and your expectations in a way. . . . You can't rush. You can't be impatient. It's such an altered state of mind! Right? Suddenly it's making me want to try again. So since

Monday when I had this realization, I pulled out all my gardening books. . . .
I decided what I would like to do is grow flowers and cut into flower arrangements in my house. . . . So I found a page in the Sunset book of cutting
flower varieties, and I went to OSH with my little two pages photocopied of
that book, and I looked at what they had.

An older, more upper-class woman explained less ambivalently, "I do
love gardens, but from an aesthetic point of view. It's just not what I do."
Her home garden featured nearly seventy rose bushes, but her husband
and Latino gardeners tended the rose garden and other plants. "I'm not
the gardener. I'm like Ferdinand the bull," she said, referring to the children's story. "He likes to smell the roses." She expressed her love of gardens
by serving on the board of a prominent botanical garden.

The home owner men that I interviewed did not express similar longings or ambivalence toward gardening. This is striking, since it is the men
who have abdicated lawn mowing. Dr. Aleman, as we saw, derived tre-
mendous satisfaction from gardening work, and from relaxing in his garden among a profusion of plants, but he did not miss the mowing. For
some men, coming home from work to putter in the garden still provides
an arena of relaxation, a cooldown moment away from public work and a
way to plug back into the private paradise. After one executive's busy day
at the office, he came home to "tomato time," a liminal juncture and bridge
between work and family that allowed him to unwind by tending an
impressive hearty patch of tomatoes, cucumbers, and peppers. Ralph
Hutchins did lots of work in his work in his exquisite garden because "the
result is so satisfying," but he also said he would easily give it up if he could
just clone himself and be assured of keeping the same garden. "I find it
very relaxing at the end of the day, but if I could just magically push a button and have everything watered and everything pruned, I'd do it."

Mowing the lawn, that iconic masculine performance of home ownership, has now become a quaint mid-twentieth-century relic in Southern
California. No one seems to be yearning for the satisfaction of mowing
one's own lawn. And who knows how to even operate a gas-powered
mower? In Hector Tobar's novel *Barbarian Nurseries*, a Southern
California software engineer who is feeling the pinch of the economic
recession fires his Mexican gardener and the nanny and decides to mow
the lawn himself. The novel opens with this engineer, who is half Mexican

and grew up mowing the lawn in the suburbs, now totally befuddled by the apparatus. He can't get even the power mower started, and the Mexican immigrant housekeeper, the one person he has not fired from his household staff, looks on wondering if she should tell him how the gardener, Pepe, used to do it. She decides, wisely, to withhold a potential moment of embarrassment and emasculation. Even his wife wonders, "It uses gasoline. How complicated can it be?"[28] It remains a scene of failed domestic masculinity, but only because he got out there and tried.

The men do not bemoan the loss of domestic masculinity in lawn care, but some home owners worry that in the age when Latino gardeners do all of the garden work their children are becoming too pampered and spoiled. Middle-class home owners recalled childhood chores of mowing, weeding, and raking leaves, and while most emphatically said they had never liked doing these chores, many believed that these activities helped to build virtue and a strong work ethic. Were their children now deprived of these character-building exercises? This was a quiet question to contemplate, not a burning anxiety. Barbara Klein, the mother of three teenaged boys, disclosed her discomfort with the situation. "I have to say one thing that really makes me cringe, is when the gardeners are here and my kids are in there watching TV," she said. "It makes me feel like I'm raising spoiled brats—even though I know they're not . . . but I just kind of wonder what those guys [the gardeners] feel like. 'Oh, well, look at those fancy pants white guys, they get to watch TV all day while we're out here busting our asses.' You know its kind of hard when class differences are that stark."

No one else spoke about class and racial inequalities in these clear-cut terms, but other respondents talked about their children's laziness with garden work. One couple had offered to pay their ten-year-old son, who was saving money for new electronic games, money for weeding, but he lasted only ten minutes. At another magnificent canyon property with many areas for running, hiding, and climbing trees, the children rarely went outside because they were so busy with homework, extracurricular activities, and computer games. Dr. Aleman said his teenagers enjoyed hanging out by the pool with their friends, listening to music over the sound system, but they didn't do any of the gardening work. The California dream garden doesn't require too much heavy lifting from anyone but the Latino immigrant gardeners.

THE GARDENERS AND THE CALIFORNIA DREAM

What are the gardeners' California dreams, and how do they experience the work? Working in private residential yards is their portal to a better life. They're in it—let's be clear on this—to support their families back home, or to make their California dream here. This dream of upward social mobility and providing better life opportunities for their children is one that *is* being fulfilled for the Latino gardeners who got into the business during the expanding boom years. These are older men, now in their fifties and sixties, who entered the occupation in the 1980s, when there was less competition. These gardeners also benefited from the 1986 Immigration Reform and Control Act, a law that allowed them to become legal residents, substantiating the dictum that legal status enhances earning potential.[29] Many of these men have since become naturalized U.S. citizens, and some of their children have graduated from college and become upwardly mobile professionals.

Gardeners in this upper tier are still doing the hard manual labor of tending other people's gardens, but they are also solvent business owners and home owners. Many of them have also built their own California dream-escape garden yards, often miniature versions of those that they tend during the week. Ramon Espinoza, the gardener who lives in Inglewood with his family of five, has a house and garden property that includes neatly mowed lawn, palm trees and white ice-berg roses lining the front walkway, and a backyard patio outfitted with a built-in barbecue and bar, where he relaxes after work or on Sundays. The most financially secure gardeners have purchased not only their own homes but also rental property, which they plan to rely on for retirement income. The twentieth-century narrative of immigrant social mobility continues in the lives of these self-employed gardeners, who are simultaneously entrepreneurs and manual workers. They are exemplars of the American dream, but the fate of their younger peers, the workers who migrated in the 1990s and afterwards, is not so certain.

The new opportunities for occupational succession look dim for the gardeners' wage employees. They are earning minimum wage or slightly better, neither of which puts them in line for home ownership, and many of them are stuck in a legal limbo with undocumented or temporary legal status. Many of these men have lived and worked without legal authorization for ten, twenty, or more years. They live in crowded apartments with kin or with other immigrant laborers. Mine is not a longitudinal study, so it is impossible to predict where they will be on the economic ladder a decade down the road, but it seems unlikely that these gardeners will be climbing the escalator to self-employment any time soon. The labor market is saturated, and competitive underbidding prevails. Some of the *ayudante* employees realize this, but they also recognize the extent to which social capital binds them to gardening. "I work for another *señor*, helping to make him rich," one *ayudante* said with wry humor. "I've only worked with people I know, brothers, cousins, friends. That's why we get along." Conflicting interests thread through these relations too. For the Central American men who have migrated since the 1980s to Los Angeles from Guatemala, El Salvador, and Honduras, fleeing civil wars and economic wreckage, it has been tough to break into employment social networks already tightly woven by men from central western Mexico. Competition is fierce.

Most Latino immigrant gardeners working in Southern California have only a few years of formal schooling and few technical skills, what economists would call low levels of "human capital." They were raised on ranchos, in the countryside or small provincial towns, where the lack of upper-grade education and family needs for their labor cut their schooling short, but they are rich in social capital, as regional ethnic and family solidarity binds them together. Their experience of the job is informed by their ranchero pasts in their countries of origin, the daily routine of their work, and their future aspirations for themselves and their families.

Ranchero masculinity, an orientation born of work experience in central western Mexico, shapes their work in gardening.[30] In Mexico, many of these men cultivated crops and controlled livestock, usually on their own land, where they were accustomed to working independently. They like working outdoors and they value what Marcia Farr has called "*el progreso* [progress] through hard work and an individual entrepreneurial effort."[31] Even though they are slogging through many gardens in one day, the gardeners still enjoy tactile, sensual connection with plant nature and the sense of freedom that comes from working outdoors in different settings. When asked what they most like about their work, the *jardineros* said they enjoy the spatial mobility, being their own boss, and working in "*aire libre*," or fresh air. A literal translation is "in free air," and this too is telling. Working outdoors in the sunshine, and moving about from one house to another, brings them a sense of freedom that resonates with their *ranchero* cultural origins. They value independence and autonomy, and working outdoors with plants. One gardener captured the sentiments of many when he said, "I like my work because I'm not inside. I like the open air. I like it because I go around here and there. And I don't report to anyone."

Working as a gardener involves a steady pace of constant outdoor physical exertion, and long work days are broken up by driving in trucks from early morning to dusk, from one job to the next. It's hard, physical work, often requiring exertion under a burning sun. Yet when asked to compare their current gardening jobs to crop cultivation work they did in Mexico, or to other jobs they have held in California agriculture, factories, and restaurants, the men unanimously said gardening was preferable. Francisco, who had previously worked in a Chicago factory, said he now felt free of factory regimentation. "What I most like about my job is working outdoors, not having to punch a time clock," he said. "I'm my own boss. Of course, if you need to get to a job you need to get up at dawn. You put in your time to arrive at a certain hour [but] you can choose." Francisco also said he liked the freedom of flexibility and said the earnings were better too, resonating with a sense of independence and entrepreneurial drive. "Here I can earn a little more if I put in more hours, and back there [in the factory job], no. You have to check in at a certain time, and they're always changing your schedule. The company decides, and you can't say anything." Ricardo, who had previously worked in a high-pressure restaurant as a busboy and waiter for fourteen years, claimed he still had bad dreams about that job. By contrast, he liked "*la libertad*" or the freedom in gardening work. "You're in charge of yourself," he explained. "You're not tied down to one timetable or schedule. You don't have that pressure to be at one place at a certain time. You plan the day so it's most convenient for you." He also liked the familiarity of being around plants, as he grew up "planting and harvesting." In gardening, working outdoors, tending plants, and roaming around in trucks, the men do not feel trapped by four walls and surveillance.

Plate 1. A well-researched drawing of what San Gabriel Mission looked like in the 1830s shows irrigated and cultivated land surrounded by vast empty plains below the San Gabriel Mountains. Michael J. Hart, www.michaeljhart.com.

Plate 2. Most Latino immigrant gardeners do not dress like this, but maybe they should, as without protection for their eyes, skin, lungs, and ears, they risk bodily injury, skin abrasions, respiratory ailments, and hearing loss. This gardener is so covered up and carries such a mega-sized blower that he resembles a soldier going to battle. Photo by Nathan Solis.

Plate 3. Many Mexican immigrant gardeners approach their work with pride and dignity and have rural, ranchero origins in central western Mexico. While the job allows some of them to earn a good living, the work is hard and causes bodily injury, as the brace on this gardener's wrist shows. Photo by Nathan Solis.

Plate 4. Most Latino gardeners dress in basic work clothes and boots and must drink plenty of water to stay hydrated as they work below constant sun. Photo by Nathan Solis.

Plate 5. Near this community garden, gentrification and new construction threatened to change the character of the neighborhood. The construction project shown in the background here was a new "low-income housing" development, but the rents and required income level were so high that none of the community gardeners would be able to live there. Photo by Robbert Flick.

Plate 6. The Suzhou-style garden, Liu Fang Yuan, at the Huntington. Photo by author.

Plate 7. Besides being a food production site and a community resource, the urban community garden is a place for ornamental beauty, play, and relaxation. Photo by author.

Plate 8. At the urban community gardens, friends help one another with planting and watering. Photo by Michael Messner.

The gardeners of Eden, however, also feel the stress of 24/7 responsibilities that self-employment brings. They feel pressed and harried for time, and they need to manage relations with both their clients and their workers. The gardening business enters their personal home life, and not always in ways they can control. When clients call on Sundays or in the evening, work intrudes on family time. Ricardo Morales explained what it's like. "You leave early in the morning and never know when you're getting back. And Sunday is the day for family, but sometimes you have to work, you have to do it." Evenings at home are not free of work: "You didn't really leave work, because you have to make calls, you have to buy material, you have to pay your worker, or you have to find another worker. You can get home at 3:00 p.m., but you're still working until you sleep."

The self-employed gardeners appreciated their coethnic employees, some of whom were relatives, but they also expressed typical employer complaints about them. "It's frustrating when people don't have the experience to do these jobs. I don't like to be after them, telling them what to do," said one *jardinero,* "[but] sometimes I struggle with the *muchachos.*" Another, commenting on his worker, said, *"Siempre es pushar y jalar. . . .* It's always pushing and pulling. It's a constant struggle, in a way, with the workers. There's days when they feel like working hard, days when they don't." Another gardener reasoned, "You can't demand more work [from them] than what you are willing to do." The gardeners feel the squeeze from both their home owner clients and their workers. "Sometimes the clients are very demanding. They demand a lot, and they pay little. And there's days when the workers know how to work, and days," he chuckled, "when they don't know."

THE BLOWERS

Pristinely manicured lawns and gardens introduced a new element to the private paradises, noise pollution caused by the gas-powered leaf blowers. In fact, this is the only facet of the Latino immigrant gardening regime that receives regular media attention—and it is always unambiguously negative attention. Since 1975, over twenty cities in California, and now more cities nationwide from Massachusetts to Long Island, have moved to

Figure 21. Latino immigrant gardeners at work with backpack
leaf blowers are common sights in middle-class and affluent
neighborhoods. Photo by Nathan Solis.

ban the blowers. In Los Angeles, the leaf blower bans of the 1990s, driven
by complaints from Beverly Hills residents such as Julie Newmar (who
played Catwoman on the Batman TV show), and Mrs. Peter Graves, represented the biggest political confrontation encountered by the gardeners,
prompting them to organize their own social movement organization, the
Association of Latin American Gardeners of Los Angeles.[32]

Southern California is a crazy quilt of municipalities, each with different regulations and resources for implementing these bans. Affluent and
predominantly white residential cities all over California have banned the
blowers, but in Southern California enforcement of these municipal bans
has been spotty or nonexistent. Over a two-year period, Santa Monica
issued twelve tickets, with fines of $250 to $1,000, while city officials
reported receiving over 2,500 complaints about blowers.[33] Even though
Santa Monica covers only eight and half square miles and supports its
own Office of Sustainability and the Environment, enforcement remains
erratic. In Los Angeles, which spans 468 square miles, the leaf blower ban
is largely symbolic.

Calls for strict enforcement of blower bans have escalated incendiary
nativist attacks on Latino gardeners. The category "Mexican," long associated with "illegality," is now extended toward a key tool of the trade, the

leaf blower. None of the home owners that I interviewed decried the noise-blasting machines used to tidy their gardens and yards, and perhaps they felt, in the context of our interview, that they couldn't really say this without appearing to be hypocritical. But other home owners have let loose on the issue. Here are a smattering of anonymously posted barrages from an online site, *The Los Angeles Forum*:

> What's wrong with these Mexican gardeners that they PERSIST on using their ILLEGAL banned gasoline leaf blowers creating noise pollution throughout LA?
> It's bad enough they can't exercise family control, but why this?
> What is there [*sic*] motive?
> Who are the idiots who are hiring them?
> —Solitude, Los Angeles

> We always hear what hard workers Mexicans are, how about they pick up a broom!!
> —Adam, AOL

> Gas powered leaf blowers in neighborhoods was made illegal in LA over ten years ago. These inconsiderate greedy gardeners claim they just want to work. . . . Its not right that the Mexicans should come here and destroy the environment and hurt people.
> —Ron, Santa Rosa, CA[34]

These rants build on colonial-era stereotypes of the "lazy" and "sleepy Mexican" and fears of the "*reconquista*" by Mexican "invaders." Throughout California, and now from coast to coast, public outcries have called on the Latino gardeners to put down the labor-saving devices and do the job the old-fashioned way: pick up rakes and brooms. But as the job is organized and remunerated today, the only way for gardeners to earn a living is to tend many yards in one day. "Without the blower, you work a lot harder and there is no compensation," said one gardener. Stagnant fees have fueled a work speedup, so the job can be performed only with the most efficient gas-powered technology. The Latino gardeners understand this well. "The blower is a necessity. . . . Without it] you would have to charge more, and they don't want to pay more." Not one of the Latino gardeners reported having a customer step forward to offer higher pay for doing all the garden cleaning with rakes and brooms.

Figure 22. While Latino immigrant gardeners are criticized for using loud power mowers and blowers, they also use rakes and other manual tools. Photo by Nathan Solis.

There is a hierarchy of California dreams operating here in Southern California, and when it comes to the immigrant gardener regime, the first priority is the creation of perfect California dream gardens with the new high standards of tidiness and perfection that everyone has come to expect. The gardeners understand this is a non-negotiable requirement, and with the way the job is organized and remunerated, so too is the blower. "Without it, we couldn't do our work. . . . People want to see their houses clean, but they don't want to pay for more time," reasoned one gardener. Another gardener, commenting on Beverly Hills, where the blowers are banned, said: "We kept using them anyway. I think there's a lot of tolerance, because they know everyone uses them. They just give out tickets once in a while."

Private residential gardens in Southern California are paradoxical places, sites of both labor exploitation and garden enjoyment. The gardens are shaped by home owners' desire for a private Edenic paradise and yearnings for comfort, beauty, and tranquillity, as well as the display of status and property value, and by the Latino gardeners' dream for "a better life," as the title of a popular movie about a Latino gardener and his

Figure 23. "Sleepy Mexican" statues were once popular garden ornaments, much like statues of black lawn jockeys. While these are no longer prevalent sights in California, campaigns that have vilified Latino immigrant gardeners as "lazy" echo racialized stereotypes. Photo by author.

teenage son in Los Angeles aptly puts it.[35] Multiple and intersecting California dreams unfold in these gardens, and labor and money are exchanged as people pursue these dreams. In the movie, the actor Demian Bechir plays a single father, Luis, who makes a valiant effort to go from *ayudante* to route-owner *jardinero* in Los Angeles when he buys his former boss's truck. "This country is the land of dreams," he narrates in the film. "It can be a hard place, a cruel place. But each day at work, I dream of a better life for my son." He yearns to move his son to better schools and soccer fields, but when his truck and tools are stolen the dream bursts and disrupts into deportation and family separation. Legal status remains a key factor separating the route- and truck-owner gardeners from their wage-earning *ayudantes.*

The new California dream-escape builds on an older Jeffersonian narrative, but instead of living on acres of land worked by hundreds of slaves, the middle class and the affluent now live on smaller plots of land, and the hired Latino immigrant gardeners arrive weekly to mow lawns and trim a vast array of ornamental plants. The gardeners are overwhelmingly Latino immigrant men, and their hard work allows Southern Californians to have private sanctuaries and express ideals of moral virtue, integrity, and status through neatly mowed front lawns and backyard dream-escape gardens. The yards are stages of conspicuous leisure, but many residents are too busy managing work and family life to fully enjoy their private paradises. While garden standards have increased to new levels of perfection and tidiness, the Latino gardeners suffer social invisibility, lack of recognition, and frozen fees, and in one city after another they have been pilloried for using the leaf blowers.

The maintenance gardening occupation is stratified, with California dreams of upward mobility and dream-escape homes and gardens available to the gardeners at the top, the route owners who got into the business when the field was still relatively open. Many of them have now bought their own homes and gardens, not in Bel Air but in cities such as South Gate, Rosemead, and Inglewood. They own the tools and the trucks, and most of them have access to dense social networks and permanent legal residency status. They collect monthly fees from the home owners and manage their gardening business. For the younger cohort of workers that these gardeners employ, who are often their kin and acquaintances from back home, the mobility opportunities in gardening look dim. Home owners do not want to pay more for services, while the route-owner gardeners must pay more for gas and machinery, so wages remain stagnant. Newcomers to the job settle for low wages, and when they try to build their own routes they accept jobs at lower fees.

Multiple visions of the California dream are operative here, but within the hierarchy, well-to-do home owners retain the upper hand and Latino immigrant men from the global South make it all possible. Rather than recognition, the gardeners of Eden face public allegations that they are not "real gardeners" because they use machinery. Global processes of immigration, intersecting with relations of class, gender, and race, are played out daily in the beautiful residential gardens of Southern California. Mexican immigrant men are the new male domestic workers, and six days a week they are mowing the lawns, trimming the hedges, and cleaning private paradises.

4 "It's a Little Piece of My Country"

Once a month on Saturday it's cleanup day at the Franklin urban community garden, just west of downtown Los Angeles.[1] Outside on the sidewalks, Latino and Korean vendors sell used clothing and household goods, transforming an intersection into an informal open-air market. Dresses and jackets hang from the trees and chain-link fences, and shoppers dawdle as they haggle and inspect used tools, blenders, toys, bedspreads, shoes, and still more items. This is a poor neighborhood, and around the block, hundreds of people line up every Saturday morning for bags of food distributed at a church by the LA Regional Food Bank. It is widely believed that no one walks in Los Angeles, but in this neighborhood pedestrians line the streets every day. Few people own cars here.

Inside the garden, about twenty-five people, most of them Central American and Mexican immigrant women but also men and children, gather for the collective *diá de limpieza*, the garden cleanup day. Everyone who rents one of the eighteen parcels at an annual rate of $30 must participate, but neighbors and friends of the garden pitch in too. We start working around 9:00 a.m., with a handful straggling in slightly later, and Monica Sanchez, a charismatic forty-four-year-old mother of three from Michoacán, greets us with her radiant smile, coffee, and *pan dulce* and hands out clippers, rakes, and brooms. Monica is the official gatekeeper, paid a nominal fee to open and close the front garden gates daily at dawn and dusk, but really she is the heart and soul of this place, welcoming newcomers, connecting people, and providing advice on everything from what herbal remedies might calm a colicky infant to the necessity of carefully reading the fine print on rental contracts. Monica thrives in nature, and as she often reminds us she entered this garden when it first opened over ten years ago and has never left. She's agile and fit, dressed in running shoes, cargo pants, and a hoodie. With her waist-long hair hanging in one thick glossy braid, Monica swiftly hands out tools, and all morning she is besieged by incessant questions, which are shouted in Spanish across the garden beds. Monica, *como quieres que corto esto?* (How do you want me to prune this?) Where do you want me to put these trimmings? Shall we move this compost? The barrage of questions never ceases, and Monica flits from one corner of the garden to another, doing hands-on work but providing vital directives and guidance, telling us when it's the right time to cut back the sugarcane or the banana leaves. She is harried, but she always makes time for children, pausing to admire the latest batch of worms they have dug up in the dirt and finding ways for them to feel useful too. Coordinating the cleanup can be a frustrating job. Some people drag their feet, and a few fail to show up. And sometimes people make mistakes, as I did with Marcos Gutiérrez, a Zapotec father of five and a respected, experienced gardener, when we were both clipping a wisteria vine dangling over a fence. He worked much faster than me, and feeling sub-par, I tried to pick up the pace. We got lost in conversation, chatting about Oaxaca, deer, flying saucers, and his job as a gardener in LA, and before we knew it we had radically and incorrectly pruned the wisteria. Monica had exclaimed, *"Ay, Marcos y Pierrette! Que han hecho aquí?! Así no se corta! Esto ya no va florecer por dos años!"* (What have you done here?! That's not the way to cut it! Now it won't bloom for two years!). I felt terrible—it's a heartfelt loss when someone cuts down your plant—but Monica quickly forgave us and soon we all gathered for a shared feast, which always followed the cleanups.

As helicopters fly overhead and sirens wail, blossoms, vegetables, herbs, and delicious *pupusas* and quesadillas are regularly produced here in the middle of urban Los Angeles—but other life-sustaining value is created too. The *mujeres* weed, water, and cook, and in the process they are also tending to themselves, creating homeland tableaus and a new place of belonging, reaffirming cultural identity and improvising solutions to their daily problems. In an otherwise bleak urban landscape, these women, and the men and children who gather here, are taking care of the earth and taking care of themselves.

I spent over one year participating in weeding, clipping, eating, attending meetings, chatting and hanging out, observing, and interviewing people at two small urban community gardens located just west of downtown Los Angeles, and I was assisted in these activities by Jose Miguel Ruiz, a young college graduate who had just returned to the neighborhood where he was raised.[2] As a child, Jose Miguel had attended Hoover Elementary School, a local school featured in a documentary about California's Proposition 187, which in a frenzy of nativism spearheaded by Governor Pete Wilson's 1994 desperate reelection campaign had threatened undocumented immigrant children with removal from public schools.[3] Jose Miguel had been one of those students, and his teachers had brought him to the Franklin garden. Now he was helping me understand the next generation at the gardens, and the research experience was helping him prepare for graduate school. He was instrumental in my entry to these urban community gardens. Together we participated in many community garden events, and our discussions enhanced the insights I present in this chapter. I use the pseudonyms "Dolores Huerta Community Garden" and "Franklin Community Garden" for the two gardens we studied. I stayed on the scene far longer than the ethnography warranted, drawn by the familylike social hub, especially at the Franklin garden, which helped me navigate my own life transitions and empty nest. Attesting to the community bonds these places foster, Jose Miguel now cultivates a plot at the Dolores Huerta garden and continues his activism at the garden with a group of Guatemalan youth.

The community gardeners here come from the southern region of Mexico and Central America and are among the poorest, marginalized residents of Los Angeles. Dislodged from their home countries by the aftermath of civil wars and neoliberal development policies, they now find themselves in a double dislocation, also excluded from many public and private spaces in Los Angeles. Their lives here are shaped by segregation, poverty, racial discrimination, and criminalization because of their immigration status. Some of them are indigenous and speak Spanish as a second language. Many of them are undocumented. Their families are fragmented, with some members here, some still there. The most well off among them work as janitors and domestic workers—and they are the only ones who regularly leave the immediate vicinity. Other residents live on the fringes of the informal economy and rarely travel on the bus to other neighborhoods. All of them are struggling to educate their kids and navigate new lives in Los Angeles, but spousal separations, bad jobs without security and living wages, and deportations disrupt family solvency and the ability to pay bills and put food on the table. Life is not easy.

They seek belonging, inclusion, and a recreated homeland. Men, women, and children gather at the gardens, but these are really women's spaces. Men can congregate elsewhere—at nearby Lafayette Park, or on street corners—but these women lack access to public space. At the gardens, they nourish and heal themselves and their families with cherished homeland plants such as *papalo*, *verdolaga*, sugarcane, *chiles*, and *hierba buena*. Sometimes the tomatoes and squash are bountiful, sometimes not as much. Even these seasoned, experienced gardeners and farmers, I learned, have mini-crop failures and disappointing harvests. But just *being in the garden*, tending to their plants or even sitting on a bench with tiny birds fluttering and chirping in a nearby tree, or inhaling the fragrance of spring blossoms and the earthy smell of wet soil, revives them and makes complicated lives seem bearable. Here they experience the restorative power of being in a garden that looks, feels, and smells like their original homeland, literally rooting their communities and culture in this part of the earth. But these are not simply gardens of nostalgia, for the gardens and sharing of information here enable community members to innovate versatile solutions to pressing problems.

Urban community gardens always arise in times of social crisis, such as war or economic recession, and with the global financial crisis that hit the United States in 2008, community gardens around the country enjoyed new resurgence. Activists, scholars, and advocacy organizations now hail their many benefits. Community gardens generate social and cultural gatherings, provide healthy foods in neighborhoods where fresh produce is not always available in stores, and revitalize communities by serving as sites of leisure where low-income adults and children may experience nature in cities lacking parks and playgrounds.[4] All of these benefits are evident at the Franklin and Dolores Huerta community gardens, but because of the deportation crisis producing immigrant illegality and marginality, the gardens serve other functions too.

First, these gardens serve as restorative spaces of belonging and inclusion, encompassing both recreation and the re-creation of homeland practices and culture. These gardens are fundamentally about belonging and social connection, with food and plants bridging Central American and Mexican immigrant gardeners to their past, to others, and to visions of the future. They are making a new home for themselves here, and homemaking, as Yen Le Espiritu reminds us, is an active process.[5] Life in these gardens is particularly meaningful because many of the Mexicans and Central Americans here cannot afford to return to their home countries for a visit or in addition cannot do so because of the dangers of crossing the militarized US-Mexico border.

Between 1997 and 2012, the US government carried out 4.2 million deportations. These were concentrated in Latino immigrant communities. Without viable routes to legal permanent residency and citizenship, millions of Mexicans and Central Americans were deported, detained, or removed from the country, while others remained stuck, literally trapped in the United States, afraid to return home for a visit because it was now more difficult to return to the United States. During this period, even immigrants with legal status felt under siege.[6] In this context, the gardens become places where elements of homeland social and material life could be re-created. The gardens served as safe, outdoor, noncommercialized sites for combating social isolation, depression, fear, anxiety, and alienation.

Everyday disappointments melt away at the gardens. People say they inhale a different air and experience a sort of momentary amnesia from the violent assaults of power that they experience on the streets, at work, and in their crowded apartments. Sometimes they share their problems with others and think up solutions. The gardens also act as incubators of democratic civic engagement and activism. These gardens are not pure Edenic paradises, but they exert a strong palliative force.

THE HISTORY OF URBAN COMMUNITY GARDENS

Urban community gardens focusing on food production have a long history in the United States, typically arising in times of social crisis with the goal of producing not only vegetables but also a modicum of community self-sufficiency.[7] In the United States, between the 1890s and 1917, social reformers of the Progressive Era promoted urban community gardens for the unemployed, driven by the belief that these community gardens would revitalize poor urban neighborhoods, ameliorate urban poverty, and Americanize new immigrants from southern and eastern Europe. This was a very top-down movement, tinged with middle-class good intentions and paternalism. "Anchored in a philosophy of environmental determinism," as Laura J. Lawson observes in her comprehensive review of American community gardens, "turn-of-the-century urban garden programs were expected to simultaneously improve both the environment and the behavior of the participants."[8]

Middle-class and upper-class leaders of the era devised school gardens and vacant-lot cultivation to inculcate agrarian values and a strong work ethic in the urban working class. By the early twentieth century, gardening was widely integrated into the school curriculum. In 1906 the US Department of Agriculture counted seventy-five thousand school gardens in the United States, and prominent leaders of the day, including the urban social reformer Jacob Riis, the landscape designer of Central Park Frederick Law Olmsted Jr., and President Woodrow Wilson heralded these efforts.[9] In Southern California, a significant school garden program began in 1898, and by 1912 there were over one hundred school gardens in Los Angeles, with special garden teachers, assisted by civic and women's groups, providing direction and support. Typically, each grade level at a school cultivated their own plot of land.[10] Gardening was also a central part of the curriculum at the Indian boarding schools, such as the Sherman Institute in Riverside. At the turn of the century Los Angeles nurseryman Horatio Rust recommended that every Indian child should be taught to "make, and care for, a garden. . . . so that when he leaves school he shall be competent to perform all the varied labors on a farm or garden."[11] By then, many Mexican, Chinese, Japanese, and white midwestern youth were already working with their families in the fields of Southern California.[12]

Nation and migration have been central forces driving community gardens. During World War I, the federal government promoted "Liberty Gardens" to augment domestically produced food. The government supported this effort through the National War Garden Commission and with a large media campaign, recruiting women and children with beautiful decorative posters and slogans declaring "Food Will Win the War" and "Liberty Sowing the Seeds of Victory." Working in individual plots in backyards and public spaces, the gardeners were, by all accounts, enormously productive in growing food, with five million gardeners producing more than half a million dollars worth of produce, thereby preserving produce for export to the US troops in Europe.[13] When the war ended, both government and business withdrew support from the Liberty Gardens, and during the economic boom years of the 1920s, both school gardens and Liberty Gardens declined.

With the Great Depression, "relief gardens" and "potato patches" emerged as a remedy for the nation's joblessness and food scarcity. These garnered momentary support from the federal government until new programs for food stamps and surplus farm products were introduced. World War II "Victory Gardens," animated by patriotic ideals of self-sufficiency and aiding the war effort, provided the next installment of food gardens. Food production reached astoundingly high levels: in 1944, Victory Gardens are believed to have produced 44 percent of the fresh produce eaten in the United States.[14] Contrary to most people's image, Southern California was a hotbed for agricultural production throughout the first half of the twentieth century—and it wasn't just Victory Gardens. Until the 1950s and the expansion of the postwar housing boom and suburban sprawl, Los Angeles County was the top agricultural county in the United States, home to approximately ten thousand small family farms and to citrus and walnut orchards that enjoyed close proximity to their consumers.[15]

A couple of decades later, fueled by the social movements and "back to nature" countercultural ideals of the 1960s and 1970s, and facilitated by the urban fiscal crises and availability of vacant lots in cities such as Boston, Philadelphia, and New York City, a new crop of urban community gardens emerged. Unlike the wartime gardens, these were formed through creative, transgressive direct action, not by federal government support.

In fact, many of these gardens were spawned by the deliberately antiestablishment politics of the 1960s. The Green Guerrillas, a grassroots group started by a young artist, Liz Christy, in New York in 1973, initially threw "seed bombs" and "green-aids" to plant sunflowers and morning glories in abandoned, fenced properties. These garden activists sustained threats from city authorities, developers, and the banks, but after direct actions and lawsuits over a thousand vacant lots in New York City were transformed into urban community gardens.[16] These declined in the 1990s but are once again on the rebound.[17] As Sharon Zukin points out in *Naked City*, these gardens have shifted from grassroots efforts to become institutionalized, professional organizations, supported by administrators who are able to apply for and oversee grants.[18] Bureaucracy and nonprofit professional organizations have become increasingly important to urban community gardens, a trend that emerged in the 1980s, with organizations such as Urban Garden Program directed by the US Department of Agriculture, and with state agricultural extension programs lending institutional support.

Detroit and New York City are now among the cities that lead the nation in urban community gardens (Newark and Philadelphia are up there too). Detroit pioneered the vacant-lot movement in the 1890s, and today, postindustrial, rust belt Detroit is once again the epicenter of the social movement for urban community gardens and farms. As the city has removed burnt-out and fallen-down houses, urban agriculture has flourished. During the first decade of this century, as sociologist Monica White has shown, a revitalized movement for autonomy and food security emerged in Detroit, connected to the movement for black sovereignty and autonomy. In other cities such as Boston, similar community garden mobilizations grew out of the civil rights movement in the 1960s.[19] The confluence of inexpensive, abandoned land and a strong African American mobilization has had a lasting impact in Detroit, which now boasts three farms and over one hundred community and school gardens.[20] Land is plentiful, and the city allows people to "adopt a lot" for free, allowing many collective gardens, urban farms, and produce markets to flourish.[21]

Contemporary global migration has also invigorated community gardens. By 2010, the United States was home to thirty-eight million foreign-born people, the vast majority from Latin America, the Caribbean, and

Asia. For new immigrants and refugees, community gardens provide thriving food growing spaces and homeland connections. Some of these gardens permit commercial sale and thus enable job creation and economic self-sufficiency. In western Massachusetts, Cambodian Khmer refugees grow melons and pumpkins on public land, and as Patricia Klindienst observes, "They give new meaning to the idea of the garden as refuge."[22] In the City Heights neighborhood of San Diego, eighty refugee families from Somalia and other nations grow radishes, chard, and tomatoes, assisted by the International Rescue Committee's "New Roots" program, which supports similar refugee community gardens in Salt Lake City, Boise, Idaho, Charlottesville, New York City, and Seattle.[23] At El Poblano Farm in Staten Island, Mexican immigrants blend Mexican farming techniques with what they have learned at a seven-week course on the requirements for commercial farming in New York, allowing them to grow and sell *papalo* and *flor de calabaza* to local restaurants and markets.[24] Throughout New York City, Puerto Ricans and Dominicans grow familiar foods and seek leisure in Caribbean landscapes of nostalgia.[25]

The most famous urban community garden, thanks in part to the Oscar-winning documentary *The Garden*, is the South Central Farm of Los Angeles.[26] Until 2006, when it was bulldozed, more than three hundred families, mainly Mexican and Central American immigrants, including indigenous people of Mixtec, Tojolobal, Triqui, Yaqui, and Zapotec descent, cultivated a fourteen-acre property in the impoverished neighborhood of what we now call South Los Angeles, near Watts and Compton. This large urban garden began in the 1990s, in that post–Rodney King moment when community activists and new coalitions were rebuilding poor communities of color in Los Angeles. With funding from both public and private parties, the organizers started with a 7.5-acre vacant lot controlled by the city and deliberately embraced the word *farm* to emphasize agricultural production and to erase any connotation of suburban, ornamental gardening.[27] The South Central Farm grew to include over three hundred substantial-sized parcels, each averaging 1,500 square feet, big enough for families to build small shelters or *casitas* where they would gather for socializing and eating.[28] Until it was bulldozed, the South Central Farm was reportedly the largest urban community garden ever documented in the United States. When geographer Devon Peña conducted a study of plant biodiversity there, he counted over one hundred species of trees, shrubs, vines, cacti and herbs, and proclaimed the replication of a veritable "Vavilov Center." Vavilov Centers are world sites where the original domestication of wild plants occurred, and there are only eight in the world. Mesoamerica is one of them, having introduced corn, beans, squash, tomatoes, chiles, chocolate and peanuts, foods now commonly ingested in our global diet. In this regard, Peña suggests that the South Central Farmers served not only as food producers but as "stewards of a significant cultural and natural resource."[29]

The South Central Farmers were sustaining their families and communities with food, but they were also involved in the project of community narration through place making, what Devon Peña calls "autotopography."[30] In one of the poorest, neglected industrial neighborhoods of Los Angeles, the South Central Farmers transformed abandoned urban wastelands to look like their homeland, often with *nopales* (cactus) and small *casitas* erected on the plots. This transformation was particularly salient for Latino immigrants denied formal legal status and US citizenship. As William V. Flores and his colleagues suggest, "claiming space" is a vital aspect of Latino cultural expression, allowing groups to define themselves and to create "a distinct Latino sensibility, a social and political discourse, and a Latino aesthetic."[31] As we will see, this process of community self-definition is also part of what is unfolding at the pocket-sized community gardens just west of downtown Los Angeles.

The South Central Farm was violently razed in 2006. Why was it bulldozed? I contend that this happened because both the cultivators and the land lacked legal permanent residency and full rights. This was essentially the struggle between the legitimacy of private property held by a multimillionaire (who continued to leave this large property vacant) and the illegitimacy of poor people's collective claims to the productive use of land. Not even celebrity support from Daryl Hannah and Joan Baez could stop the bulldozers. The original farm was lost, but today South Central Farmers are thriving, thanks in part to strong organizational leadership and community autonomy, *and* to their integration into local capitalist markets. Many of the farmers continue to grow vegetables in South Los Angeles at the Stanford Avalon Community Garden, a nine-acre space under power lines in Watts, where individual families cultivate nearly two hundred large plots

(40′ × 60′) for both personal consumption and sale to local restaurants and taco trucks. Restaurant owners and catering trucks arrive early in the morning to purchase fresh produce, and food writer Jonathan Gold has even profiled the garden in an upscale food magazine, *Saveur*.[32] A small group of the original South Central Farmers have taken this to another scale, and as a nonprofit 501(c)(3) organization they now lease land near Bakersfield in the Central Valley, producing bountiful fresh organic produce that they sell at trendy farmers' markets and at Whole Foods stores in Southern California.[33] These inner-city Latino immigrant community gardeners have brought organic farming to the heartland of California agribusiness, innovating business models and new forms of land use.

The global financial crisis of 2008–12 and the interest in organic foods spurred a resurgence of urban agriculture around the country and in Southern California. Urban community gardens are part of this movement, and there are now between seventy and one hundred community gardens operating in the Los Angeles area.[34] A combination of public and private funding supports these gardens, and while the urban community gardens in Los Angeles include diverse demographics and different kinds of neighborhoods, the gardeners are mostly low-income, older, and Latino.[35]

·   ·   ·   ·   ·

The Franklin and Dolores Huerta community gardens are situated in the most densely populated areas of Los Angeles, the Westlake District (popularly called MacArthur Park or Pico Union), just west of the high-rises in downtown Los Angeles. This is a poor urban area where the majority of the households earn less than $20,000 a year.[36] Many of the community gardeners are getting by on half that amount.

This was once a high-end part of town, but the classic postwar city transformations of the late 1940s and 1950s—suburbanization, white flight, and the expansion of the freeway system—took affluent residents out of the neighborhood, to the West Side or to suburbs in the valleys.[37] Westlake's grand single-family homes were divided into apartments and residential hotels or were bulldozed for new buildings, and as the well-heeled white residents exited, the neighborhood became much poorer. Salvadorans fleeing civil war and Guatemalans fleeing militarized violence and attacks on

Figure 24. The Franklin garden gate is open from dawn to dusk. Photo by author.

Figure 25. The Dolores Huerta garden gate is open only to parcel renters and their family and friends, creating a kind of gated community. Photo by author.

indigenous communities began arriving in Los Angeles in the late 1970s and the early 1980s, and they settled into the Westlake District, principally around MacArthur Park and near the intersection of Pico and Union Avenues. Mexican immigrant families also settled in the area, and although Mexicans here today outnumber Central Americans, the area became the official Central American neighborhood of Los Angeles, with *taquerías*, *pupuserías*, check-cashing services, and courier services specializing in sending money and goods to Mexico and Central America. Nonprofit community organizations such as CARECEN (Central American Resource Center), El Rescate, and CHIRLA (Coalition for Humane Immigrant Rights in Los Angeles) opened their doors in this neighborhood. In the 1990s more organizations, such as SALEF (the Salvadoran American Leadership and Education Fund) emerged, and in 2002 the UCLA Downtown Labor Center opened offices across the street from MacArthur Park.[38] Westlake remains a key center of Latino immigrant life in Los

Figure 26. La casita, as it often looked while everyone was working in the garden. Photo by author.

Angeles, and it provided the anchor site for the May 1, 2006, immigrant rights marches that brought thousands to the streets to demand comprehensive immigration reform.

The two community gardens here are very different. The Dolores Huerta Community Garden is located in the Pico Union area, and it is less welcoming and less public than the Franklin Community Garden. First, it's a closed-gate garden. It has over thirty *parcelas*, but the only people who can freely enter are the key holders who rent the plots (for $30 a year), and their friends and family. The *parcelas* are slightly bigger than at Franklin, and there is more heterogeneity, with a few plots holding monocrops of corn or cilantro, one holding a giant *chayote* supported by a trellis, and others planted with a variety of herbs and vegetables. The Dolores Huerta garden boasts beautiful amenities for socializing, such as picnic tables and benches under citrus trees, a brick barbecue grill, a shade cover, and an open circular area that might be used as a large meeting or play space, but these often remained underutilized. This is another difference with Franklin, as the collective cleanups and activities at Dolores Huerta are scarce. The garden is managed by a community center, and Don Jorge, a longtime local resident and elderly former bracero, is paid a

nominal fee to oversee things, but neither he nor the organization sponsors community events or programming. Some garden members here
complained about this lack of engagement.

The two community gardens are flanked by very different street scenes.
The Dolores Huerta Community Garden is on a busy avenue traversed by
buses, cars, and pedestrians, and in the middle of the day small groups of
men sit outside the garden, drinking from brown paper bags. One afternoon I counted eight people. A few were slumped over, and two lay
sprawled on the sidewalk. Across the street at the gated soccer field on late
afternoons, Latino dads coached their five-year-old sons, creating a portrait in contrasts: wholesome youth soccer on one side of the street, and
homeless people self-soothing with intoxicating substances on the other.
Three liquor stores sit within two blocks of the Dolores Huerta garden,
and when Jose Miguel Ruiz came alone in the evening, small groups of
young men eyed him menacingly. Don Jorge complained that *cholos* (gang
members) hopped the fence at night to party in the garden, breaking
faucets and plants. One of the most active and devoted gardeners at
Dolores Huerta was a diminutive indigenous Guatemalan woman in her
fifties, Doña Nilda. She told me that one day while tending her plants she
spotted a *boracho* (a drunk) defecating outside the garden gate, right there
in broad daylight and on a busy avenue. Undeterred, she took her hose
and sprayed him with water, and he quickly pulled up his pants and ran
off. These types of incidents did not occur at the Franklin garden, where
the street scene was vibrant and exuded more positive energy.

The gardens also had very different gatekeepers. Don Jorge did not fill
the same community builder role that Monica Sanchez did at the Franklin
garden. For starters, he was not a model gardener. Don Jorge's *parcela*
usually looked dry and untended, with half-dead plants. One woman commented, *"No sé, pero parece que no le sale nada. No tiene buena mano"* (I
don't know, but it seems like nothing grows for him. He doesn't have a
green thumb), and others repeated this assessment. No one came to him
for advice on what to plant when, as they did with Monica Sanchez at
Franklin. Moreover, he rarely socialized or lingered in the garden, but he
lived nearby, on call should any problems arise. One Sunday I was helping
Doña Nilda and Juan Franco with their gardening chores, while Maura,
another garden member, hosted a birthday party for her twenty-year-old

nephew. Relatives and young people listened to hip-hop out of a boom box and gathered around picnic tables to eat carne asada tacos and drink soda (liquor is prohibited at both community gardens). When a five-year-old girl trampled some plots and ruined some fledgling radishes, Juan Franco whipped out a cell phone to call Don Jorge, who came within minutes to restore order. There was community life at Dolores Huerta, but it remained a gated community, not fully public. Outside the gates, the streets are tough, but less than one mile east from the garden is the new glamorous entertainment zone of LA Live!, the Nokia Theater, and Staples Center. The shimmering JW Marriott/Ritz Carlton tower, which features luxury penthouses and a Wolfgang Puck restaurant where diners might plunk down $500 for a meal with wine, hovers in the sky nearby but worlds away from the Dolores Huerta garden.

The Franklin Community Garden is also in a poor part of the city, but more churches than liquor stores surround it, and vibrant minimalls with *marketas* and *pupuserías* too. The garden sits in the borderland zone between two infamous rival gangs, Mara Salvatrucha (MS13) and Dieciocho (Eighteenth Street), so it is not unusual to see gang members, with their trademark tattoos and baggy, oversized clothing, walking down the streets side by side with parents taking their kids home from school, *paleteros* selling mango- and *chile*-flavored popsicles, and local residents traipsing to and from the bus stops. Gang graffiti covers nearby apartment buildings and store walls, but gang members have refrained from vandalizing the garden here. "*Respectan el jardín,*" people say. The street scene at Franklin, located closer to the more prosperous Wilshire Boulevard and Koreatown, displays more vitality than the streets around Dolores Huerta.

The Franklin Urban Community Garden is open to the public from dawn to dusk, 365 days a year. (The back section of the garden with the individual *parcelas*, however, opens only for the key holders). The front section serves as a plaza, a minipark, an informal gathering spot, and the site of many community meetings. On late afternoons, *comadres* (co-god-mothers and female friends) gather to chat on a bench or under the shade of the *casita*, the roofed dirt-floor patio that serves as a communal gathering spot.[39] Time takes on elastic, expansive quality in late afternoons, with storytelling, gossip, and laughter. Children run around chasing birds, hopping on sacks of compost, or digging up roly-polies. During weekday

Figure 27. La casita, during a small community meeting focused on the problems of neighborhood gentrification and the scarcity of low-income housing. Photo by author.

mornings and early afternoons, Soon Young, an elderly Korean widow who used an empty baby stroller as her walker, regularly came to sit in the sun (she was the only Korean person who came here regularly during this period). When I first visited during the summer of 2010, on a hot afternoon, I found clucking chickens and a spectacularly plumed rooster roaming freely. Around the perimeter of the garden, bananas, sugarcane, a mango tree, and three small papaya trees gave the garden a tropical feel, and the *parcelas comunitarias*, a sort of green commons, held culinary and medicinal herbs. In this neighborhood of cement, to step in this garden was to feel refreshed and momentarily transported by the clucking of the chickens and the sights of the sugarcane and the bougainvillea.

Inside the Franklin garden, Monica Sanchez was the nucleus of community life. Members from the local Unitarian church had helped the residents build it up from an abandoned lot, and the nonprofit organization Green Spaces (a pseudonym) had bought the property in 2007, offering three reforms: (1) land security (there was no risk this garden would be bulldozed); (2) resources for programming and for paying Monica to open and close the gate and oversee the garden; and (3) new rules and tighter administration of the garden. These reforms were necessary to help preserve the

Figure 28. Inside the Dolores Huerta Garden. Photo by author.

garden, and while the financial resources fortified community life, the top-down administration caused conflict. Participation at monthly community meetings and in monthly collective cleanups was required of all the gardeners, but other neighbors helped out too and attended meetings and classes here.

The Franklin garden was like a multipurpose community center and playground. On Saturdays, there were free guitar lessons and art classes for kids, and Patricia Veliz Macal, a Guatemalan life coach, community educator, and motivational speaker, taught a popular women's empowerment class in the garden, which a few men attended (and from which I graduated, twice). The class motivated the women to launch various projects that they organized from gathering in the garden. They made soap, tamales, and jewelry to sell for much-needed income, started a collective bank account, and arranged for zumba and aerobics classes, held at the Unitarian church. At least three more explicitly political groups met periodically too, one organized around low-income housing, another affiliated with the Mexican leftist organization Morena, and another run by a minister on Sunday mornings.

Green Spaces also dispatched one of their staff members, whom I shall call Teresa Tobillo, as the official community organizer. A huge vacant lot sat empty and adjacent to the Franklin Community Garden, and in an effort to expand the garden, Green Spaces tried to buy it from the owner for nearly half a million dollars, but the owner, a Korean doctor, refused to sell it. That lot remained vacant and fenced off, but with gentrification looming, the property will likely be developed for lucrative profits. Up and down nearby avenues, gentrification loomed in the form of new upscale condominiums and Korean minimalls, but with the recession construction had stalled. Both of these urban gardens served as creative sites of social life for Latino immigrant communities in need, but they did so under very different terms.

HOMELAND RE-CREATIONS AND RECREATIONS: "ARRIVING IN LOS ANGELES FOR THE FIRST TIME, IT'S LIKE IT BREAKS YOUR HEART, NO?"

Labor migration is a heartbreak. People muster up courage and optimism to pick up and leave everything they know in El Salvador, Guatemala, or southern Mexico, traversing perils and risks on the road, and at the end of the physical journey Los Angeles does not exactly roll out the welcome mat. Newcomers expected a new beginning, but LA feels like a dead end. Homesickness and often second thoughts about the wisdom of migration ensue. Ceci Portillo, one of the few community gardeners from El Salvador, is now a confident, loquacious thirty-two-year-old student, a part-time employee, and a mother of two children, but she said her initial arrival in Los Angeles in 1997 was "the disappointment of my life." As a nineteen-year-old, after traveling for over a month and crossing multiple borders as a *mojada* (undocumented migrant), she found only tentative support from relatives in a crowded, dilapidated apartment near MacArthur Park. "I had imagined a more futuristic city," she said, but once here she wondered, "So much suffering to get here? Maybe I should have stayed in my familiar nest, where people help one another, even if they fight amongst themselves." Others reported similar second thoughts and disillusionments. People who had settled in the Westlake, MacArthur Park, and Pico Union neighborhoods in the 1980s and 1990s recalled the grim gang violence that had ruled the streets then, forcing them to live *un encerramiento* (a lockup), where they alternated only between work and apartment, swiftly traversing the dangerous streets.

Añoranzas, deep longings for people, places, and collective practices, are part of the experience of immigration, and for undocumented immigrants in the 1990s and first decade of the millennium the United States had become a new carceral environment, with a militarized US-Mexico border separating them from everything and everyone they knew. Participating in transnational circuits by traveling back to visit family and home in Guatemala or Mexico was no longer possible as it had been for earlier cohorts who either had access to legal status or had migrated during a time when border crossing was less risky. Without the possibility of returning home for visits, a kind of permanent homesickness takes hold. In the urban community gardens, immigrants rebuild their lives and link the lives of their past with their new realities. The gardens become linking objects to lessen the pain of lost social worlds.[40]

While commercial places and ethnic enclaves can serve as comforting links to the homeland, it takes money to engage in these sites. At the urban community gardens, people without cars or much pocket money informally gather and feel connected to place and people. Many of the regulars here described the garden as an intimate place of belonging, as a second "home," or like "family." Gustava, a transnational mother of four adolescent and young adult children in Guatemala, had started working the fields at age seven, with plow and bull, and now she tended a small *parcela* here with her partner, who hailed from Puebla, Mexico, and their young son. She sent housecleaning earnings back to Guatemala for her kids' education, while she worked through the sadness of transnational separation by volunteering with a youth group at the local Catholic church. But the garden rooted her. "It's as though it [the garden] was my home," she said, "with people and with nature." She claimed the garden even looked like her home in Guatemala. "I come here, and I feel like I'm back there in my country," she said. "Here in this little patch, I see the dirt [floor] in the *casita*. I see the flowers at the entrance and it seems like I could just be sitting back there in a pathway." Her friend Elodia, an undocumented single mother, came to the Franklin garden daily. Although she had never farmed in her native El Salvador, she said, "Everything here reminds me of my country. Like that corn, also the nopales. My grandfather had a lot of those, even though we didn't eat them. Even these benches," which were in a rustic state of disrepair, "remind me of home." Not all of the women had a background in farming, but the garden seemed familiar to them nevertheless.[41] Another woman who was now infrequently at the garden because she had to work extra jobs to cover bills during her husband's detention, softly and affectionately recalled, "We would sit here, just like we were in our own home."

Men were in the minority here, but Marcos Gutiérrez felt it was a second home for him too. He lived with his family in an apartment down the street, and he worked as a gardener tending the suburban yards of the San Fernando Valley. He was one of the most accomplished community gardeners, widely admired for his fertile, lush, and always well-tended plot of cilantro, strawberries, and myriad vegetables. I often saw him there, weeding and turning soil, and he claimed he never went more than two days without watering his plot. He loved coming to the garden, claiming, "It's as though I have another home here." His voice cracked, revealing emotional ties as he spoke about this. "You can't distance yourself [from the garden] so easily. No? No, you can't distance yourself."

Even when they were physically away from the garden, the community gardeners still felt deeply and emotionally connected with people and plants. Ceci Portillo cultivated a plot, but not too diligently. Her plot was the opposite of Marco Gutiérrez's. It was usually kind of dried out, occasionally filled with bountiful *verdolaga* (purslane), but often it contained only a few scraggly *chipilín* (a popular Central American herb) and *chile* plants. As a single parent, she had a busy life during the week, but she was at the garden every weekend, drawn by supportive friendships. "I'm not a member of this garden," Ceci clarified. "I'm part of here. And even when I'm not here, I'm thinking about the people who come here. These are images that come to me like photographs or videos, memories. Whatever conversation we have here, I'm later thinking about these at home, sometimes laughing, sometimes worried, worried for others. Like right now, Natalia is sick, so suddenly I'll think, 'Is she better now? Is her spine still hurting?' So one cannot disengage. You can separate physically but not emotionally."

Food is a critical part of community and cultural memory for immigrants. And growing and eating food together, "breaking bread" or sharing

Figure 29. Growing, sharing, cooking, and eating food together created a sense of community. Photo by author.

tortillas and *pan dulce* (sweet bread), created community and homeland affiliation at the Franklin Community Garden, where social activities revolved around shared fruit harvests, meal preparation, potlucks, and familylike feasts on weekends. There was no sink or countertop at Franklin, but tomatoes were rinsed off with bottled water in plastic bags, and onions, chiles, and squash were skillfully minced and sautéed over small propane burners (which were later stored in the toolshed, along with a few utensils and paper plates). Collective meals centered on carne asada tacos with beans, rice, and salsa unfolded at Dolores Huerta too, facilitated by better infrastructure of a brick barbecue and tables and chairs below a big citrus tree. People contributed what they could. As anthropologist Teresa M. Mares has noted, "Sustaining and re-creating the cultural and material practices connected to food are powerful ways to enact one's cultural identity and sustain connections with families and communities who remain on the other side of the border."[42] This is exactly what people were doing, reclaiming traditional foodways in the new here and now, collectively, and under conditions of food scarcity.

These neighborhoods are not food deserts, as local markets, street vendors, and discount grocery stores sell plenty of produce here. I found, however, that the quality of produce was spotty, and sometimes astonishingly bad. At Liborio, a large supermarket, I saw tomatoes with mold, fungi, and literally rotten potatoes offered for sale, nothing like the produce at my suburban supermarket. A rumor circulated that the public health department had even shut down the supermarket for a few days, but I could not corroborate this. Every community gardener agreed that what they grew tasted far better than purchased produce here, and most said their garden produce tasted just like home. In the middle of urban Los Angeles, the community gardeners were creating new definitions of what it meant to eat locally and globally, growing familiar homeland foods of Mesoamerica.

Humor always accompanied the meals and garden gatherings. Sometimes I brought a pot of rice, a dish that I make with onions, carrots, peppers, and Italian turkey sausage. The *mujeres* at Franklin liked the rice, and the Italian sausage was a new food that inspired no end of thinly veiled phallic references, as they chortled with raised eyebrows to jovially query one another, "Oh, have you ever *tried* the Italian sausage? Do you *like* Italian sausage?" As we worked in the *parcelas* among a seemingly infinite variety of *chile* plants, there were many quips about the size and potency of *chiles*. At another Saturday afternoon meal, people were biting into big grilled jalapeños, and they urged me to try one. I was cautious, but when I finally bit into one, I liked it, and announced, "*Esta sabrosa, pero no espantosa*" (It's tasty, but not scary). I am no wit in Spanish or English, but I scored some chuckles with that rhyme. Or maybe I just looked funny. Either way, this contributed to the jovial conviviality of the moment.

At the Dolores Huerta garden, the built-in barbeque pit served as the hearth of the urban garden home. After a garden cleanup or a spontaneous gathering, Don Jorge or Alma would stoke a fire, using tree limbs stacked by the toolshed, and as people ran home for ingredients a potluck meal would materialize. One bitterly cold February afternoon—it is sometimes cold in Los Angeles—when snow had fallen at 2,500-foot levels on nearby mountains, after enjoying one of these impromptu meals, we brewed tea from lemon leaves and drank out of Styrofoam cups. Suddenly, José Franco, who described himself as "*hiperactivo*" and who seemed always to be full of energy, leaped up and began stomping around in his *parcela,* compressing the soil, which was rich with humus and decomposing leaves. Somehow, he convinced four of us to join him, claiming this was good for the soil, and so we ended the day by marching and stomping around in the dark and cold evening, laughing heartily at our own silliness, and staying a little warmer before parting to start whatever Monday morning would be bringing our way. I left feeling replenished and fortified by food, friendship, and shared activity in the garden, and I think the others did too.

Growing food and preparing and sharing meals forged new familylike relations. One afternoon at Franklin, a dozen of us had finished yet another delicious meal, and we were sitting around two folding tables pushed together and draped with a vinyl tablecloth. At that moment, Don Fernando, an affable, elderly Argentinean who gave free guitar lessons here on Saturdays, revealed some personal and painful details about his current family life. The details of his story were particular, but the raw emotional disappointments of fragmented family life were shared by just about everyone there, calling to mind Tolstoy's opening line about how "every unhappy family is unhappy in its own way." In this shared moment of melancholy, Don Fernando remarked, *"De la manera que estamos aquí, parece que somos una familia"* (The way we are here, it seems as though we are a family). Most of us murmured and nodded in agreement, but Monica hastened to correct him, emphatically declaring, "No, we *are* a family."

"YO SIENTO QUE ME CURO AQUÍ"—
I FEEL I HEAL MYSELF HERE

The community gardens also serve as neighborhood homeland pharmacies. A wide variety of Mesoamerican herbal homeland remedies grow both inside the individual *parcelas* and in the commons, the space around the garden perimeter. Some herbs were universally embraced to cure tummy aches or ear infections or to calm colicky infants, and neighborhood residents frequently asked for *hierba buena, albaca, ruda, ximpachuli* (mint, basil, rue, marigolds) to make home remedies. The gardens became round-the-clock pharmacies—but unlike the local CVS or Rite

Aid, they provided these remedies free on demand. At the Franklin garden, Monica sometimes received urgent phone calls in the middle of night from desperate parents of sick children, and unbegrudgingly, she would come to unlock the gates and dispense *ximpachuli* (marigolds) or *ruda* (rue) from the garden. "We rely more on the medicinal herbs and plants than we do on the vegetables," Monica had told me when I first met her, and this seemed to be true. During the day, women sometimes strolled around the garden together in a very purposeful way, their eyes focused on the ground, closely examining the different medicinal herbs planted along the edge of the fence. These were social and cultural exchanges between women from different regions of Mesoamerica who shared multiple medicinal uses of the same plant and various healing practices. At the Dolores Huerta garden, pedestrians spoke to the community gardeners through the chain-link fence and received handfuls of requested mint or rue.

The women at the community gardens relied on both traditional herbal remedies and access to Western medicine. As Menjivar (2002) has shown, Latina immigrant women regularly use local and transnational social networks to obtain medical treatment for their families, including prescription drugs and traditional remedies. At the community gardens, I saw the women regularly exchange information about clinics and local resources, but I did not see them sharing or exchanging pharmaceuticals, although it is possible that they did this and I just didn't see it. More commonly, a neighbor might appear and ask one of the garden members, "*No me regalas ruda?*" (Won't you give me some rue?"). Or friends and acquaintances would share tips on preparing herbal medicinal remedies.

Not everyone shared the same herbal remedies. Next to the locked gate guarding the *parcelas*, in a small corner at the Franklin garden, was a vine called *chichicastre*. It was tied up with twine, and everyone cautioned one another not to touch its spiny leaves, which would act like stinging nettles. This was neither a shared homeland remedy nor a valued plant for any of the current community garden members, who often snickered when they discussed how it was purportedly used. Monica had explained that the application required stripping down to one's underwear and then whipping the body, especially the back and the legs, with the stinging vines. Several years back, a woman from Oaxaca had planted it because it was said to cure *susto* or fright, and although no one at the garden used it, not even the Oaxacans, people wondered: Maybe someone else in the neighborhood might need this strange cure? Garden members spoke of it as a slightly bizarre, out-of-the-norm tradition, yet the vine kept its place in this new shared composite homeland pharmacy. Keeping it in the ground memorialized someone who had passed through the garden at an earlier time and still allowed the community gardeners to bond in their shared aversion toward this purportedly healing vine.

The women also introduced new healing practices. One Saturday, I brought bamboo cuttings from my backyard, where we have a small grove of thick oldhami bamboo that requires constant thinning. Right away, the women began suggesting ideas for different uses—for a fence, tomato stakes, or a structure to support a *chayote* vine. Children used the bamboo as toys, running pebbles through the hollow middle, or in mock battle. Then Natalia, who suffered from crippling back pain, started using the bamboo to massage her quadriceps, and within moments we were all doing the same, kneading our tired muscles as we momentarily fell into a trance. The bamboo turned out to be more useful as a source of self-massage and relaxation than as a vegetable support. And that's how it was at the garden, where nothing went to waste. If someone harvested a bad crop of corn with missing kernels or tiny dried-out ears, they still found utility and even joy in the bounty, using the corn silk to brew a remedy or delighting a child with a tiny, pickle-sized ear of corn.

Tending plants in the garden was also a restorative and sometimes a playful practice. At the Dolores Huerta garden, José Franco loved overwatering his plots of cilantro. I shuddered at the amount of water he ran from the hose—it seemed wasteful here in arid Los Angeles—but his cilantro always looked lush and he was delighted with the water play. One Sunday afternoon after we had spent several hours with Doña Nilda in composting, weeding, and moving flower pots, we started taking posed photos of each other wrapped up in vines, sometimes posing seriously, staring off in the distance like statues. During these revitalizing moments of play and recreation, social problems and private troubles melted away.

Beyond medicinal herbs, the satisfaction of cultivating your own food, and just the fun of playing around among plants, urban community gardens also provide places of relaxation for solitary reflection and therapeutic tranquillity. There is now quite a significant subfield of landscape architecture devoted to understanding the therapeutic and healing effects that gardens have on physical health and psychological and emotional well-being.[43] The Franklin and Dolores Huerta community gardens were not intentionally designed for therapeutic purposes, but they served as healing sites, providing places not only for sociability but also for reflection on personal problems and for recovery from the fatigue of challenging daily demands.

At the Franklin open-gate garden, women gathered in the late afternoons to relieve the stress and strain of their lives. At home, in their small crowded apartments, they felt as though the walls and their problems were closing in on them. Some women were caring for family members with serious illness or had husbands and sons in detention, facing deportation or prison, and all of them worried about the bills. The garden offered momentary relief as a healing oasis of tranquillity and as a spot of friendship and social support. Those who worked outside the home felt the time-squeezing pressure from rushing all over the Los Angeles Basin evaporate once they set foot in the garden. Victoria, the mother of five children, and herself one of the most accomplished gardeners, sometimes spent two hours traveling home on the bus after cleaning a house in Venice or Santa Monica. After work, she sought a moment of peace puttering in her *parcela* or chatting with friends. "Sometimes I get home really tired from my job and I tell my husband, 'Ay, I'm going to go rest a while at the garden.' And then I come here, and I feel calmer," she explained. Elodia, a Salvadoran single mother of four, worked only a few hours outside the home, taking care of other people's kids in the neighborhood, but at her apartment she often felt, she said, as though "I'm going to have an attack." Coming to the garden relieved her worries. "Where I live I sometimes feel asphyxiated [*asfixiada*] from thinking about things, all my problems, and when I come here, I relax really well. I feel really good, and sometimes I don't feel like leaving. I'd like to sleep here!"

The garden served as a social capital incubator, connecting women to the information and resources that would help them navigate and consolidate their family lives here in Los Angeles. Sitting on benches relaxing in the late afternoon, or sometimes while weeding and clipping, they shared vital information about critical resources for their families. Which ones are the good charter schools, and which ones to avoid? What dental clinic should you visit when you have a toothache?

The women credited the garden with getting them through their trials and tribulations. Gustava had left her four children behind in Guatemala when they were young, between the ages of four and thirteen. Ten years had passed; the children, she said, were now thriving educationally, and the eldest would soon be going abroad for a religious mission. She was rebuilding her life, in a new relationship with Armando, and happily raising their exuberant second grader, and she had found fulfillment as a volunteer with a church youth group. But along the way, Gustava had faced bouts of depression and *nervios* (anxiety), and she credited the garden for helping her achieve emotional well-being. "When I come here, all my cares fade away. Yes, I'll tell you that when the *nervios* hit me, I would always seek this out, I sought out the garden." She credited both the experience of being in nature and the supportive friendships for helping her. Armando also testified that he found stress relief at the Franklin community garden. "One comes here to calm down [*tranquilizarse*]," he said. "It's a pleasure to be here, no? It gives you tranquillity. . . . The air you breathe here is cleaner, you feel it's purer, fresher. And stress, well, you just forget it [when you are here]."

Over and over, the community gardeners emphasized how the garden had become a restorative and therapeutic space, helping them with physical ailments, emotional challenges, and depression. Doña Griselda, a Zapotec woman who hailed from San Marcos Tlapazola, Oaxaca, suffered from diabetes, and she had undergone bladder surgery in Tijuana with poor results. She also carried a heavy load of family problems, including a formerly abusive husband who was now on dialysis, which required accompanying him on the bus daily; an adolescent mentally disabled son at home; and a twenty-four-year-old son who supported the four of them on his wages earned as a dishwasher in a Chinese restaurant. When I interviewed her, she claimed the garden helped her live through all of these trials and tribulations. "*Ahorita mucho mejor.* . . . Now I'm a lot better now that I have my parcel. From my point of view," she said, "it's helped me a lot, because before I was falling apart, sick, and my sister-in-law had passed away, and that made me even sadder. So I'd say to myself, I'm going to go sit in the garden, even though I didn't have my own parcel, I went to emotionally let go [*desahogarse*] so that I wouldn't just be thinking about things."

This was a common refrain, the idea that leaving the four walls of the apartment allowed them to momentarily forget their problems. "The garden helped me a lot with that," Doña Griselda said. "And now even more, because thanks to God, at whatever hour I wish, I have the key and I can enter and take a stroll and sit here for a moment." Another woman, Doña Natalia, claimed that the clucking chickens helped relieve the pain of her migraine headaches. She knew others laughed at this notion, but she insisted it was true.

The community gardens also served as the setting for recovery from acute trauma. For months Ceci and I had worked side by side on many garden cleanups, and had laughed at the same jokes over shared meals, but toward the end of our formal interview she revealed a confidential incident to me and to Jose Miguel. The previous year her seven-year-old daughter had been raped by the babysitter's husband, a Christian minister who lived in their apartment building. There are many terrible details of this assault, and although the assailant was not put behind bars, he died of a heart attack not long after, giving them a sense of protection and justice. Ceci and her daughter ultimately sought recovery at Stuart House, a UCLA rape crisis center for children. Only a few friends at the garden knew about the sexual assault. Her therapist advised her to continue coming to the garden for therapeutic relaxation, and Ceci credited the garden as a healing space for both her and her daughter. "When we started coming to the garden again, she forgot about all of that, and she played with her friends," she said. "They make little mud cakes. And they water the plants, and she forgets. She now wants to be here at the garden all the time." Ceci also felt *desestresada*, relieved of stress when at the garden. "Here I feel like I am in a little part of my house in my El Salvador," she said. *Verdolaga*, or purslane, a green that grows like a weed, was the only plant that ever truly thrived in her plot, but really, she and her daughter came to the garden so that they could flourish. They were healing and cultivating their own well-being. The community gardens had not been designed as therapeutic, healing gardens, but this was the purpose they served for so many who gathered there.

FLUID AND IMAGINARY HOMELANDS:
"I FELT LIKE IT WAS INSIDE ME"

At the gardens, no one clung to authentic replication of homeland foods and plants. People hailed from different countries and regions, so they shared regional traditions and a kind of intraethnic *Latinidad* unfolded on the table and in the soil. Rather than preserving homeland culture in some rarefied way, as if in a museum, the garden members liked tasting and growing new plant foods (kale, broccoli, brussel sprouts) that they didn't know about back home, generating a vibrant, porous, shared culture. Corn, squash, beans, tomatoes, and chiles remained the unalterable foundation for this shared food canvas, but they added new ones.

Most of the gardeners came from rural areas where they cultivated land, but a few community gardeners had connected with their cultivation traditions only here in Los Angeles. Armando, one of only a handful of men who regularly participated at the Franklin garden, was one of them. Because he grew up poor and landless and had lived on his own since age thirteen, he had never prepared the soil or grown his own crops in Puebla, Mexico, where his grandfather had cultivated sugarcane. He grasped onto this fact as though it might restore a place-based dignity that he had been deprived of himself and that he might now pass on to his son. Land, *tierra*, was the principal rallying cry during the Mexican Revolution, and it continues to be fundamental to the national vision of Mexican sovereignty. With rural-urban migration and the growth of cities, Mexico is now a predominantly urban society. Moreover, NAFTA and neoliberal policies adopted in 1992 modified the *ejido* system, a form of communally held land that was institutionalized after the Mexican Revolution and that had defined land tenure for indigenous people cultivating maize since before the European conquest.[44]

For Armando, who had never grown his own crops in Mexico, the garden filled two gaping holes in his life. First, the garden was a setting for becoming a devoted dad, something that he regretted not doing with his first son, now a young adult who lived in Mexico. Second, the community garden allowed him to connect with ancestral traditions that he himself had missed out on. He found deep satisfaction in passing on this ancestral legacy to his seven-year-old son, Oscar. "I want him to learn how to work the soil, how the trees bear fruit, so that he can see where it all comes from," he explained, "and how enjoyable it is to harvest and eat what you grew ... so that he can see what the earth can give us." For Armando, growing and eating these foods became an experience not unlike religion, a practice that connected the *tierra* (earth) of the homeland past with the present lived geography in Los Angeles, California. Although he had never grown his own crops or held land back in Puebla, harvesting his crops here in the garden, he said, "gives me that sensation that I'm back there in my *pueblo*, and that I'm harvesting something there in my town. . . . I think we are rescuing something of what we were back there in our country, right? We are rescuing these roots, these values."

According to Armando, homeland traditions and rights had been lost even in the homeland. "I am one of those who did not have land back there," he explained. "But in spite of that, I'm here at the garden. I think many of those men [in the neighborhood] have forgotten where we come from, and what we did back there in our countries." He also openly discussed *vicios* (vices) that he had overcome, alcoholism in particular, which still plagued many people, but especially men, in the local neighborhood. The Franklin garden allowed Armando to live in the imagined homeland that he had been deprived of in Mexico. Armando had been denied participation in ancestral traditions in Puebla, Mexico, but he reenacted them here in middle of inner-city Los Angeles, and most importantly, he saw his son restoring the tradition in the future. This was important. The Franklin garden was a material bridge to link this imagined past to the present, and to a legacy that he hoped his young son would carry forward.

One of the most talented gardeners at Franklin was Fernanda, a shy, soft-spoken twenty-four year-old mother who always brought her preschool age daughter, and often her mother, to help tend her plot. She was the youngest community gardener and the only person who did the interview in English, the language with which she was most comfortable. Fernanda had come to Los Angeles from Oaxaca City as a toddler, and while her mother told her that they had never cultivated land in Oaxaca, Fernanda still remembered Mexico as a garden space. "I guess I was only in Mexico for three years or something, but I remember in Mexico some garden," she said. "I remember plants like this. But my mom says we never had that, but I remember things like that." For Fernanda, the Franklin

Figure 30. Lush banana trees gave the garden a tropical feel and reminded immigrants of their homelands in Guatemala, Honduras, and southern Mexico. Sometimes neighbors requested corn or banana leaves for wrapping tamales. Photo by Robbert Flick.

garden was a way to restore and materialize the Mexico that had been lost to her but that she felt deeply in her bones. "I felt like it was in me or something, I don't know where exactly. I forgot, I forgot a lot when I came here [to LA]," she explained. These homeland yearnings were realized in the garden. "I had a craving to plant something, and I did it. I had a craving to just pick a fruit out of a tree. And I finally did it. Or just to sweep, you know, the leaves, the water, [to experience] the smell."

In the fields of Oaxaca, Fernanda's great-grandparents had cultivated beans, corn, melons, and watermelon, but Fernanda was now three generations removed from this experience. As her mother said when I interviewed her, *"Todo lo que hemos aprendido lo hemos aprendido aquí. O sea como se abona la tierra, como se siembra, como se pone la semilla"* (Everything we've learned we have learned here—how you fertilize the soil, how you cultivate, how you plant a seed). On one of the cleanup days, I worked side by side with Fernanda. I followed her lead in clipping garden cuttings into tiny half-inch bits until my wrists ached, getting a good lesson on composting and insights into why my own efforts at home had produced so little, and so slowly. Later I asked Fernanda how she got to be so good at composting, and gardening in general. "Online," she said. "I research so much. How do you do this? What is that? Everything, online." Composting had become her forte, and on the garden cleanup days Monica always assigned her to this task. "I was in love with it, you have no idea," she gushed. "Every week, you know, I made myself come here . . . and I would go and mix it, and it started smoking and it didn't stink." When other community gardeners carelessly threw trash into the pile, she said, "I was like, heartbroken." It wasn't always easy getting along with others here, but the community garden restored the ancestral legacies she had craved, allowing her to cultivate the imagined homeland and practice devotion to the earth by making fertile soil. She felt this connection to Mexico was inside her and could sprout here at the garden.

This was no romanticized, insular homeland, though, as the community gardening experience enabled Fernanda, a shy, introverted young woman, to become an assertive advocate for neighborhood change, challenging the second-class city services and unkempt look of the Westlake area. After participating in so many collective garden cleanups, she began noticing the stark difference between the verdant, trash-free Franklin garden and the littered streets and sidewalks outside the garden gates. "I hated this area so much, she said, "'cause it's always dirty." As a student traveling on the bus to Santa Monica City College, she made another comparison and noticed that the streets in the predominantly white, Westside neighborhoods were not littered with trash and discarded furniture. Why shouldn't the streets here be that way, she wondered. She recalled feeling "embarrassed [by the neighborhood]. People come here and they think, goodness, they're pigs or something . . . Hispanics. But then I noticed, first of all, there's no trash cans. Where are people going to put all the trash?" Inspired by collective work at the garden, and by civic ideas and tools she had learned at the community meetings, Fernanda took it upon herself to call the Bureau of Sanitation to request trash cans, and she called 311 for graffiti removal and pickup of abandoned furniture.

Through her actions, Fernanda was not invoking some nostalgic vision of homeland, but she was claiming the right to a better city, and taking action to create a new improved homeland, inside and outside the garden. "Before I felt like, who am I? No rights. But I'm like no, you're here," she asserted. "We have the right to call these numbers." Tools she learned at the garden spurred her civic action. Now, she took pride in the Franklin garden as an inner-city gem, and she likened it to the sweet core of an apple. "If you come to the garden, you know, it's like a rotten apple and you cut it in half, and it's nice inside. . . . I'm no longer ashamed."

THE CHILDREN'S GARDEN

Mothers regularly brought their children to the Franklin garden on afternoons and weekends, and while the kids might sit still for a moment to enjoy a snack, they were usually in constant motion, swirling among the different public spaces in the garden. During community meetings or the women's empowerment class, there might be thirty boisterous kids. This was their playground. There were no swings, but they invented their own games, playing hide-and-seek behind tall succulents and hopping on compost sacks piled near the shed, or taking turns sliding on a tiny plastic vehicle down the paved driveway. Their irrepressible energy, stifled in small, crowded apartments in this park-poor neighborhood, got uncorked here. Both MacArthur Park and Lafayette Park were blocks away, but neither was considered a safe place for kids, so parental concern for safety and the long walk to get there precluded those options.[45]

This was a neighborhood with few play spaces. This fact was underscored for me one evening as I was leaving a community meeting at the church around the block. It was already dark, and I walked a few steps behind Reynalda and her three young children. Reynalda pushed a stroller, and her little daughters eagerly ran over to a piece of broken concrete ruptured by tree roots. Clearly, the kids had rehearsed this activity many times, and each one took her position. The toddler sat on one end of the broken concrete while six-year-old Katrina stood on the other end, energetically jumping and thus bouncing and delighting the giggling toddler with this makeshift urban seesaw. Without swings and slides, they were making do with broken concrete.

At the Franklin garden during the meetings, there were as many as thirty children running around and playing, but the children sometimes

Figure 31. After school and on weekends, children ran around the garden, hopped on sacks of soil, played hide-and-seek, and enjoyed peering at insects and worms. Chomping on sugarcane was a special annual treat. Photo by author.

slowed down and were mesmerized by the wonders of nearby nature, falling into dreamy worlds as they gazed at butterflies, hummingbirds, and giant beetles. One day while I was clipping banana leaves, I noticed a boy of about six or seven, standing alone at the edge of a small *milpa* (corn patch), staring at a big, black beetle. He mimicked the "buzzzz" sound, and soon another child stood next to him, not talking but also staring at the beetle and making the same sound. They stood hypnotized and immobilized, each in his own meditative moment. On another day, I sat and ate popsicles with three young children, and when a butterfly flew by, the two five-year-olds shouted excitedly, *"Mira, mira, ahí va!"* (Look, look, there it goes!). This was their park, their backyard, and their place for magical encounters with plants and insects.

Parents brought their young children to work in the *parcelas*, and in the *parcelas comunitarias* (the commons). On Saturdays, some kids took free guitar lessons from Don Fernando, and while their mothers attended the women's empowerment classes, children assembled garden collages and painted wooden birdhouses under the supervision of an art teacher paid by Green Spaces. Kids "aged out" of the garden when they reached their early teens, but the garden drew many children between the ages of infancy and about thirteen. At Dolores Huerta, the locked gate allowed entry only to the children who were friends and family members of the parcel holders.

A combination of the open gates and Monica Sanchez allowed the Franklin garden to serve as a refuge for children with home troubles. I got my firsthand glimpse of this one sunny Saturday while Jose Miguel Ruiz and I were waiting to interview someone. An eleven-year-old boy, Justin, arrived at the garden with his mother. The boy seemed anxious, his big brown eyes frantically scanning the garden. "Where is Monica?" he asked. There is a rule at the garden that kids cannot be left unattended, so I told the mother, who said she was on the way to visit her son in juvenile hall, that I would watch Justin until Monica arrived. We had never met before, but she left her son with me and did not return until five hours later. Justin immediately charmed us. He was chatty and eager to describe the many wonders he had experienced in the garden when he was eight and nine years old and had lived in the brick apartment building overlooking the garden. Monica, he said, had let him and the other kids build a clubhouse under the banana trees. His vivid descriptions blended childhood inno-cence with astute, adultlike observations, and he related these with an articulate self-confidence that belied his age. He excitedly recalled chasing chickens, practicing soccer kicks by the gate, sharing in tasty meals—and he told us the sad story of how a big green monster had eaten the bunny the kids had kept in the clubhouse.

Later, when I spoke alone with Monica, I learned that Justin had only recently reunited with his Honduran mother after spending six months in the foster care system. Family trauma and disruption had included domes-tic violence, which had prompted Justin and his mother to flee from the apartment one night. An older brother was in jail, and his sister had been adopted by a white family in another state. Justin had been frantic to find Monica because he wanted her to help him use the Internet to locate his sister. I don't know if this ever happened, but clearly the Franklin garden was a safe sanctuary and still a place of promise for this boy.

Once they hit adolescence, the kids stopped coming to the garden. Monica worried that time was running out with Justin. "He is still open to the garden," she said, "but that changes when they get to be around twelve or thirteen." Monica recalled how a group of her son's friends, now in their late teens, had gathered at the garden daily when they were young. In the sum-mer, they had enjoyed water balloon fights, built forts, and eaten peaches off the trees. She had even let them sleep overnight in the garden, roasting marshmallows, just like children on a suburban backyard campout. Now these same kids passed her on the street and acted as though they had never met. They were still in school but standing on a slippery slope, getting high and riding around on skateboards in a neighborhood where gangs actively recruited. "I know it's a difficult time for them," she said. "They're navigating everything that's going on in their head, and all around them in this neigh-borhood." The community gardens did not appeal to teens here.[46]

THE ALLURE OF ENCHANTMENT

Urban community gardens are routinely celebrated for the food, commu-nity, and democratic empowerment that they produce, but they have not been appropriately acknowledged as places for quiet contemplation and direct appreciation of nature. We normally think of these moments in some rarefied, privileged way, as in the tradition of Thoreau going off to the wilderness to experience a romantic, idealistic retreat in nature, or someone hiking alone on distant mountain trails. But these sorts of engagements were happening in the middle of the city at the urban community gardens too.

Perhaps more than anyone, Monica Sanchez felt at one with nature, and she experienced an oceanic feeling of dissolving ego boundaries at the garden. "I just enter it," she said, "and I feel it's like a refuge. From here to there, it's another air, it's another house, since I feel protected here, and I'm in what I am [*estoy en lo que yo soy*]." For months, we had spent so much time together working on cleanups and shared meals, in community meetings and in the women's empowerment class, but when I conducted the first part of an audio-recorded interview on a busy afternoon at the Franklin garden, she chose for us to go sit in the dirt, next to a big *chayote* vine in the back garden, on a communal space next to the *parcelas*. This was her favorite private spot in the garden, and she confessed that she longed to come here in the afternoon and take a nap, and sleep here in direct contact with the earth (she avoided doing this out of fear). But as we sat on the soil on that warm January day, she took her shoes off and wiggled her toes in the earth and spoke breathlessly of the garden, as though reciting a Neruda poem:

Siento que es mio . . .
I feel it's mine—mine, not like my private property,
but mine like my planet.
I think it's mine.
Just like the sun, I say it's mine too.
And like the air is mine.
And the stars are mine.
That's how I feel about the garden.
And then, the people are part of it—of me, of the garden.

This was a stunning declaration of love and attachment to the garden, and it struck me not only as eloquently poetic but also as an accurate representation of what she felt. One of the first times Monica had walked me around the Franklin garden she took me to a spot near the perimeter of the vegetable plots. There were about a dozen pots in a corner with plain-looking, slightly unkempt ornamental plants. Frankly, I was unimpressed, but then she directed my attention to one spindly succulent. Once a year, she explained, this plant produced a spectacular blossom, *La Reina de la Noche* (the Queen of the Night). She had been keeping a watchful eye on it, checking it every few days, and she thought it would blossom soon. It did, and later that week, around 11:00 p.m., she called her friend Natalia, and together with Natalia's pregnant daughter-in-law the three of them had come to the garden, with flashlights, to see the special flower. They were still extolling its beauty when I saw them the following week. Monica had snapped a photo on her cell phone, and as we were chatting at the *casita* with several other women she passed it around for all of us to see. It looked a bit like a multiple-petaled calla lily, but I'm afraid that description doesn't quite do it justice—it was something to see. The following year Monica caught the ephemeral night blossom again, and this time she texted the snapshot to me with this message: *"Esta es la flor del jardin que abre solo en la noche y Pierrette la quiere ver"* (This is the flower in the garden that opens only at night and Pierrette wants to see it). Monica always had her eyes open and ready to appreciate the minute miracles of nature. On another occasion after a garden cleanup, Monica had directed us to watch butterflies that were swooping down to lay their eggs on the *ruda* (rue). A small group of us had stood together in respectful silence and awe.

Other people experienced moments of solitary enchantment as they tended their plots. When I asked Marco Gutiérrez what he most liked about the Franklin Community Garden, his eyes and entire face lit up with enthusiasm, and without hesitation he replied, *"Pos, estar aquí en mi parcela, revolviendo la tierra"* (Well, being here in my parcel, moving the earth). He used the word *cariño* (love, affection) to describe the tenderness he felt taking care of little seedlings, and in a loving, almost maternal gesture he moved both hands as though he were caressing a small imaginary plant. Armando also described the deep satisfaction of producing food this way. *"Es muy agradable. . . ."* It's really nice to harvest what you sowed, truly. You sowed it, you took care of it. You put in your time, you put in your interest. And when you harvest, well, it's truly delicious," he said. "*Te saboreas lo que te costo a tí.* . . . You relish what you worked for."

Urban community gardens are celebrated as sites of food production, but the gardeners at Dolores Huerta and Franklin also craved the beauty of flowers. At both gardens, fragrant roses and citrus blossoms perfumed the air, and an array of other flowers mesmerized. At Franklin these included a tall poinsettia and spiny euphorbia, bird of paradise, cannas, bougainvillea, roses, and one of my favorites, a datura with fragrant pink "angel's trumpet" flowers.

At Dolores Huerta, a small group of the gardeners had started their own "city beautiful" project with shoestring resources. José Franco and Vanessa propagated multiple pots of geraniums and impatiens from cuttings in little pots, and these were eventually scattered around the tables and ledges. Vanessa's long bejeweled, blue-lacquered fingernails, also speaking to the longing for adornment and beauty, served as the perfect planting tool for making stem-sized holes. Doña Nilda, seemingly indefatigable in her weekly work schedule of cleaning twenty houses and two churches, used her steady income to purchase many brightly hued ornamental flowering plants at the local Home Depot. In clay pots and plastic containers, she displayed marguerites, Icelandic poppies, pansies, azaleas, and multicolored tulips on a plant stand made of cinder blocks. This was a flower sculpture of pure beauty. She loved flowers and she enjoyed receiving compliments and admiration, adding, "Oh, people say it looks like a shrine, and that all that's missing now is a statue of the Virgin of Guadalupe." No religious statues adorned these gardens, but the flowers and ornamental plants imparted a feeling of sacred space and the desire for transcendence. Community gardens are pretty places, with productive and ornamental plants, but they are not paradise, as the section below makes clear.

THE DIFFICULTIES OF DEMOCRACY

Urban community gardens have been celebrated as "acts of political redemption" and as the "communal expression of a community's political

Figure 32. The Saturday morning women's empowerment class drew community gardeners (including a few men) and other neighborhood women. Photo by author.

power."[47] But how much self-governance and democratically exerted power do community gardeners wield? A mixture of government resources and sponsorship from nonprofit organizations now supports the community gardens, and today even corporations such as Scotts MiracleGro Company offer grants to community gardens, including one awarded to a community garden in East Los Angeles.[48] New costs and tensions have emerged in tandem with the institutional support, prompting questions about the relationship between community autonomy and institutional support.

At the Franklin garden, institutional financial support from Green Spaces allowed for a rich array of workshops, classes, and celebrations, as well as for shared garden tools and sacks of soil amendment and mulch. These enhanced community life and allowed for the women's empowerment class, where Patricia Macal led us in discussions of critical social issues and encouraged us to leave behind our *"papas podridas"* (emotional baggage, but literally "rotten potatoes") so that we could set new goals, both individual and collective ones. Green Spaces paid her a fee to teach these Saturday morning classes, and to keep the children from interrupting their mothers while another woman offered the kids arts and crafts classes in another area of the garden.

Green Spaces collected information on how many people participated in workshops such as these and required all plot holders to attend monthly community meetings. Like other NGOs, they needed to supply information to their granting institutions, showing how many people they had served.[49] The community meetings focused on governance at the garden (e.g., Was everyone following the rules? Participating in the cleanups?), and several conflicts emerged between the Franklin community gardeners and Green Spaces, suggesting that the project of community empowerment and democratization was at best compromised and at worst a sham. Below, I focus on two.

First, there were problems around the selection of new parcel holders. This is a familiar issue at urban community gardens, where demand often outstrips supply of parcels open for cultivation. At Franklin, the vegetable beds were small, but many of the *mujeres* found that competing demands with family and work often precluded them from regularly coming to water and weed their parcels, so they agreed to informally share, with say two or three friends sharing a small vegetable bed. When one woman had a crisis in the family, then her friend could take over tending the plot. This seemed reasonable enough to the community gardeners, but it was against one of Green Spaces' many rules, and the community organizer, Teresa Tobillo, had cracked down on this practice.[50] Community garden members tried in vain to fudge the issue, but it became "illegal" to be cultivating a plot if your name was not on the official contract, and some community gardeners ultimately lost the parcels they had been cultivating.

The Green Spaces staff and the Franklin community gardeners held competing visions of justice about who should receive a little of plot of land to grow vegetables and herbs. For Green Spaces, the garden was a public space that had to be open to all, even those who did not live in the immediate neighborhood, or who might have never previously set foot in the garden. Formal organizations want to avoid the formation of cliques in community gardens. They need to apply for grants and show that the garden is open to a wide diversity of people. As a nonprofit organization initially funded by the City of Los Angeles and now supported by foundation grants, Green Spaces had to ensure that garden membership was not personal or particular but rather followed certain procedures, which included abiding by the rules of conduct and signing a formal contract. The contract defined membership rights.

The community gardeners had a different vision. For them, it was all about connection with land and people. This was their community backyard, their new homeland. They had so little, and now even the land they tended in this little oasis might be ripped away from them. In this case, unlike the case of South Central Farm, it was not rapaciously greedy real estate developers and bulldozers but an organization ostensibly in the service of community empowerment that threatened to take their land from them. When several community gardeners were banished from their plots, other garden members departed too.

Another conflict emerged when Green Spaces obtained substantial public funds for infrastructural improvements on the garden.[51] In anticipation of spending a jaw-dropping $350,000, the official community organizer asked the garden members how they wanted this spent. Over and over again, in endless community garden meetings, the gardeners said they wanted just three things: a toilet, chickens, and a brick barbecue, preferably with a faucet for rinsing vegetables and a counter surface for preparing food. During 2010–11, we met monthly on Wednesdays from 5:00 to 7:00 p.m. to discuss these matters, and during the winter the meetings moved from the garden to a church basement. Sometimes landscape architects came to the meetings, offering different ideas and options for new garden amenities. In the end, here is how the democratic design process went: we were handed Post-it flags and were asked to walk to the front of the room and cast our vote by choosing between red or brown brick pavers, and between picnic tables with yellow or blue trim. The chickens, the toilet, and the built-in barbecue never appeared on the ballot.

The Franklin garden shut down for nine months beginning in January 2012, and when it reopened it included new pavers, electricity, four-foot cinder block walls and electric lights for the *casita*, terracing to allow for better water drainage, a new shed, picnic tables with yellow trim, and folding chairs. A toilet, a built-in barbecue, and chickens—the items that the community gardeners in this neighborhood had said loud and clear that they wanted—were nowhere in sight. The garden now has a sort of cleaned-up, institutional look, and while a few of the original members

Figure 33. View of the Dolores Huerta Community Garden. Photo by Robbert Flick.

remain, a new crop of garden members has replaced those who left. There's now a new cycle of life in the Franklin urban community garden.

·   ·   ·   ·   ·

Urban community gardens are sites of belonging and healing, and for immigrants these places offer opportunities for connecting the homeland of the past to the homeland of the future. The Mexican and Central American community gardeners in Los Angeles do not necessarily feel welcomed to a new nation, but they do feel as though they belong to a new community on a plot of earth. They live in a city where their major source of employment is tending to the needs of others—as nannies, cleaners, janitors, restaurant workers, car valets, tree trimmers, and painters. In this sea of service work, the community gardens are oases where they can tend to their own needs, laughing and gossiping with friends, nurturing their children, finding out about neighborhood resources, and growing wholesome food. As one of the gardeners said, alluding to both the ethereal and the material, "Where else can we touch the earth?"

In inner-city Los Angeles, many of these Mexican and Central American workers feel stuck in bad jobs and drowning in problems, but the garden transports them to a place of healing and growth. The power of the nation and large bureaucracies and the daily challenges of being poor and undocumented are made tolerable by the moments of pleasure, togetherness, and enchantment they find in these gardens. The community gardens provide possibilities for transcendence and improvement, as this final quote suggests: *"Cuando uno viene al jardín, como que se transporta uno a otro lugar....* When you come to the garden, it's like you are transported to another place. It's like you are no longer in the city.... You forget even that building that's right there, you don't even see it. You just concentrate on the garden. And you feel differently."

5 Cultivating Elite Inclusion

One of the largest Suzhou-style scholar's gardens outside China opened to much fanfare in the San Gabriel Valley in 2008, at the Huntington Library, Art Collections and Botanical Gardens. The project brought together diverse donors, scholars, and landscape architects in a complex transnational collaboration, and in this chapter I discuss the social process and context in which this Chinese-style garden emerged at the Huntington. Like many museums around the world, the Huntington now seeks to include exhibits that will better reflect contemporary societies formed by globalization and migration.[1] The Liu Fang Yuan, or the Garden of Flowing Fragrance, marks a significant addition for this Eurocentric garden, and the garden-making process provides a window for understanding the shifting social position of Chinese Americans and Chinese immigrants in Pacific Rim cities.

The Chinese Exclusion Act is now a legislative relic of the past, but Chinese homes, gardens, and buildings have emerged as sites where new forms of restrictionism occur. Even as working-class Chinese immigrant workers toil in low-wage jobs in California, in many Pacific Rim cities of the West Coast post-1965 Chinese immigrants now include sectors of highly educated professionals who entered the United States with significant financial capital, social capital, business ties, and often a "flexible citizen-ship" that may include access to more than one passport. They come from diverse places, including Taiwan, mainland China, and Hong Kong, and as sociologist Min Zhou notes, they are "disproportionately drawn from the highly educated and professional segments of the sending societies."[2] Rather than working up from the bottom, they have created what my col-league Leland Saito calls "an economy from the top."[3]

At the upper ends of the class spectrum, wealthy and highly educated Chinese American immigrants and transnational business elites have influenced the material culture of the Huntington gardens by contribut-ing to a Chinese-style garden in what was previously a Eurocentric space. This is a marked departure from the recent past of exclusions of Chinese people and built environments in California. The garden signals the inte-gration of Chinese elite resources and cultural traditions into an elite botanical garden located just east of Los Angeles, in the expansive eth-noburb.[4] The project has required the joint action of groups that have not always worked well together, including Taiwanese and mainland Chinese immigrants. In this respect, it echoes earlier processes that led different ethnic groups, say Lombardians and Sicilians, to work together as Italian American immigrants.

Gardens are powerful instruments for showcasing status and power. That is why kings, queens, and industrialists have invested so heavily in grand gardens. The Huntington botanical garden is a place of spectacular beauty, but it is also a platform for the presentation of cultural refinement, leisure, and status. As Thorstein Veblen observed in his late nineteenth-century book *The Theory of the Leisure Class*, abstention from pecuniary productive work and engagement in "conspicuous leisure" are hallmarks of elite social life. Conspicuous leisure is sometimes mistaken for doing nothing, but as Veblen wrote in the 1890s it includes "quasi-scholarly or quasi-artistic accomplishments and a knowledge of processes and inci-dents which do not conduce directly to the furtherance of human life."[5] A lot of this occurs at the Huntington, which offers a lively schedule of lec-tures and exhibits designed to teach knowledge that will enhance enjoy-ment of fine art, literature, and gardens. In anticipation of the 2008 open-ing of the new Chinese-style garden, the Huntington inaugurated an endowed lecture series on the origins, philosophy, and symbolism of

Chinese Suzhou gardens and on related arts, such as Chinese landscape painting, calligraphy, poetry, and courtyard garden furniture. Not all Chinese gardens are Suzhou-style scholar's gardens, but this type of garden, which originated with upwardly aspirant merchants and scholar officials in the fifteenth to seventeenth centuries, remains the garden style most widely identified with China.[6] The Huntington's stated intent was to generate financial donations and interest in the Chinese scholar's garden, but the lecture series also legitimated the Chinese garden and Chinese culture as appropriate terrain for contemporary conspicuous leisure.

Affluent and highly educated elites are certainly not the only ones who can enjoy the garden, but they are central figures at the Huntington. Writing many years after Veblen, sociologist Pierre Bourdieu taught us to see that culture provides an important mechanism that allows elites to reproduce class superiority over others. This process is often obscured by the ideology that high culture (e.g., what is considered refined aesthetic expression) simply reflects innate talent and taste. Bourdieu asserted that elites use cultural production and consumption as a way to maintain their dominance and hegemonic status.[7] This observation, of course, does not negate the pleasure and passion that one may truly feel for high-status arts. One may feel passion as an "opera fanatic" or plant collector, yet still rely on these activities to show class supremacy.[8]

In this chapter I examine how the premier elite botanical garden of Southern California invited the inclusion not only of Chinese material culture and plants but also of Chinese people into what had been an arguably Eurocentric cultural space. Chinese donors, landscape architects, calligraphers, docents, and visitors became involved in this project. What does it mean for this long-standing white, Eurocentric institution to open the doors to Chinese culture and people? Are the doors truly open? What does the Huntington gain with the introduction of the Chinese garden, and what do Chinese Americans and Chinese immigrants gain in the process? I address these questions using data obtained from in-depth, audiotaped interviews with key figures in the planning and building of the garden, ethnography conducted in the garden and the related lecture series, and analysis of Huntington documents, such as brochures, promotional DVDs intended to cull new donations, and news reports about the garden.

First, a caveat: Chinese American immigrants are diverse, and at lower and middle points on the class spectrum Chinese people and cultural traditions are also shaping the way public gardens and parks are used in Southern California. For example, at public parks in the San Gabriel Valley, working-class and middle-class residents gather daily to collectively transform parks into places for quotidian Chinese aerobic exercise, flute playing, and early morning tai chi. With these practices public parks take on new Chinese meanings and uses during the morning hours, but their material culture and plant life remain intact. Transforming the material culture at the Huntington botanical garden has relied, not on quotidian practices, but on the substantial resources of upper-class Chinese and Taiwanese newcomers.

BOTANICAL GARDENS AND THE HUNTINGTON

Modern botanic gardens are rooted in the migration of conquest and colonialization.[9] European imperial powers developed botanic gardens in the eighteenth and nineteenth centuries as both the mechanisms and the products of expanding economic empires, as places to display colonial acquisitions and to propagate economic growth through plant cultivation.[10] The Dutch started botanical gardens, and France, Spain, and Germany followed, but these operations found fullest expression in Britain at the Kew Royal Botanic Gardens.

British plant hunters and botanists traveled around the globe and brought back seeds, cuttings, and plants to discover which ones might be useful economically. Kew Royal Botanic Garden served as their scientific testing ground. Potentially profitable plants would first be cultivated at Kew, and if they showed promise they might be grown in an entirely different region of the British Empire, with say, tea plants from China grown in India. Joseph Banks (1743–1820), the most famous plant hunter of this era, believed that Kew should serve as "a great botanical exchange house for the empire,"[11] and Kew came to serve exactly this purpose, supplying seeds, crops, and horticultural advice to large-scale cultivation projects in the colonies. By the turn of the twentieth century, there were over one hundred colonial botanic gardens dispersed throughout the British Empire.[12]

European botanic gardens eventually supplied a new array of ornamental plants for private residential landscape gardens, and collecting exotic ornamentals become a status activity. Until the introduction of plants from colonies scattered around the globe, Europeans had a paucity of colorful ornamental plants. Gardens must have looked very dreary in winter. By the 1780s, gardening had become part of the national identity in Britain, and trees and plants from North America and other parts of the globe became increasingly accessible. Plants and gardens entered a new crisscrossing nexus of global migration in the eighteenth century.[13] This resulted in an ironic juxtaposing of plants and national identity, as the so-called "naturalistic" British landscape gardens were in fact populated with non-native plants from around the globe. When Thomas Jefferson visited England, he apparently recognized many American trees and knew immediately that these would thrive at his estate in Monticello.[14]

In early twentieth-century Southern and Central California, prominent industrialists developed ambitious estate gardens to project their own personal power and status. Along the rugged California coastline and in an inland valley, these one percenters of the day acted as imperial nations, carving spectacular vanity gardens to convey their cultural refinement and status. They did so by looking to Europe, emulating aristocratic European and ancient Roman garden traditions.

In 1903 Henry E. Huntington, a railroad and real estate mogul, purchased six hundred acres of sprawling orange groves that he transformed into his private European-style estate home, complete with an avocado orchard and a massive garden collection with rare and exotic ornamental plants and imported statuary in San Marino, California, forming the basis for what is today the Huntington Library, Art Collections, and Botanical Gardens. A few decades later, William Randolph Hearst, heir of a mining fortune and a yellow journalism tycoon, transformed a 250,000-plus-acre property that he had inherited on the central coast of California into what is now known as Hearst Castle, a Spanish-Moorish Revival estate compound that by 1947 included 165 rooms filled with tapestries, antiques, and art that had belonged to European royalty and cathedrals, as well as 127 acres of Spanish- and Italian-inspired gardens, pathways, fountains, terraces, and pools (including the famous Neptune pool complex, featured in *Spartacus*, and another tiled, indoor pool with statues of Roman gods and goddesses). As a young boy, Hearst had accompanied his mother on a grand European tour, and he purportedly drew inspiration for his private California castle from the chateaus, aristocratic gardens, and cathedrals that he had seen at age ten while on that trip. In the 1950s, the oil industrialist J. Paul Getty commissioned an elaborate Roman garden and gallery to house his collection of Roman antiquities art, built near his home in Pacific Palisades, just south of Malibu. Like the Huntington estate and Hearst Castle, the Getty Villa, which aspires to recreate an ancient Roman garden, complete with fountains, hedges, a narrow reflecting pool, and marble and bronze statues, is now open to the public and is visited by thousands of people each year.

Huntington, Hearst, and Getty were trying to tame the landscape of the wild West. When they imagined their private garden paradises, they all looked to European models of imperial beauty. Consequently, the gardens at the Huntington, the Getty Villa, and the Hearst Castle compound were built to convey civilization, power, and grace by copying aristocratic European and ancient Roman garden traditions. The Huntington did add a Japanese-style garden, initially called the Oriental Garden, which I discuss below as both similar to and different from the Suzhou-style garden. Today, these once private estates serve as public institutions of conspicuous leisure.

THE HUNTINGTON

> A visit to the Huntington is like taking a trip to a grand
> estate in Europe, a top-notch university, a world-class art
> museum, and an around-the-world botanical tour—all in
> one day!
> —promotional letter for Huntington membership renewal, 2008

Railroad and real estate magnate Henry E. Huntington purchased the ranch property for his estate in 1903. Relying on a small army of labor supervised by the German-born and Austrian-trained landscape gardener William Hertrich (hired as his "superintendent" in 1905), Huntington transformed a working ranch into a series of distinctive gardens with rare and exotic ornamentals. The Huntington opened as a research institution for scholars in 1913 and as a viewing destination for the public in 1928. Today it encompasses a complex of galleries, archives, and gardens situated on a sprawling 207 acres, 120 of which are landscaped and open to visitors. Besides the garden, the Huntington includes important collections of eighteenth- and nineteenth-century British, American, and French painting, sculpture, decorative arts, and antiques, and approximately six million rare books, photographs, and manuscripts in the library. Special lectures, conferences, and exhibits are regularly featured at the Huntington, and the gardens are part of this elite cultural compound.

The Huntington gardens speak to the ambition of the western industrialist for whom it is named. It includes his Beaux Arts mansion and expanses of lawn, terraces, lily ponds, a rose garden, a Japanese garden with a teahouse (which Huntington purchased from a Pasadena commercial venture), palm and desert gardens, an Australian garden, a bamboo forest, a Shakespeare garden, an herb garden, and statuary. If you are visiting and wish to see it all in one day, you must be prepared to walk several miles, and this requires a good deal of stamina, especially on a warm day. In recent years, a successful fund-raising campaign allowed the Huntington to add a sixteen-thousand-square-foot Conservatory for Botanical Sciences, which includes a mini-rain forest, a cloud forest, a bog, and a plant laboratory, and attached is a charming outdoor children's garden with fountains designed for splashing. Everywhere you look, the scale of the Huntington botanical gardens is monumental. The desert garden alone includes ten acres planted with five thousand species of cacti and succulents, including giant saguaro cacti, golden barrel cacti, and aloes and agave set artistically among winding paths. Many of these plants were brought by railroad from the Southwest and Mexico in the early twentieth century, and the largest cactus is now said to weigh fifteen tons.

The Huntington is a major destination point for well-heeled tourists, locals, and scholars. Each year, over half a million visitors come to the Huntington Library, Art Collections, and Botanical Gardens, including fifty-five thousand international visitors and the children who come on field trips just about every weekday, and two thousand scholars or readers are in residence or use the archives.[15] I feel lucky to live nearby, and I enjoy strolling the gardens and being a reader at this significant library and archival collection. Located just a dozen miles from downtown Los Angeles, it is tucked away in San Marino, a wealthy residential municipality of mansions and manicured estates below the San Gabriel Mountains. No one stumbles on the Huntington. When I first moved to Southern California, I was always confused when trying to find the main entrance. The signage is negligible, so in spite of its size, it seems somewhat hidden.

Southern California's climate allows for year-round visitors at the Huntington, and people slowly stroll the garden and galleries and observe. Entrance is not cheap—it cost $23 to enter on weekends (there is one free admission day a month, but reservations must be made in advance). There are many educational programs, and during the weekday mornings school buses bring children for field trips. Most people visit as couples, as families, and in small groups. Many carry cameras and take photos as they stroll contemplatively, perhaps stopping to point out and observe a plant or sculpture of particular interest. Social behavior at the Huntington gardens resembles the way one would behave at a museum rather than a park. Picnicking is not allowed, although there is a cafeteria and a formal British-inspired teahouse, which serves tea, scones, and crustless cucumber sandwiches. It was in this serene environment that the Chinese-style garden debuted in spring 2008. The introduction of the Suzhou-style garden into the Huntington represents a significant rupture in the vernacular landscape of botanical estate gardens, as well as with respect to social processes of inclusion. To understand the true significance, we must revisit the history of Chinese exclusion.

CHINESE EXCLUSIONS

Chinese immigrant workers were recruited for labor by the railroads in the nineteenth-century American West, but they met with overt exclusions, legal discrimination, and hostility from the late 1880s until 1965. The mid-nineteenth-century scapegoating of Chinese workers by white male labor union leaders, combined with the eugenicists' warnings against Chinese contamination and moral degeneration, produced the Chinese Exclusion Act of 1882.[16] Until its repeal in 1943 and the passage of the

Immigration and Nationality Act of 1965, Chinese immigrants faced restrictions on entry, legalization, and naturalization. As recently as the mid-twentieth century, Chinese immigrants were excluded from U.S. citizenship.[17]

In the late twentieth century, restrictions moved to built environments. On numerous occasions, when Chinese people have developed religious, commercial, and residential built environments marked as distinctively Chinese they have encountered hostility.[18] Chinatowns were once reviled as dens of iniquity and policed by a barrage of "pigtail ordinances" (e.g., San Francisco's 1876 queue ordinance, or other municipal laws passed to drive the Chinese out of the laundry business). Today Chinatowns are seen as quaint, picturesque, self-contained enclaves, as destination spots for dining and acquiring inexpensive tourist items.[19] The new contested terrains are outside Chinatown, mostly in affluent suburbs.

Monterey Park, a bedroom community located eight miles east of downtown LA, is now famously known as the "first suburban Chinatown." As Los Angeles became an important node in Chinese transnational business networks, post-1965 Taiwanese immigrants and Chinese investors redeveloped a sleepy commercial area into a municipality of vibrant Chinese shopping malls and condominium complexes. In response, an anti-Chinese backlash emerged in the 1970s and 1980s, fueled by the rise of the English-only movement in the 1980s and by localized reactions to Chinese-oriented businesses, commercial signs, and store names written in Chinese characters.[20]

Built manifestations of Chinese commercial life—commercial shops, signage in Chinese characters, and shopping malls with Chinese businesses—became the focal point of controversy. By the 1980s, along the main commercial arteries of Atlantic Boulevard and Garvey Avenue, Chinese was spoken in most businesses, and Chinese developments of new luxury homes and condominium complexes dwarfed the old Craftsman homes, drawing the ire of old-time residents. As sociologist Leland Saito noted, this led to the racialization of architectural disputes in the building of a shopping mall, Atlantic Square. White and Latino residents ultimately pushed for pseudo-Spanish style buildings—stucco, with arches and red-tiled roofs, a vernacular that is widely reproduced throughout Southern California—in order to tamp down overt displays of Chinese material culture and symbolic power.[21] Today, these types of Chinese commercial districts extend throughout the San Gabriel Valley, far beyond the confines of Monterey Park. And the controversies over building and gardening styles continue in residential homes and gardens, as shown below.

Affluent Chinese Americans have also encountered contentious politics over residential styles in the Pacific Rim cities of Vancouver, Los Angeles, and San Francisco. In the well-heeled suburbs of LA's San Gabriel Valley, in the Silicon Valley that stretches between San Francisco and San Jose, and in suburban residential areas of Vancouver, some Chinese Americans have been accused of building tasteless McMansions, "monster houses" devoid of appropriate landscaping. Home owners in Vancouver have long adhered to English landscape traditions—lawns with curved borders and naturalistic-looking clumps of trees and bushes—but as geographer Katharyne Mitchell has shown, many of these white home owners reacted antagonistically toward their affluent neighbors from Hong Kong, who preferred rectangular, symmetrically shaped houses with big double doors, two-story entrance ways, and yards with straight-line borders and little foliage. These were perceived as ostentatious and lacking in good taste. Animosity against these built environments, Mitchell contends, is part of a legacy harkening back to when Chinese were seen as moral inferiors who had to remain perennial outsiders.[22] The homes and gardens, Mitchell argues, disrupt the identification of Vancouver with English residential and landscape traditions. By contrast, as we saw in chapter 1, when Taiwanese immigrants adopt US-style detached homes and gardens with sprawling green lawns, they blend into affluent suburban landscapes and conflict is avoided.[23]

Chinese people in other Pacific Rim cities have also been criticized for building houses out to the maximum square footage. Design review committees in affluent residential suburbs around the Huntington, such as San Marino and South Pasadena, are charged with ensuring that all buildings follow strict municipal zoning regulations, and they regulate house size, construction specification, and front-yard appearance. Sometimes there are explicit references to "Chinese houses," as when one realtor told me years ago, when we were shopping for a house in this area, "This isn't bad for a Chinese house." I was a little stunned, but I knew what she meant—a large, open, modern design rather than the vernacular Craftsman style.

More often color-blind language is used, as in this angry letter to the "Home" section of the *Los Angeles Times*:

> I'm sorry that Vanessa Choy and Andrew Wong were unable to find a house in Brentwood or Westwood, because it would have spared our neighborhood of their oversized house. . . . Although the house may cover "only a quarter" of the lot, its appearance is much greater because it sits on a corner lot with minimal landscaping to mitigate its size. The statement that they chose the peaked roof to blend with the neighborhood is laughable. It's a 6,200 square-foot house in a neighborhood that has historically had houses in the 1,500–2,000 square-foot range and its transitioning to 3,000–3,500 square-foot houses. The mark of good architecture is to build a structure that harmonizes with the site. Theirs doesn't.
>
> Bruce Horn, Studio City, *Los Angeles Times*, F-6, March 20, 2008

New "taste wars" unfolded in Pacific Rim cities, and it was affluent immigrant and ethnic groups, rather than lower-income Mexicans and Central Americans, who were perceived as the violators bringing the wrong cultural preferences into the built environments of middle-class and affluent residential communities. Chinese immigrants and transnational elites are not the only ones who have been accused of these transgressions: wealthy Iranians who resettled in Beverly Hills and other wealthy enclaves of West Los Angeles in the 1980s have met with similar accusations. But the Chinese, as the second-largest immigrant group in the United States, far outnumber Iranians, so the impact is more widespread.

Another example of restrictionism against Chinese built environments is the Hsi Lai Temple, a $25 million, fourteen-acre Chinese Buddhist monastery located in Hacienda Heights, an unincorporated suburban area in the San Gabriel Valley.[24] In the 1980s, when the temple was first planned, residents in this community feared that a compound with foreign-born, non-Christian Taiwanese Buddhist monks and nuns would severely disrupt the community with noise, traffic, and cultlike practices.[25] The temple was eventually built, but only after six public hearings, over one hundred meetings, and concessions regarding building size, parking, incense use, and even the color of the robes that lower-ranked monks and nuns would wear.[26]

The social animosity and restrictionism directed against Chinese commercial developments, "monster houses," and religious temples is allied to fears and anxieties about the new Yellow Perils: the global economic commercial power of China and the competitive Chinese student and math/science/engineering/computer professional.[27] One controlling image that circulates widely today is that of China as a superpower ready to rule the world. In these renditions, China is posed as a new threat not because of communism but because of excellence in global capitalism. Manufacturing pollution, human rights violations, and the export of unsafe toys and poisonous foods are sometimes included in this scenario, but the title of a *New York Times* best seller succinctly gets at the dominant anxiety: *China, Inc.: How the Rise of the Next Superpower Challenges America and the World.*[28] It is in this contradictory context that we must understand the debut of the new Chinese garden at the most elite garden in the western United States.

THE NEW CHINESE GARDEN, LIU FANG YUAN

It would be hard to live in Southern California and not know about the Liu Fang Yuan, or Garden of Flowing Fragrance. Featured stories about the new garden ran in local newspapers, Chinese newspapers, and regional publications such as *Sunset*, a glossy commercial magazine devoted to "living in the West," and the Automobile Club of Southern California's *Westways* magazine, where it graced the cover of the November/December 2008 issue. The Huntington has published a beautiful coffee table book, *Another World Lies Beyond*, with photographs and essays on the making of the garden.[29] Because all of this media publicity, annual visits to the Huntington increased 20 percent after the Liu Fang Yuan opened. More Chinese people seem to be visiting than before.[30]

The garden is built in the tradition of the classical gardens of Suzhou, which are today a UNESCO World Heritage Site. These gardens date from the Ming dynasty (1368–1644), when merchants and scholar officials from fifteenth- to seventeenth-century China sought status by building residential gardens that would recreate the natural landscape through strategically placed rocks, plants, and pavilions. Money alone did not signal status, so merchants and the scholar-gentry built gardens and pavilions around their homes where they welcomed scholars and the literati to tutor their children and to write poetry and philosophical reflections. These were aesthetic sites intended to inspire the literati.[31] The Suzhou scholar's garden, then, is based on a tradition not unlike the origins of the Huntington garden, where a railroad and real estate baron used his wealth to acquire status-enhancing art, botanical specimens, and rare manuscripts that would attract renowned scholars from around the world.

Today, Suzhou City has been described as "a veritable museum of classical gardens." The *New York Times* art critic Holland Cotter underscores the extent to which these were the products and oases of elites. The scholars and merchant elites of these gardens "wanted no contact with the larger world," he writes. Rather, the Suzhou gardens and pavilion culture represented a "willed retreat from social realities."[32] Birds, fish, and plants were included to provide inspiration for meditation, reflection, and metaphysical meaning.

At the Huntington, the Liu Fang Yuan includes graceful willow and elm trees, camellias and nandinas, and, around the courtyard, plantains. There are smaller shrubs too, but this garden is less about plants than about the built structures that surround the manmade lake. These structures were painstakingly planned by a complex transnational design team that imported materials from China and brought in sixty Chinese craft workers to help with the construction. The garden includes meticulously crafted pavilions (featuring roof tiles that were fired in China and then shipped to the Huntington), decorative mosaic pebble paving, hand-carved bridges, and 850 tons of huge, craggy Taihu rocks that are vertically and sculpturally displayed along the lake's edge (these were imported from Lake Tai in China). Botanically inspired lattice windows (also fired in China) were inserted into an undulating wall that forms part of an intimate corridor, the Corridor of Covered Clouds.

The symbolism is subtle and quiet. By design and at the insistence of the Huntington planning team, there are no dragons or phoenixes in the garden, but the gently undulating wall subtly alludes to a dragon. The structures invite contemplation, and viewing the garden through moon gates, round doors and windows, seems to invite one to enter another world. The title of the Huntington's official book on the Chinese garden, *Another World Lies Beyond*, underscores this aspect of the garden. Great care was taken to situate the garden to take advantage of views of the nearby San Gabriel Mountains. Respecting the natural site in which a

Figure 34. Fifty artisan workers were brought from China to work on built elements of the Suzhou-style garden, such as the mosaic stone patio. This item is reproduced by permission of the Office of Communications, at The Huntington Library, San Marino, California.

garden is to be built is a Suzhou tradition, and here the mountains and native California oak trees located at the northeastern perimeter help create the composed scenes that are viewed from the pavilions.

Chinese-style gardens are relatively new in the West, but Japanese-style gardens have been widely embraced in the United States and western Europe since the turn of the twentieth century, when Japan emerged as a powerful nation and actively promoted Japanese garden aesthetics at the World's Fairs in Europe and the United States. In fact, scholar Kendall H. Brown claims that in the twentieth century "more large scale public 'Japanese gardens' were built outside of Japan than within . . . particularly along the Pacific Coast."[33] As we saw in chapter 2, Japanese-style gardens, together with Japanese art, literature, and architectural styles, were adopted as favored aesthetics in the United States, signaling fascination with Orientalism. In the early twentieth century these often featured Japanese women dressed in kimonos and serving tea. As a teen growing up in the Bay Area, I visited the Japanese tea garden in San Francisco's Golden Gate Park, where I loved the rice crackers, almond cookies, and green tea served by Japanese women in kimonos, but I never reflected on what exactly I was consuming or how it came to be. That stance reflects in part the extent to which Japanese gardens have become so thoroughly incorporated throughout the West.

The Japanese-style garden at the Huntington remains among the most beloved gardens there, but it began as a commercial Japanese tea garden operated by the Australian immigrant entrepreneur George Turner Marsh, who invested in over half a dozen Japanese-style gardens in the early twentieth century and used them to sell souvenirs and Oriental antiques. This was a type of commercialized Orientalism, and when one of the three-acre ventures in Pasadena was not faring well, Henry E. Huntington bought the whole thing, including plants, statues, and a two-story house, parts of which had been constructed in Japan. Huntington was courting his widowed aunt Arabella, one of the wealthiest women in the country at the time, and the exotic gardens are said to have helped woo her to the West. The Goto family, who had worked for Marsh, moved to the Huntington estate and maintained the Japanese-style garden. They were required to dress in kimonos when visitors came, providing an animated Oriental cultural enactment in the home and garden of Henry and Arabella Huntington.

The Liu Fang Yuan at the Huntington signals a departure from this sort of Orientalist display. Chinese culture is not appropriated as a costumed, colonialist fantasy. As I will show below, Chinese designers, donors, and scholars were intimately involved in the process of planning and building the garden, and great care was taken to understand the garden in the terms of Chinese literary and artistic traditions.

Special knowledge is required to fully appreciate the garden too. As Veblen underscored, conspicuous leisure requires time invested in knowledge acquisition. The meanings of the Suzhou-style garden are fully available only to those who understand the richly layered symbolism and the inscriptions derived from Chinese landscape painting and literary texts. As T. June Li, the curator of the garden, explained when I saw her present a spring 2008 lecture to the Chinese American Club in South Pasadena, "The Chinese garden, like Chinese painting, is a mini-representation of the universe." Decoding the garden involves more than simply knowing that the rocks symbolize stable mountains, or the water, changing elements in life. Fully understanding the garden elements and decoration requires formidable scholarly erudition in Chinese philosophy and aesthetic traditions. In the official Huntington book on the garden, T. June Li elaborates on the depth of literary scholarship required: "Many of the architectural ornaments and landscape details in Liu Fang Yuan reinforce the themes of the garden. For example, the carved fish finials decorating the ends of the zigzag Bride of the Joy of Fish, Yu Le Qiao, recall the playful discussion between the Daoist Zhuangzi and his friend the logician Huizi. This famous exchange centered on the enigma of whether it was possible for Zhuangzi to know that the fish in the river were happy, pitching the free-spirited Daoist ideas against the more pedantic arguments of logic."[34]

This sort of esoteric knowledge is not accessible to the vast majority of garden visitors. Even highly educated Chinese and Chinese American visitors may be only remotely familiar with Suzhou gardens, or even with their own ancestors' gardens. One Oregonian professor, for example, discovered in a Huntington lecture that a famous Suzhou garden had belonged to his great-great-grandfather.[35] It is true that the garden is like a piece of art that is open to interpretation, but there are clearly varied abilities of appreciation and interpretation.

Language is one medium through which the garden is interpreted. Chinese calligraphy offering poetic reflections on nature is literally inscribed on the rocks and buildings, and the garden structures and elements bear names (e.g., "the Lake of Reflected Fragrance," "Pavilion for Washing Away Thoughts," "Love for the Lotus Pavilion"). An advisory panel of scholars carefully chose these names during the planning phase of the garden, and the names echo those from famous seventeenth-century Chinese texts, such as *The Story of the Stone* (also known as *Dream of the Red Chamber*). The Huntington planning team carefully consulted this novel of the mid-eighteenth-century Qing Dynasty, widely revered as a detailed account of the daily life of the Chinese elites of that era, in order to best approximate an authentic Chinese-style garden. They also consulted *The Craft of Gardens,* a seventeenth-century garden-building manual written between 1631 and 1634 by Ji Cheng.[36] According to Alison Hardie, who translated this book, "The late Ming was a time of social and economic change when the emergence of a wealthy merchant class with aspirations to join the cultured upper class created a strong demand for manuals of self-improvement and advice."[37] Scholarship, elite Chinese traditions, and literary erudition are literally materialized and inscribed in the garden.

Figure 35. Chinese grape harvesters at work in the Shorb Vineyards (ca. 1800s), site of the Huntington today. While Chinese people were once allowed in San Marino only as truck farmers, servants, and grape pickers, today they are well represented among city leaders and home owners in the affluent city of San Marino. Courtesy of California Historical Society, CHS2010.233.

The Chinese-style garden currently covers 3.5 acres, but when stage 2 is completed, it will account for 12 acres within the 120 landscaped acres of the Huntington. According to garden designer Jin Chen, it will be larger than any other scholar's garden in China. It will then occupy a physical space larger than the Japanese garden—which is significant, given the historical animosity between Japan and China—and it will be larger than any of the other gardens at the Huntington.[38]

These developments are striking not only given the legacy of exclusion in the United States but also given the history of Chinese immigrant "coolies" who performed the hard and dangerous work of blasting the mountains and laying the railroad tracks that would connect California to the transcontinental railroad. Collis P. Huntington (1821–1900) was one of the big four California railroad barons, so the basis for the Huntington fortune began with the railroads and the labor of Chinese and Mexican labor. Chinese people were once allowed in San Marino only as vegetable peddlers or as grape pickers and haulers in the vineyards that prevailed here in the late nineteenth century.[39]

Why Here and Now?

Discussion about building a new Chinese garden began in the late 1980s, but the Huntington leadership did not pursue this project until Peter Paanakker left a $10 million bequest in 2001.[40] Paanakker, a cosmopolitan businessman whose mother had created the Anthropology Museum at the University of Pennsylvania, had served as a Huntington Overseer, and his gift was earmarked explicitly for the Chinese garden, with half going toward construction costs and half toward an endowment. The Huntington already had impressive collections of Chinese flora, including one of the world's top camellia collections, as well as bamboo, azaleas, and magnolias, and this formed part of the rationale for building a Chinese garden, but the Huntington was also responding to changing demographics. As the director of botanical gardens Jim Folsom told me, "The botanical stores alone made it worth building a Chinese garden, but . . . [given] the growth of the Chinese community in California and the opening up of China—what you end up with is an almost unavoidable compulsion to build a Chinese garden."

The Huntington still needed to raise another $20 million for this project. Philanthropic donations to elite cultural institutions, such as the ballet, the opera, or botanical gardens and museums, typically come from local elites. By the 1990s, the Huntington could hardly ignore the changing face of its local neighbors in San Marino. This had once been an exclusively WASP residential enclave where black, Jewish, and Chinese people were prohibited from purchasing property, but by the year 2000 43 percent of San Marino's population was Chinese.[41] Today the mayor of San Marino is Chinese, as is half of the city council. It remains a residential enclave for the affluent. With the booming economy of the early millennium, and in spite of the economic recession of 2008, San Marino's median household income increased to $154,318 in 2007–11, with 53.5 percent of the population having Asian origins. The median value of a house here is over $1.5 million.[42] While home values plummeted in other wealthy communities during the housing slump, they rose here, in part because of the popularity of this neighborhood with Asian buyers. Many buyers here pay full cash, forgoing mortgages. The proportion of Chinese home owners in other San Gabriel Valley residential communities also expanded throughout the 1980s and 1990s.[43]

Prestigious private universities, museums, and cultural institutions are now courting Asian American philanthropy from California to New York.[44] The fund-raising campaign for the Liu Fang Yuan began in 2003. Until this moment, there were two parallel cultural universes living side by side—the mostly white, Euro-oriented Huntington and the growing Chinese communities. Examining the process of planning the garden and incorporating Chinese donors and landscape designers reveals the challenges the Huntington faced in gaining the trust of their Chinese neighbors and the chasms that had to be bridged.

Fund-Raising

First, the Huntington had to learn the rules of Chinese philanthropy. Donor recognition is common in both American and Chinese contexts, but as the vice president for advancement explained to me, eliciting donations in the United States is all about "making the case" or proving the worthwhile nature of a particular project, while Chinese philanthropy operates on the principle of who has already given money. Previous donors lend credibility, and if the "right" names are on the list of donors, then more people will give. This involves *guanxi*, or the social capital, connections, and trust embedded in social relations. Who has already given and who is asking are very important. When I interviewed her, this top professional recalled sitting down with potential donors who would ask, "Who is on the donors' list? Who is already supporting you?" As she explained, "In the Chinese context, it's the person that asked, it's about who."

The Huntington's first hurdle was to recruit initial donations and endorsements from well-respected Chinese and Chinese American entrepreneurs. It started slowly, with a gala party organized by Chinese women in the "Friendship Fund Committee," press coverage, and the recruitment of well-respected members of Chinese communities to ask for donations. The first major donation was in kind—free shipping of a hundred containers of rocks from China, provided by COSCO, the Chinese Overseas Shipping Company. Donations increased once real estate and banking tycoons began giving. The Huntington was able to publicize major donations from Roger Wang, a transnational Chinese businessman, who made the Forbes list of notable billionaires in 2007 and 2008; Dominic Ng, an immigrant from Hong Kong who famously went from being a drug store manager in the 1970s to becoming the president of East West Bank; and Wilbur Woo, the member of an older Cantonese Chinatown family and one of the key founders of Cathay Bank. Each of these men, along with their families and businesses, gave donations of $1 million or more to the Huntington's Chinese garden project.

Philanthropy is a way of giving back, but it is also a way of acquiring and displaying privileged cultural status, and the Huntington developed mechanisms to publicize the names of donors and the amounts of their donations. The Huntington developed a "donors' list" brochure with different amounts of donations categorized by the names of prized gems and stones, now also available on the website.[45] Donors who gave $100,000 to $999,999 were recognized as Jade level, those who gave $50,000 to $99,999 as Ruby level, and so on. The donors' names were published in brochures and on the website, and the largest donors were acknowledged with small plaques on pavilions, bridges, and other structures in the Chinese garden. Many donors approached this competitively, trying to outdo one another.

As the Huntington began to recruit well-regarded donors and to prove the authenticity and seriousness of the project by having many of the materials shipped in from China, confidence and trust grew. As the vice president of advancement explained, "Initially, the donations were kind of modest votes of confidence." Good press in both Chinese- and English-language newspapers helped to increase that confidence.

The Huntington also developed a lecture series on Chinese gardens, and this simultaneously authenticated the garden project and provided aesthetic education to Chinese and non-Chinese alike on the traditions of Suzhou-style scholar's gardens. These were classes on how to fully appreciate the garden. And in 2005, the Huntington also brought four Chinese members to the Board of Overseers. This was publicized in the *Chinese Daily* and the *Sing Tao Daily* newspapers, which are widely read in Southern California.

Fund-raising for the new Chinese garden required overcoming long-standing political and regional differences that had impeded prior collaborations. For instance, donations from mainland Chinese and Taiwanese immigrants had to be delicately balanced. A large donation from a Taiwanese person had to be followed by a similar-sized donation from a person with origins in mainland China—the Huntington could not afford to alienate one group in favor of the other. This led to two processes of immigrant integration, one interracial and the other intraracial.

When the contract to design the garden went to Jin Chen of Suzhou Landscaping, a mainland China company, potential Taiwanese donors had to be reassured. As the vice president of development at the Huntington explained to me, "We needed partners in China, and the operations people chose this Suzhou design and construction company to partner with us. Once we made that decision we had to protect our interest in mainland China. So we couldn't let an exceptionally wealthy Taiwanese businessman, for example, if he was renowned for being green, which is proindependence, come in and slap ten million dollars down and buy the garden. Couldn't do it, 'cause we would have lost our partnership with Suzhou, the mainland would have just pulled 'em out." According to the vice president of development, "The COSCO commitment was important because it saved us over $200,000 in shipping costs, but it also was a really important gift from mainland China. And that helped to counterbalance a lot of the $100,000 gifts that we were getting from many of the local Taiwanese community."

Throughout this process, the Huntington's key fund-raiser had to act with great sensitivity. In her office, she showed me one of the designer's early drawings of the garden; to the side were Chinese characters that read "the China Garden." Some prospective Taiwanese donors did not like this, as it suggested a PRC affiliation, and she said prospective donors would have preferred something like "the Chinese Garden." But one Taiwanese man saw the design to be configured in the shape of Taiwan, and this perception allowed him to buy into the project. Was the garden deliberately shaped like Taiwan? She sensibly offered that "people see what they want to see."

What Class and Racial Projects Are Achieved?

The process of creating the new Chinese garden at the Huntington reveals three major shifts in class and racial projects. First, new alliances emerged between elite groups who had previously experienced little contact with each other. These included interracial partnerships between white professionals and leaders of the Huntington and their wealthy Chinese neighbors, and intraethnic alliances connecting Taiwanese, mainland Chinese, and old Chinatown families in a shared project of projecting and displaying an elite, premodern shared Chinese cultural form in a mainstream venue.

Transnational Taiwanese and mainland Chinese elites with residential bases in the San Gabriel Valley, together with established Chinese American families, entered into new cultural and financial relations with what has been, until now, an exclusively white, Eurocentric cultural institution. This new collaboration between an American white cultural institution and Chinese elites represented a shift away from what some had perceived as an insular "bunker mentality" among Chinese Americans immigrants—thought to be sequestered in ethnic enclaves—and transnational professionals and entrepreneurs, more attuned to transnational global connections than local ones in the United States.[46]

Global elites donated money for the Suzhou-style garden. Many of the Chinese who own homes in San Marino and other affluent San Gabriel Valley neighborhoods have achieved their wealth and status in ways that allowed them to maintain themselves in entrenched communities. Several studies have noted their transnational family formations of "parachute kids" who are dropped and anchored in the United States while their "astronaut" parents with multiple passports shuttle across borders on trans-Pacific business. Flexibility and mobility are critical for transnational business and may require the ability to maintain social interactions that are more integrated into Chinese transnational spheres than American social institutions. Now integration into Huntington allows some of these elites to gain new symbolic cultural capital in Southern California.

The Suzhou-style garden at the Huntington was a project of class consolidation, not immigrant assimilation. As noted above, it required delicate intraethnic negotiations and collaborations between Taiwanese and mainland Chinese elites who had established residential and business anchors in Southern California. The need to balance mainland Chinese and Taiwanese influence continues. A 2012 Huntington brochure, for example, declares that "when Chinese dignitaries arrive in Southern California, one of the first stops on their itinerary is often The Huntington for a tour of the Garden of Flowing Fragrance. Interest in the garden is high among Chinese officials." On the same page, we learn about a Taiwanese doctor's monetary and cultural contributions of exquisite flower arrangements that are sometimes on display for Chinese New Year celebrations at the Chinese garden; the doctor shares that she and her husband enjoy their membership privileges with early morning walks through the gardens.[47] China and Taiwan still lack diplomatic relations, but here in the garden, they coexist.

Not all Chinese people in the San Gabriel Valley or Southern California are wealthy enough to be in the donor class. How does the new garden affect nonelite Chinese Americans? They may visit, and they are also incorporated as docents, trained volunteers who stand in the garden and offer visitors information. According to Mikki Heydorff, who manages the substantial volunteer program at the Huntington, 70 percent of the docents in the Chinese garden are of Chinese origin. These docents, like the visitors, include students and those of more modest middle-class means, and according to her they take great pride in the presentation of a built garden environment that represents their cultural origins and identity. The new Chinese garden provides an alternative aesthetic representation to the kitsch of Chinatown, the pollution of Beijing, noisy commercial streets, and tasteless monster houses. And in fact, this narrative is part of what the docents narrate.

At a personal level, the Chinese garden at the Huntington has served as an emblem of cultural pride. One of the docents, a thirty-seven-year-old artist from Hong Kong, reported that she had previously felt ashamed of her accent and heritage and that she had been more drawn to Western forms of design in her art. Now, she said, "These Chinese impulses are bubbling out of me. . . . I'm able to accept myself and who I am, and it's a lot more healing."[48] On opening day, a woman from Taiwan gushed, "It is so wonderful to have Chinese heritage at the Huntington. We're so excited."[49]

Not everyone in the local Chinese American community, however, expresses such enthusiasm for the new Chinese garden. My interviews with Chinese Americans not affiliated with the Huntington reveal not only measured but also distant, uninterested, and even openly critical views of the new garden at the Huntington. For example, Yan Wong, a 1.5-generation teacher, felt very strongly connected to her Chinese heritage and expressed this through her own reconstructed homeland garden. When I visited her home, I found a tiny front and back yard brimming with a lush array of Asian fruits and vegetables, including a spectacular Pakistani mulberry tree, Chinese yam, Thai lemongrass, starfruit, lemon verbena, four bay trees, and many other edibles and pretty ornamental plants, such as cordyline, blue fescue, and creeping thyme. It was one of the most beautiful and enchanting gardens I had ever visited, and I found it particularly inspiring because it produced so much food and diverse plant beauty on a small property. Although Yan had come to the United States as a young child, her plants, she explained, were inspired from memories of her childhood in Southern China, where her parents worked in peasant agriculture. "We had a garden, and everyone grew their own food and vegetables in our village," she said. She recalled running and hiding among sugarcane fields and eating guava, peaches, and medicinal herbs. "Grandpa was growing carnations on the rooftop," she added. Her family migrated to Los Angeles, where they took immigrant working-class jobs, her mother as a seamstress and her father as a busboy, and when they settled in Highland Park they grew their own vegetables in the backyard. Now Yan Wong had her own Edenic Chinese homeland garden, and she promoted school gardens through her job as a high school teacher. Yet when I asked what her response was as a Chinese American to the new Chinese garden at the Huntington, she did not hesitate to say, "To be honest with you, I didn't like it. . . . It wasn't lush. I knew they had spent a lot of money on it, but it did not impress me. . . . The garden I grew up in in the southern part of China did not look like that." The formal landscaping, the preponderance of hardscape, and the lack of edible plants did not evoke the orchards she had grown up around and only served to underline class distance and elitism. When I asked if the new Chinese garden made her feel proud, she replied, "No, not at all." She elaborated: "I did not feel particularly connected to it [because] we were from, I mean, we were poor. Poor people did not have gardens like that, but in 2007 I did a tour of China with my parents and we did go to the North. In the northern part of China we have gardens like that, but the wealthy had that, because the wealthy had hid their wives and their concubines in that. They were not allowed out, and they had to be enclosed indoors in garden areas like that. I couldn't relate to it."

Other Chinese Americans have expressed a lack of interest in the Liu Fang Yuan. Dr. Woo, a third-generation Chinese American physician and a true garden enthusiast with a substantial-sized residential property that she has planted with many trees and ornamental plants, also told me that she was unmoved by the new Suzhou-style garden at the Huntington, which she found harsh and dominated by concrete architectural features rather than plant nature. Dr. Woo, a longtime admirer of Japanese aesthetic traditions and the beauty of Zen simplicity, hung Japanese woodblock prints in her home and had planted her front yard with delicate Japanese maple trees. These looked slightly sunburned and were perhaps too thirsty for the interior canyons of Southern California, but they matched the rustic Craftsman style of her home. When I asked her about the Huntington's new Chinese garden, she explained, "I don't really identify so much with the Chinese, 'cause we don't even speak Chinese . . . but I love their Japanese garden. It's very beautiful, very peaceful." And another woman, a Taiwanese immigrant professional who lived only minutes away from the Huntington, told me that she was not even aware that the Huntington had introduced a new Suzhou-style garden.

Clearly, not everyone identifies with or appreciates Suzhou-style gardens. Chinese and non-Chinese people who visit the gardens must learn the codes and symbolism required for interpreting the garden, and as they do, they too experience themselves as participating in an elite "scholarly" activity. A new endowed lecture series accompanies the garden and helps accomplish this. Renowned scholars of East Asian languages and culture from top universities lecture on topics such as Chinese landscape painting, poetry, and Chinese garden furniture. At an October 2009 symposium entitled "Poetry and Textual Memory in the Chinese Garden," I listened to an esoteric lecture, "Petrophilia and Its Anxiety," covering the history, symbolism, and abuse of labor involved in excavating Taihu rocks, while dozens of images of rocks, calligraphy, poetry, and scholar's gardens were projected on a screen in a dim lecture hall. The professor spoke in English, with a thick Chinese accent, but the audience remained fully attentive. I described the audience this way in my field notes:

> It's the crowd I've come to expect. On a sunny, warm, Saturday morning in Southern California, not one person is wearing jeans and a T-shirt. The crowd is old, and overwhelmingly white and Chinese. I spot two women who could possibly be in their thirties, but most people seem to be in their fifties, sixties, and seventies—lots of gray hair and glasses. There are a few men in bow ties, many more in navy blue blazers and ties, and women in "casual business attire." No bright colors, although the Chinese woman sitting next to me is wearing stunning gray glossy patent leather platform wedges that match her gray outfit. There appear to be no blonds, and no brightly colored clothing in the room, until I spot two wildly dressed people in different corners of the room . . . but these eccentrics are the exception: it's a conservative crowd.

A serious, earnest group gathers at these lectures. The participants are becoming erudite on the topic of Chinese scholar's gardens, but they are simultaneously creating a particular kind of community engaged in the conspicuous leisure that Veblen described. They are performing and deepening their understanding of the esoteric, complex knowledge that is required to fully appreciate and decode the Chinese garden. An authority on landscape architecture has observed that gardens "may locate ideas, themes, and reference . . . [and] to the prepared, that is to say, to the knowledgeable and educated visitor, these 'codes' or 'messages' can be recovered and, if appropriate, strung together into an iconographical program or narrative."[50] In this regard, the lecture series seems to work as a "decoder." Together with the specialized books sold in the Huntington gift shop and the docents' tours, the lecture series makes available the tools for participating in elite conspicuous leisure. And one needn't be rich to attend the lectures. Most of them are free, supported by donations for this expressed purpose. The fee for attending the lecture on rocks was half that of the entrance fee to the garden itself, as it was funded by the Justin Vajna Memorial Fund for educational programs in the Chinese garden.

What does the Huntington gain through all of this? Obviously, it takes pride in the addition of a new, beautiful themed garden. There is palpable pride in the Liu Fang Yuan among the staff, and a sort of institutional pride is evident in the brochure and documents. Beyond that, however, the Huntington gains access to two things: a new donor base and multicultural legitimacy.

First, the new money is important. Certainly Chinese capital is not the only or even the major source of funding for the Huntington institution's expansion, but this new donor base, particularly considering the local geography, is crucial. Cultural institutions generally rely on local donors. With Asians accounting for nearly 54 percent of San Marino's population, this new source was necessary. As one administrator said, "We set out initially, as a policy, to raise the money from a new constituency, from Chinese Americans living nearby. We were not going to tap our traditional donor base because we needed their support for other things. . . . Nothing is as important as this [the Chinese garden] because it connects us to a new set of neighbors."

Second, the Suzhou-style garden allows the Huntington to slowly recast itself into a twenty-first-century institution in tune with globalization, transnationalism, and multiculturalism. Eurocentrism is now perceived as provincial and especially out of step in Pacific Rim cities, and the Huntington is refashioning itself. The Huntington has long been identified with its European collections and grand portraits. For years, Gainsborough's grand-manner portrait *The Blue Boy* was considered the signature acquisition. The Chinese garden and the corresponding exhibits and seminars on Chinese calligraphy and landscape painting are changing that perception of the Huntington, offering multicultural legitimacy and challenging the representation of monolithic European culture. As Steve Koblik, the president of the Huntington, told the *Los Angeles Times*, "We used to have an image of being inward-looking. We let you think the only thing here was 'Blue Boy' and 'Pinkie,' when we are one of the most important libraries about the history of California."[51]

New acquisitions and exhibits suggest that the Huntington is changing. The same year the Chinese garden opened, the Huntington acquired the archives of *La Opinion* (the largest Spanish-language newspaper in the United States) and the papers of Charles Bukowski (the bohemian poet and writer of debaucheries). It also expanded the Virginia Steele galleries holding American art. The American art collection at the Huntington is still relatively new, but it expanded significantly in 2009 with the opening of a new 16,379-square-foot gallery dedicated to American art. And in 2009 the Huntington acquired the archive of black science fiction writer Octavia Butler and had exhibits on Langston Hughes and the Central Avenue jazz district. These are efforts to help erase the image of the Huntington as a European cultural shrine. With these additions, Koblik says, "People can't tell you we're not interested in change."[52]

There are multiple constituencies involved in the production and consumption of the Liu Fang Yuan, and they are exchanging status, money, and power. With the Suzhou-style garden, the Huntington can better resemble a place that represents multiculturalism, the diversity of Los Angeles and the San Gabriel Valley, and more particularly the global connection to premodern Chinese aesthetic traditions and contemporary superpower finance. Observers and critics might point to the limitations of this expression, but it strikes me as a significant addition of multicultural legitimacy for the Huntington.[53] That is part of the work the Suzhou garden accomplishes for the Huntington.

What do the diverse Chinese communities gain? They gain legitimacy and the benediction of having Chinese culture represented and included in one of the most famous cultural spaces in the western United States. At all parts of the class spectrum, they gain status and distinction, and a venue for the exhibition of Chinese aristocratic, premodern cultural forms and artistic traditions.

Chinese donors and participants in the Chinese garden project are not trying to reconstruct or remake a "homeland" garden for themselves. They are adamant that they are simply trying to teach others about Chinese culture and to gain respect for these traditions. Here it is important to place this is in the context of the contemporary "Yellow Peril," in which Chinese science professionals and engineers are seen as devoid of cultural and humanistic traditions and values. As Betty Wang, one of the fundraising volunteers on the Friendship Committee, put it: "I thought it was a very meaningful project because it can be used as a bridge between East and West. That is how I feel. . . . It can be used as an educational tool, and I thought, you know, kids go to the Huntington library in the morning as a field trip and the docents there tell them about Chinese history." Similarly, one of the staff related that this too was how one of the major donors felt: "Dominic Ng said, 'I'm giving this not so much so my mom and dad can come here and feel like they're in China, but I'm giving so that the kids from East LA, from the LA Unified School District, can come here and learn about Chinese culture." Displaying a premodern cultural heritage and donating money for the construction of an elite Chinese garden are ways to obtain symbolic capital and recognition. A representation of Chinese garden culture is now showcased in the most elite botanical garden in the West, and this has been accomplished with the input and resources of Chinese Americans and transnational Chinese and Taiwanese immigrants.

Are the Doors Open?

What does the garden say about the social position of the Chinese in Pacific Rim cities? The social position of transnational Chinese and Chinese Americans is usually described in one of two ways: they are assimilated, financially successful entrepreneurs, or they are professionals who remain conditionally accepted as transnational "flexible citizens." Looking at the social processes surrounding the introduction of the Chinese garden at the Huntington suggests immigrant integration without assimilation. Chinese donors, docents, and designers are reshaping the landscape. At the Huntington, their valued expertise was solicited and accepted so long as the conditions of the built environment remained in line with the Huntington vernacular, reflecting refined, "tasteful" grand representations. The Suzhou garden style chosen for representation is a premodern aesthetic form associated with the private retreats of an elitist society. The new garden is technically open to the paying public, but as we have seen, it is not easily accessible for everyone, even those who can pay the entrance fee. Through the Chinese garden, there is an exchange of status and distinction between the Huntington (which, for California, is an old-line Eurocentric institution) and a diverse array of affluent Chinese groups. The Huntington's Chinese garden is the material manifestation of the interracial and intraethnic consolidation of distinctive elite sectors that would not normally interact and collaborate. The Huntington doors have opened, but not wide enough to allow much of a Chinese presence on the ruling boards. There is scarcely any diversity of leadership.[54]

The development and promotion of the Garden of Flowing Fragrance at the Huntington have provided Chinese elites a venue in which to capture a form of legitimizing high culture, status, and distinction that is in distinct contrast to the Yellow Peril scenarios embodied by the monster houses, the noisy signage of Monterey Park, and the foreign temple. In contrast to the pervasive ruling images of the highly competitive Asian American engineering student or the global superpower competition of China, the Chinese garden offers a new embraceable form of Chinese-ness for white Americans and other visitors to the Huntington. Museums are always trying to court new elites as potential donors, and here the process resulted in the cultural representation and "tasteful" humanistic contribution of premodern, elite Chinese culture. The Chinese garden simultaneously allows contemporary elites and less elite Chinese the possibility of expressing cultural pride and cultural symbolic capital in the dominant society, and it allows the Huntington to capture a new source of social relevance, revenue, and the appeal of multicultural legitimacy.

6 Paradise, Future

After the Franklin Community Garden closed for infrastructural improve-ments, Monica Sanchez, who had served as the paid gatekeeper and hub of community life there, lost her job and was banished from her inner-city Eden. Without an income and access to the garden, she fell into a depres-sion. She thought she might move to Texas, where a relative owned a plant nursery, but instead she and her children first moved in with a niece in Chinatown, and then went to East LA. On Mondays through Fridays, she now worked as a live-in nanny for a Nicaraguan woman, and like many live-in domestics Monica was unhappy with her job. When I spoke with her on the phone, she seemed like a wilting flower.

I had invited her and Jose Miguel Ruiz to the Huntington, and we finally went on a Saturday when they would open "the ranch" to visitors. This is a new garden project that aims to connect sustainable agricul-ture with the Huntington's historic roots as a producer of commercial fruits and agriculture. On this much-anticipated outing, I had expected Monica not necessarily to swoon but at least to say something about the spectacular sweeping panoramas, stunning foliage, and giant cacti at the Huntington. But all day her focus and commentary lingered on the smallest, microsensory features of the gardens. As we strolled through a camellia forest, with twenty-foot-tall camellias in bloom, Monica zeroed in on one scraggy shrub with tiny, delicate blossoms. At the ranch, I showed her the fruit trees that had been rescued from the South Central Farm, but she was more interested in noting how the Greek oregano growing there smelled different from Mexican oregano and in observing the deep furrows where peas and asparagus grew. When no one seemed to be looking, she snatched a pomelo that had fallen on the ground and surreptitiously peeled it, and the three of us savored an extraordinary bright, tart citrus with honeyed sweetness. We wandered into other gardens, with me rattling on with what I now know about the Suzhou-style garden, but she remained unimpressed and far more absorbed by a monarch butterfly that we saw laying eggs in the herb garden. We stood and watched it a long time, and she picked a tiny blossom and tasted the nectar. At the cactus garden, where I am always in awe of the psychedelic display of golden barrel cactus, she stared at the tiniest odd succulent from Namibia, a plant that looked like small brown stones. At every spot, small won over big.

For Monica Sanchez, these botanical gardens were a place to appreciate nature over culture. In a gesture of defiance, she spurned the visual aesthetic of privilege and conspicuous leisure in favor of minuscule insects, fragrances, and small, fragile buds. This was a tough time in her life. She had lost her own zone of garden autonomy at the inner-city community garden, so she took this visit to the botanical garden as an opportunity to reenact micromoments of restorative connection with nature. She no longer had a plot of land to tend, but even her way of being in this garden was an act of agency, self-care, and communion with the earth.

.   .   .   .   .

Monica Sanchez's trajectory sums up the larger story that I have told about migration and the making of Southern California gardens, illustrating how successive migration cultures and migrants occupy and cultivate plots of land, and how the tensions between power and the quest for transcendence shape our engagements with gardens. In this concluding chapter I revisit themes developed in this book and discuss possibilities for rethinking and reinventing new models of garden making in Southern California, and metropolitan regions more generally. This requires reconciling practices of environmental sustainability with cultural sustainability.

Can small-scale solutions solve challenges posed by global migration, seemingly intransigent immigration policies, high-consumption lifestyles, and industries that rely on exploitation, polluting machinery, massive water waste, and the commercialization of chemical fertilizers and herbicides? These challenges are as big as the world. My stance is that we need to implement change at multiple scales, from one seed to the whole earth. We need individual action and structural policy changes, rearranging how we do things upstream and downstream, globally and locally. The more radically attuned reader may dismiss some of the models I propose as liberal boutique Band-Aid solutions, but I would wager that even a Band-Aid can stop bleeding. Small reforms can empower communities and rebuild soil. I feel it would be irresponsible to end this book without discussing alternative visions of the future, and I offer these suggestions humbly, as I know that environmentalists, activists, urban planners, and policy makers have already offered creative solutions and will provide still more.

The region as we know it begins with migration, conquest, and more migration. Southern California gardens have been made by people, plants, seeds, and water that have come from elsewhere, and in turn the gardens have drawn newcomers and shaped the society that formed here. Social inequality and power exemplified by successive waves of conquests, colonization, property disputes, land development, and labor exploitation, together with the newcomers' desire for fantasy, beauty, and enchantment, have etched the garden landscape. A recurrent feature of garden life everywhere, and keenly evident here, is dominant groups' imposing their own ideas about garden beauty and productivity and forcing subordinate groups to work the soil, with everyone searching for his or her own transcendence and sustenance in the gardens. Spanish, Mexican, and Anglo elites imported seedlings and seeds from around the globe and dictated sequential paradigms of garden design, while first Indians, then Mexican, Chinese, and Japanese immigrant men dug irrigation trenches and tended plants, channeling water from distant places.

The biblical Eden was a paradise because lush fruiting gardens required no labor. But that too is a fantasy, as gardens on earth require work and effort of "the constant gardener." Even then, the best gardening labor is no guarantee against blight, drought, insects, and garden pests. The immigrant gardener labor system, innovated in Southern California by Japanese men in the early to mid-twentieth century, allowed affluent home owners to surround their dwellings with swaths of lawn and ornamental plants, protecting home value and projecting conspicuous leisure. Ethnic succession passed to Mexican immigrant gardeners, and today some of them, the route owners who have combined manual work and entrepreneurship, have achieved the immigrant dream of financial mobility, solvency, and better life opportunities for their children. Their wage-earning employees, often kin, or those gardeners who came later to the game and encountered saturated labor markets, have not fared so well. They are living the immigrant nightmare of depressed wages and long days of intensive bodily exertion and injury, labor exploitation, and health hazards. In this two-tier system of labor, there are winners and losers.

The immigrant gardener labor system has taken root elsewhere too. Today Latino immigrant gardeners are tending residential gardens in suburbs and metropolitan regions of North Carolina, Georgia, Florida, Illinois, New York, New Jersey, and other states. The extent to which the occupation will produce living wages and mobility opportunities in some of these newer destinations remains an open question, but the possibilities for advancement in these jobs are likely to be better than those found in agricultural fields, meat-packing plants, and the remaining factories.

In the inner city some of the poorest, most disenfranchised immigrants find their way to urban community gardens, where they have reshaped plots in downtown Los Angeles into lush welcoming places that look, feel, and smell just like home. This too is not just an LA story. Community gardens have formed in immigrant neighborhoods from New York City to Seattle, drawing not only Mexican and Central Americans but also newcomers from Russia, Vietnam, Laos, Somalia, and elsewhere. As they gather to grow familiar foods, these gardeners reaffirm cultural identity and improvise solutions to their many problems by sharing information and resources and creating new sites of healing and belonging. They are actively reshaping the landscape, producing food and reinventing possibilities for themselves and their families and communities. While all the participants at the inner-city gardens that I studied in Los Angeles were

Mexican and Central American, other urban community gardens include people from diverse corners of the globe coming together to establish new roots, and in the process they share transcultural exchanges and new dialogue. Urban community gardens take different forms and draw different constituencies. Community gardens may serve as bridges connecting diverse newcomers with more-established residents, binding them together in a shared space of conviviality and civic engagement and organizing themselves around the basic, elemental activity of tending plants and soil and harvesting food. Others, such as the urban community gardens that I studied, eschew the mosaic model and take root in poor, segregated neighborhoods, where they provide a sense of community cohesion and belonging. As metropolitan areas and cities across the nation grapple with welcoming and integrating new immigrants, I believe both models are valuable.

Modern botanic gardens are products of migrations of conquest and colonization, first developed by Holland, Britain, and other European powers as mechanisms for expanding economic empires around the globe. Today, contemporary botanic gardens are still instruments of power, science, and status, organized around botanical knowledge and the prestige of plant collections. At the leading botanical garden on the West Coast, the Huntington Botanical Gardens, new Chinese and Taiwanese elites, many of them with strong immigrant and transnational ties, have come together in a common project and are widening the scope of gardens considered to be of museum quality. In the process, the resources of new elites and an upper-class premodern Chinese cultural tradition, the Suzhou scholar's garden, have been integrated into a previously Eurocentric cultural institution. The extent to which Chinese and Taiwanese elites are invited to serve in directive capacities at the Huntington, however, is still limited, suggesting that alterations in the physical landscape come about quicker than those in the power structure.

The introduction of the Suzhou-style garden at the Huntington reflects the rise of power of Asian Pacific Rim nations and transnational immigrant elites. Other immigrant groups also have rich cultural traditions that might enhance gardens in our metropolitan regions, but groups such as Cambodians or Mexicans do not bring the kind of socioeconomic resources that allows for their cultural veneration in aesthetic garden displays. This is a missed opportunity in promoting cultural and environmental sustainability.

· · · · ·

What is the future of gardens and gardening in Southern California? Southern California has always been a place of reinvention, and I believe it remains a place of promise and potential. Rather than trying to create a paradise, we can strive for diverse gardens that promote environmental sustainability and a kind of cultural sustainability that promotes social equality, upholds fair labor standards, and recognizes the need for green spaces of beauty in all neighborhoods and communities.

Here is our starting point: the Southern California metropolis is today home to twenty-two million people who live spread out in a horizontal, low-to-the-ground built environment. In this population, roughly the size of Australia, nearly everyone is an immigrant or a descendant of one, but the immigration of Latinos and Asians over the last forty years means these are particularly critical populations. The Latino and Mexican influence is particularly important, and as we saw in chapter 2, this entire region *was* Mexico until 1848.

Southern California, like other Sunbelt areas, is routinely denounced for its sprawl, smog, and freeway congestion—all very real problems—but unlike the vertical cities of skyscrapers, it still has many remaining pervious surfaces. That is largely because of the single-family home model. Beginning in the early twentieth century and accelerating in the postwar years with the GI Bill and the Federal Housing Administration, single-family detached homes with private yards developed all over Los Angeles, San Diego, Orange County, the San Bernardino-Riverside "Inland Empire," and Santa Barbara, and in the valleys and coastal areas that connect these cities. Hundreds of thousands of private backyards and front yards dot the landscape, holding countless patches of lawn and soil that could be replanted in more imaginative, beautiful, productive, and sustainable ways. Potential garden spaces also lie in wait in parkways (the area between the street and the curb), vacant lots, alleyways, boulevard meridians now often landscaped with lawn and palm trees, and plots of soil around schools, office parks, apartment buildings, minimalls, and even gas stations.

To outsiders, Los Angeles and Southern California may look like one giant serpentine freeway system, but small strips and plots of earth abound in this region drenched in sun and with a climate mild enough for year-round growing possibilities. In the city of Los Angeles alone there are more than nine hundred miles of alleyways that might be revitalized as parks and garden spaces.[1] The sprawling Southern California suburban metropolis, rather than the antithesis of nature, is the ideal terrain for garden renewal.

We may have a second chance to reorganize Southern California gardens in ways that promote social justice and paradises of the future. This requires heightened environmental awareness and the social will to move toward immigrant inclusion and integration. The headlines reporting on climate change and ecological devastation, including catastrophic droughts, hurricanes, and rising sea levels, have raised public recognition of these problems. Meanwhile, there is a growing consensus that we need immigrant integration policies and practices and that we must use less fossil fuels and produce less carbon. We need to keep patches of earth that can feed people and absorb carbon, and that is part of the work that plants and trees do.

Meanwhile, food has emerged as a critical vector in this conversation, with critiques of the industrial food system popularized by authors such as Michael Pollan, Marion Nestle, Eric Schlosser, and others. A food justice movement is connecting the dots between the industrial food system, hunger, childhood diabetes, and obesity among the poor. Food policy councils have sprouted in cities around the nation, with the goal of providing healthy, affordable, fair, and sustainably produced food for all, and as part of this movement urban farms, school food-producing gardens, and community gardens have multiplied.[2] When Michelle Obama opened the White House organic vegetable garden in 2009, the cause gained a new platform. The Great Recession did much to stimulate this among individuals and families too. The number of American households growing their own vegetables jumped 40 percent from 2007 to 2009, and Burpee seeds, the world's largest seed company, reported their sales increased nearly 30 percent in 2009.

The regional resources and the initiative to rethink and reorganize Southern California gardens are rich, and these efforts echo what is occurring elsewhere too. Throughout the United States, and in nations as different as Jamaica and Spain, urban and suburban agriculture and community gardens are gaining ground.[3] In the United States people are embracing shared backyard gardening and challenging restrictive municipal codes and policies that mandate lawn. There is a new enthusiasm for organic vegetable gardening without pesticides and herbicides, for wall gardens in cities where space is tight, and even for removal of lawns. Below I review some of these projects, looking at new efforts in private residential gardens, urban community gardens, and public spaces, all with an eye to keeping immigration and the Southern California region in focus. Far from the scary scenarios of an apocalyptic, evil paradise, I believe that the Southern California built environment, the immigrant and ethnic diversity here, and the new urgency to change status quo practices provide a new window on the paradise of the future.

REFORMING THE PRIVATE RESIDENTIAL GARDEN

> Spread thick like margarine over the landscape from sea to
> shining sea, the lawn—more than cows, corn, or blue
> hydrangea—is the key ingredient in the Stepford-like
> biological monotony that defines suburban America.
> Wade Graham, "The Grassman," *New Yorker*, August 19, 1996

Some people are ready to replace the monotony and the ecological costs of lawns. As we have seen, the cultural mandate for meticulously manicured lawns surrounding private homes has created a vast labor market niche for first Japanese and now Latino immigrant men. Hard work, entrepreneurial savvy, much sacrifice, self-exploitation, and exploitation of coethnics have afforded some of these men and their families opportunities for social mobility and better lives, but this sector has also created stagnant labor markets with dead-end servitude, especially for the men who lack legal authorization and driver's licenses.

The immigrant gardener labor system enables home owners all over Southern California to continue with the American addiction to residential gardens dominated by swaths of lawn, an ill-suited, nonecological gardenscape for this semiarid region. Lawns are thirsty, and in Southern

California they are quenched by imported water, chemicals, and immigrant labor. Over half—some say as much as 70 percent—of the domestically consumed water in Los Angeles goes to residential landscaping. The immigrant gardener labor system has allowed home owners to expect nothing less than verdant air-brushed lawn and garden tidiness and to equate garden beauty with this aesthetic.

For several decades now, suburban home owners, pundits, and local politicians have decried the noisy gas-powered blowers and mowers, enacting leaf blower bans in municipalities all over California, as we saw in chapter 3. But the noise is just one minor surface problem. The more serious problems are labor exploitation and the environmental consequences—including the particulate pollution of dust and dirt debris that kicks up in the faces of the gardeners, and gas emissions from the two-stroke and four-stroke gas engines that float in our shared air—and at the root of all of this is the love affair with the idealized perfect green lawn, which can thrive here only with poisonous chemicals, vast amounts of imported water, and regular mowing. None of this is sustainable.

Some home owners and landscape designers are swapping out the lawn for California native plants, succulents, and cactus, or new "meadow" types of lawn that do not require as much water or mowing, and they are planting more organic vegetables, herbs, and fruit trees. In front yards and backyards, a new morality is taking hold. But who will do the work to keep up these gardenscapes? Labor is still required in the garden. Some landscape designers who install lawn-free, less thirsty gardens do garden maintenance on a fee basis, retaining their own gardening maintenance crews, who are trained to care for these more environmentally appropriate landscapes. This is an expensive alternative for home owners, and it typically follows an already pricey garden installation that may have cost $20,000 to $30,000, even in a small yard. One popular "eco" landscape design/installation firm in the Los Angeles area will not consider taking customers for any job paying less than $150,000. When these firms follow up with maintenance crews, the arrangement erodes the autonomy and earning power of route-owner immigrant gardeners, as the landscape designers retain the contracts for service with the home owners. It removes one of the few routes to upward mobility and socioeconomic integration that is available to immigrant men from rural backgrounds.

Many home owners in Southern California do not want to do the regular garden upkeep in their yards. People are time-strapped and are now accustomed to having immigrant workers do everything from wash the car to mow the lawn. Increasingly, as baby boomers age, more home owners will be too old to stoop over and shovel, rake, prune, or mow in the garden. In the section below, I profile three new business models of residential gardening that have responded to environmental concerns in Southern California. I discuss how immigrant labor fits into these alternatives, and I suggest how these ideas and practices might be implemented differently, to allow for environmentally sound gardening practices *and* fair standards and living wages for gardening labor, ones that recognize and maximize immigrant gardening knowledge and autonomy. A discussion of public gardens follows.

When a lawn maintenance company, Whisper Landscape, made its debut in the *Los Angeles Times* with a prominent feature article on Earth Day in April 2008, the lawn stayed and Latino gardeners were demoted from being entrepreneurial workers to being wage employees. The main innovation here was getting rid of the gas-powered machinery. At this business, started by Michael Gould, a young psychologist, the maintenance crews arrived in Priuses, armed with soothingly quiet solar-powered blowers and mowers. They serviced the posh residential neighborhoods of LA's Westside, the San Fernando Valley, and the Pasadena area until the route was acquired by a larger company, Seabreeze Landscape. When I interviewed the founder of Whisper, he told me that he had started the business to help develop new, clean, zero-emission landscaping technology. While high-decibel noise provoked the various municipal leaf blower bans, Michael Gould realized that the gas emissions posed a far more significant environmental danger. Together with several partners, Gould put together a small landscape maintenance business that promised environmentally friendly fertilizers, techniques, and technology. Whisper Landscape hired primarily young Latino men, many of them sons of Latino gardeners, at the rate of $9 to $12 an hour, and at the height of business they had five employees driving two Priuses to service approximately fifty properties, both residential and commercial. Gould had planned to franchise the business, but with workers' compensation, taxes, and municipal business licenses the business did not prove to be as profitable as he had hoped—

even though it charged clients more than the average maintenance fee. "We did everything [taxes] exactly right," he said, "and it cost almost double for consumers to pay for the services." He sold the business but continues to develop new landscaping technology, a topic we will examine at this end of this section. The Whisper and Seabreeze model enhances air quality but disempowers Latino immigrant gardeners. These businesses do not disrupt the lawn as a central feature of residential gardens. In fact, the business model is premised on retaining the need for lawns and tidy, leaf-blown landscapes.

Another model of sustainable gardening labor, a workers' cooperative called Native Green, emerged in Los Angeles in 2010 after thirty-one Latino immigrant men graduated from a "green gardeners" training program focused on the care and maintenance of drought-tolerant native plants, drip irrigation, and the reuse of rainwater. This innovative program began with the Low Impact Development Ordinance, which the City of Los Angeles passed to promote landscapes that conserve water resources and mitigate water runoff.

Advocates in several public and nonpublic organizations partnered to provide training, certification, and support for this worker-owned and -operated cooperative.[4] The idea was to promote sustainable residential gardening labor services and to acknowledge and value the skills that many Latino immigrant men bring from their rural backgrounds to Southern California gardening. An early business plan stated, "The genesis of this experience comes from the places many of us were born where we needed to harvest rainwater with buckets, cisterns, aluminum tanks."[5] With the technical assistance of the Instituto de Educación Popular del Sur de California (IDEPSCA), a community organization with a long-standing commitment to organizing immigrant workers, but without any public or municipal subsidy, Native Green functions as an outlet to empower Latino immigrant men to upgrade their skill level and to earn living wages while doing ecological gardening labor. These practices go beyond simply maintaining lawn with zero-emission lawn mowers and blowers. While Native Green services residential gardens around Los Angeles, it has not generated as much business as anticipated, in part because it lacks professional business management. According to Victor Narro, a Los Angles lawyer and public advocate specializing in immigrant

labor issues, this is a familiar problem with immigrant worker cooperatives operating in a competitive capitalist market.[6]

Organic vegetable gardens are now all the rage, prompting one popular
writer to quip, "You're either growing vegetables, or you are a vegetable."
But growing vegetables is not always easy for the novice or the time-
strapped. Tapping into the current enthusiasm for fresh, organic local
grown produce, small firms have emerged around the nation, ready to
grow organic vegetables for customers in their own backyards. One of the
businesses in Portland, Oregon, advertised this: "You don't even need to
do any gardening at all. But if you want to we can assist you and your family in learning to grow your own food." Another business in North Carolina
promised nothing short of a return to Eden: "Yes! Zero work, worries, or
weeding."[7] Some of these gardening services offer to coach home owners
on how to raise vegetable plots, while others do all the gardening maintenance work. When my close friends in South Pasadena contacted
Farmscape, they booked an introductory evaluation with the resident
landscape architect. My friends are a middle-aged, affluent Mexican
American couple, busy professionals who love gourmet restaurants and
who are splendid cooks, always inviting us over for three-generation
Sunday suppers. They called Farmscape because they were interested in
both a landscape design for their sizable flat suburban lot (approximately
seventeen thousand square feet) and an organic herb and vegetable garden. Since they knew I was researching this book, they invited me too.
Before the meeting, I checked the on-site advertising, which promised a
"kind of a push-button subscription service for gardening" and showcased
the "farmers," who were mostly white, college-educated women and men
in their twenties and thirties, introduced as having interests in yoga, hiking, and playing in bands. The site advertised providing a personal connection with your personal farmer.

A representative of the firm came to my friends' home, and we walked
through the yard together, discussing the relative sun and shade in different areas of the yard and suitable plant combinations. Theirs was a big
yard, with many mature trees, hedges, nearly forty camellia bushes, and a
back lawn that they had long ago stopped watering. Mexican gardeners
arrived weekly to mow the remaining strip of front lawn, trim hedges and
bushes, and blow out fallen leaves. The Farmscape representative said

that three 4′ × 12′ redwood beds would run $3,000 for installation and that a weekly maintenance visit from one of the "farmers" would cost $60 a week. As we strolled in their backyard, no one raised an eyebrow or tallied this up aloud, but I think we were all silently doing the math: this would be a lot of money for homegrown veggies, over $6,000 the first year. Several years ago, someone wrote a book called *The $64 Tomato: How One Man Nearly Lost His Sanity, Spent a Fortune, and Endured an Existential Crisis in the Quest for the Perfect Garden*, a humorous horticultural memoir of challenges in the garden.[8] Now, with the commodified backyard vegetable gardening service, some of the gentry are paying one hundred times more to have someone else grow their "personal" homegrown tomatoes (my friends decided not to make that purchase).

A new crop of landscape architects and designers now specialize in designing and installing low-water, more sustainable gardens, but contracting for these services is expensive. For about 95 percent of the population, it is simply not an option, and this became even more pronounced after the implosion of the housing bubble. As real estate value went down, home owners spent less freely on home and garden improvements.

Some idealists may question the ethics of paid garden labor altogether. In one version of utopia, to paraphrase Marx, we might all hunt in the morning and fish and farm in the afternoon. In reality, however, not everyone with a plot of property wants to do garden work. Even those who say they would *like* to stop, smell, and maybe prune the roses are overwhelmed with other matters. Many people, especially working families, are time starved. Some scarcely spend any time outdoors. The famed post–World War Southern California leisure time in the garden may now be an unattainable dream for many, as a recent UCLA study found that some families in Los Angeles with two working parents and living in single-detached homes spent less than fifteen minutes a week in their yard, and the children just forty minutes.[9] Other people are too elderly to do garden work. Many others are just not interested or are simply stumped and inexperienced. Yet many people are rethinking their home garden. They want to get rid of the lawn and dispense with the noise and pollution of the blowers, and more people now crave homegrown vegetables and recognize they should have more drought-tolerant plants. What are some ways of reorganizing residential garden labor in this context?

For home owners who must retain the lawn, whether for children's play spaces, for aesthetic reasons, or for fear of declining property resale values, the promotion of a regional transition to solar-powered blowers and mowers is now emerging as part of environmental reform. Public and private corporate partnerships or a small tax on new real estate development could hasten the transition from gas-powered to solar-powered mowers and blowers. More home owners in sunny Southern California are having solar panels installed on their rooftops—with existing tax incentive programs it is already possible to lease and install solar panels with no upfront costs—and the gardeners could then fuel up, as quietly as the home owners wish, before they proceed to do their quiet zero-gas emission work. City governments could also do this on a larger scale, and more proactively, placing solar panels on city-owned buildings to serve as solar fuel-up stations for the gardeners. Some cities are exploring the creation of "green zones" where municipal employees would use only electric-powered equipment.

Solar-powered mowers and blowers do not eradicate the problems of particulate pollution and the vast chemical- and water-absorbing lawn. Still, these would produce a smaller carbon footprint, provide the peace and quiet that home owners desire, and, importantly, remove toxic gas fumes from the faces and lungs of the Latino immigrant gardeners and perhaps offer the gardeners new environmental cachet that could translate into better pay and social recognition. A public-private promotion of this type of reform would allow Latino immigrant gardeners to maintain their independently owned businesses, which, as we have seen, serve as an important ladder to social mobility for the route owners and promote educational and occupational mobility for their children.

The financial success of self-employed immigrant gardeners has many positive social and economic repercussions. As we have seen, many of them have become tax-paying home owners, and their children have attained college degrees and jobs in business and the professions. In Northern California, one Mexican immigrant gardener, Catalino Tapia, not only saw his son graduate from University of California–Berkeley's Boalt Law School but went on to found an educational fund, the Bay Area Gardeners' Foundation, which now provides college scholarships to low-income youth of diverse ethnic backgrounds. Catalino Tapia has received some positive press, but the more typical media story casts Mexican immigrant gardeners as social problems, blaming them for the nuisance of noise produced by the blowers.

When immigrant gardeners have been attacked for using the tools of their trade, they have collectively mobilized to defend their interests. In 1955, Japanese gardeners organized the Southern California Gardeners Federation (SCGF), and in the late 1990s Latino immigrant gardeners, supported by a handful of UCLA Chicano student activists, formed the Association of Latin American Gardeners of Los Angeles (ALAGLA) to defend themselves against LA's leaf blower ban; some of them experimented with methanol-based blowers and machinery.[10] ALAGLA became a critical political organization in the 1990s, but it withered away as the leaf blower bans were not enforced throughout the region.[11]

Currently, gas-powered lawn mowers and blowers are not covered by the stringent California emissions standards that apply to automobiles. Environmental gardening practices will require low gas emissions, and the South Coast Air Quality Management District (AQMD), the air pollution control agency for Orange County and major parts of Los Angeles, San Bernardino and Riverside counties, now sponsors a lawn mower and leaf blower change program, allowing home owners and professional landscapers and gardeners to exchange old, gas-powered equipment for new, lower-emission machines at a lower price. The program began with a lawn mower exchange program for home owners, and now four thousand cordless electric lawn mowers are available at discounted prices each year. The AQMD sponsors several exchange events throughout Southern California annually, and for several years now they have also offered four thousand lower-emission, quieter gas-powered leaf blowers to professional gardeners and landscapers.

Contrary to the idea that Latino gardeners are reluctant to adopt newer, cleaner technology, the AQMD representative that I spoke with told me that there has been a positive reception throughout the region, with Latino gardeners eagerly embracing these opportunities for leaf blowers that are efficient but quieter and less polluting than the older gas models.[12] At this point, the AQMD does not find the electric lawn mower strong enough for sustained commercial use. New technology-sharing models are still in development (e.g., a battery pack that could be recharged at different sites).

Several groups of technological innovators are bringing entrepreneurial fervor to develop new clean landscaping machinery. These include small outfits, like Michael Gould and his engineering partner, who are working on adapting Stihl electric landscape equipment to run on solar-powered lithium ion batteries, or the Santa Monica firm the Greenstation, which has also developed solar-powered batteries for cordless electric lawn mowers. One of the big weapons manufacturers, AeroVironment Inc., the firm that developed unmanned military drones, is also a major player in this emergent field. Substantial profits await the firm that develops the commercial-grade equipment on a mass scale, and there are already many compelling claims about the environmental benefits of solar-powered electric equipment.

Some environmentalists claim that we have a consumption crisis, not an energy crisis, and that these sorts of "productivist energy solutions" are simply greenwashing and perpetuating our problems.[13] That may be true, but I think we have to be realists too. The California Air Resources Board 2009 Almanac offers evidence that switching from gas-powered lawn and gardening equipment to zero-emission electric machines would have the same impact as converting 39 percent of all passenger cars in California.[14] The promise of energy savings and diminishing pollution is significant, but powerful obstacles remain. The research, development, and manufacturing of zero-emission solar and electric-powered gardening equipment require substantial investment and must overcome obstacles from the gas engine lobby to get new technology into production and dissemination at reasonable costs. Meanwhile, the public tends to blame those at the bottom: the Latino gardeners. This is an old worn pattern, in which relatively privileged people who are living high-consumption lifestyles blame new immigrants for creating pollution and overpopulation.

Lessening consumption is part of the solution, and a more far-reaching reform is to rip out the lawn and replace it with ecological alternatives. In *Redesigning the American Lawn*, environmentalists and landscape designers discuss substitutions for what they call the "industrial lawn" promoted by the lawn care industry and offer suggestions for replacing it with a low-mow lawn free of chemical fertilizers.[15] Lawns started in moist England and migrated to the United States, eventually settling even in arid areas of the West. Today, the lawn care industry takes in more than

$40 billion annually and relies on poisons and petrochemicals. While antilawnism prevails in the yards of Berkeley, it has not caught on in Southern California, even when cash has been offered as an incentive.[16] The LA Department of Water and Power "cash for grass" program met with some modest success, but a glance at residential gardens from Beverly Hills to the San Fernando Valley shows that conventional front-yard lawns still reign.

People cling to their lawns out of inertia. Many home owners lack the knowledge and time to redo their gardens. It also takes money to replace lawn with beautiful native and drought-tolerant plants. There are websites and books that help guide people with this process, but this requires time, initiative, and financial resources. Landscape designers told me their clients recognize the need to eradicate lawn but fear the disapproval of their neighbors. Some people are emotionally attached to their lawns.[17] A very smart, environmentally conscious home owner whom I interviewed told me that she wanted to switch out parts of her expansive lawn, but she assumed that the Latino gardeners would then require more supervision and directives, that they would not know what to do. I think we need to question that assumption: if we do, new opportunities arise.

One significant reform that might enhance garden ecology in Southern California is a reorganization of residential gardens and recognition of the human capital that many Latino immigrants bring with them from rural backgrounds. As we have seen, Latino immigrant gardeners are currently deskilled and dismissed as "mow and blow" labor, but in fact, many of them have extensive horticultural knowledge and experience from Mexico, Honduras, and Guatemala. Some of them began working the soil and tending plants when they were six or seven. This is not a heterogeneous group. Mexicans are by far the largest immigrant group in the nation and the Southern California region. Many of them have deep, untapped resources of horticultural knowledge, although this is less true of more recent cohorts of Mexican migrants who hail from urban and industrial backgrounds.

Gendered garden labor is also ripe for rethinking. Residential gardening does not have to remain a man's job. If residential gardening in Southern California became less focused on lawn care and hedge trimming, which now relies on the heavy, gas-powered machines, and instead centered more on growing organic vegetables and drought-tolerant shrubs and flowers, Latina immigrant women could be working in this sector. In fact, as I discovered while interviewing the women at the urban community gardens who worked as paid domestic workers, some of them are already doing this work free of charge. Here's how it currently occurs: these women take the buses to suburban neighborhoods to clean homes and care for young children, and while they are there on the job they do some informal gardening in the backyard, say, planting and tending a few tomato or cucumber plants. I say "informal" because they are not compensated or recognized for this labor. They do it freely at only a few of the houses where they work, places where they have established enough trust and familiarity to do this.

Many Latina immigrant women and men in Southern California have extensive horticultural knowledge and experience from their rural, agricultural backgrounds. A job development program might be organized as worker cooperatives, like Native Green, so that private residential maintenance gardening would include the tending of organically grown and pesticide-free herbs, vegetables, and fruits. Programs that offer classes and certification in organic gardening and in the building of bio-swales or other water catchment systems could be part of this. Certification would officially recognize training and lend legitimacy. At the inner-city community gardens, many of the gardeners are underemployed and need living wages, so this type of job development project could address both environmental and economic problems. In addition, this type of employment could be developed in public, commercial, and municipal gardens.

Time may be of the essence here, as all demographic predictions point in the direction of the end of the long era of US-bound Mexican migration. A middle-aged and older generation of Latino immigrants who hail from rural areas are already living here in Southern California, and this knowledge and leadership should be tapped now.[18] Many immigrants and refugees from Cambodia, Laos, Vietnam, and parts of China have rural origins and also possess valuable horticultural knowledge. Smaller numbers of African refugees from Somalia and the Congo are practicing urban farming in several US cities. They could serve as knowledgeable teachers and practitioners of sustainable gardening practices. I am not suggesting that only immigrants should be doing this work. In fact, we can imagine a national mandatory volunteer service for high school and college graduates, with "Garden for America" joining current options such as "Teach for America" or military service.

Immigrants do not form a singular, monolithic group, but many recent immigrants are a vital untapped resource of horticultural expertise for expanding sustainable gardens in the United States. In venues such as school gardens and universities, or if we ever institute a "Garden for America" program, immigrants from varied backgrounds could be compensated not only as gardening laborers but also as garden educators. Currently, this expertise remains untapped and simply not recognized. Economists and sociologists refer to immigrants with college credentials and technological skills as having "high human capital," but there are forms of valuable skills, knowledge, and experience that other immigrants bring that could readily enhance the garden ecology of the metropolitan region, as well as the self-reliance and socioeconomic integration of diverse immigrant communities.

GROWING PUBLIC GARDENS

We might also reorganize residential gardens in ways that make the private garden public. This is not for everyone, but it is already happening. In some cities, people are using the Internet to request or offer the borrowing of yard space for cultivation. Sometimes this is a matter of not having a plot of earth in the sun, and sometimes it is a matter of not having any land at all. In Southern California, we see a mismatch between densely populated neighborhoods such as Pico Union and MacArthur Park, where many people who wish to grow plants are crammed into apartments, and the sprawling suburbs, where many do not make use of their land. In San Diego, the International Rescue Committee, a refugee resettlement organization, offers yard share and land bank programs to make unused land available to refugees who need garden space for growing food.[19]

Some people in suburban neighborhoods are also experimenting with smaller-scale garden workshops, yard sharing, and public community gatherings in private gardens. In Diamond Bar, Rishi Kumar has transformed his parents' suburban home and yard into "The Growing Home," a new model of productive suburban agriculture based on the principles of permaculture, inspired by what he learned on Vandana Shiva's farm in India.[20] He grows enough food to feed family and friends and to sell at a local farmers' market. In perhaps the most radical move, he has opened the residential garden to tours, workshops, evening potlucks, poetry readings, and drum circles. "You know," he said, as we chatted in his farmlike backyard, "I've interacted with more people in the last year at this house than I have in the eighteen years that I grew up here. There are so many people here all the time. . . . We're making our own little village out here." In Diamond Bar, this private suburban home garden has become a place not only for plants but for people, who create music, congregate, and converse with others. Communal life in a private suburban space is another vision of shared paradise in the garden.

People in poor neighborhoods are also in search of better gardens. A grassroots community organization, Los Angeles Green Grounds, organizes daylong volunteer "dig ins" on private yards in South LA, a poor area of the city where many single-detached homes are surrounded by lawn. The organization brings together a diverse group of volunteers, people of different ages and racial-ethnic backgrounds, who gather to transform someone's front yard from lawn to an organic edible garden. The program was started in 2010 by Master Gardeners Florence Nishida and Ron Finley, and volunteers report that they learn cultivation techniques and experience the satisfaction, sometimes even euphoria, of connecting with others as they dig soil, rip out lawns, and propagate new vegetable gardens. Compost and mulch are made available by the city, and the key organizers visit the properties ahead of time and ensure that the yards receive sufficient sun. "We try to locate people who want to grow vegetables but don't know how," explained Nishida. The residents invite friends and neighbors to pitch in, and after the volunteers leave, the residents are responsible for keeping up the garden. The idea is to build community *and* spread edible gardens.

South Central Los Angeles is now home to diverse Latino immigrant communities and to African Americans, many of them members of families who migrated from the South to work in wartime industry in World War II. Growing vegetables in the parkway between the sidewalk and the curb is now happening here too, and after Ron Finley got a citation from the City of Los Angeles and then a warrant for his arrest for planting vegetables in his 150′ × 10′ parkway—vegetables that he offers free on the vine to any passerby—he went public and rallied public support. Media attention led to his TED talk, where he urges "gangsta gardeners" to replace the drive-in fast-food joints of poor urban neighborhoods. He promotes growing food in unexpected places. "Gardening is the most therapeutic and deviant act you can do," he says, "especially in the inner city."[21]

Also working in South Central Los Angeles at the interstices of public and private gardens is Community Services Unlimited (CSU), a program founded by the Black Panther Party in 1977. Today under the leadership of Neelam Sharma, CSU addresses the failed promise of "forty acres and a mule," reparations, land theft, and inequality through gardening and food justice. With a small, youthful staff and energetic volunteers, CSU sponsors a myriad of programs for youth and urban farming, an inner-city produce market, an urban farm, composting, cooking, and tree-pruning workshops that draw Latino immigrant and African American families, youth and elderly, incorporating these communities' valuable knowledge and building it up so they produce food in plots of soil or apartment balconies where they live. They also blend private and public gardening. A "tree of life fruit pick" event partnered with Food Forward and home owner residents to identify, harvest from, and help care for fruit trees on private properties in South Central Los Angeles.[22] The focus is not on immigrant communities per se, but immigrant families and their kids are regular participants in this needy neighborhood. "Community self-reliance and autonomy is our goal," Neelam Sharma explains, and "food is the entry point."[23]

Therapeutic engagements with nature, homeland culture, and community are also occurring in urban community gardens. At the Dolores Huerta garden in Pico Union, Jose Miguel Ruiz now cultivates parcels of land with a group of indigenous *Guatemalteco* youth. These are young men, many of them still in their teens and early twenties, who migrated here on their own, on freight trains, mostly without legal papers. These *jovenes* (youth) are the descendants of the Mayan communities that suffered the military massacres in Guatemala in the 1980s, and here in the United States they lack family support and the resources that flow in established immigrant social networks. When their employers in the garment sweatshops or restaurants refuse to pay them, or when they are assaulted by local gang members, they cannot report the crimes to the police or the labor commissioner because of their immigration status. They don't have kin here that can refer them to better jobs. Other Latinos sometimes look down on them because they are small, dark, and indigenous.

Through an informal group, part mutual aid society and part self-help group, they are reorienting themselves and building new resources of support. Many of them began cultivating the earth in the Sierra Madre in Guatemala at the age of six or seven, and now in urban Los Angeles, just blocks away from the glitzy downtown LA entertainment zone, they are resuscitating ancestral traditions, planting according to the Mayan calendar. To combat their feelings of distress and despair, Jose Miguel asked them to write their fears on a small piece of paper that they shredded into compost, and as each one of them planted a mound of corn, beans, and squash seeds sent from Guatemala, they used their shredded fears as compost fertilizer, transforming fear and hopelessness into homeland plants and a new flourishing place. The corn grew high but failed to set ears of corn, yet the collective act of tending a plot connected them with each other and Mayan traditions and has nourished them and given them new resolve. One afternoon when I visited, we joined hands around the *milpa* (the corn patch) as they reflected aloud on their life challenges, dreams, and aspirations. We had been sitting at the picnic tables, casually chatting and eating tacos and drinking soda, but as we gathered around the *milpa* there was a kind of solemn, sacred tone to this moment. The *jovenes* meet on Friday afternoons and evenings after work, and when the days are long they sit and stroll in the garden, reading books (the Bible and self-help books are popular). These are informal, fluid gatherings, but they point to the potential for developing therapeutic connection in public gardens among the most marginalized newcomers. These gatherings and practices of self-help have also expanded to include the seeking of legal remedies, as several of the young men have stepped forward to pursue wage claims, and all of this starts in the garden.

More public gardens and gathering spaces are needed, especially in this park-poor region. Poor neighborhoods with concentrated Latino, African American, and Asian-Pacific Islander communities face a severe deficit of parks and green spaces in Los Angeles.[24] Throughout Los Angeles and Southern California, as in many other metropolitan areas around the nation, land remains distributed unequally, but there are now efforts under way to transform vacant, unused land into flourishing gardens that will produce food, serve as sites of civic engagement, and provide green places where people can gather, contemplate, and socialize. There is fierce market competition, however, for land in Los Angeles, with the forces of gentrification and development looming. Land is a place for growing gardens, but as Harvey Molotch reminds us it is also "a market commodity providing wealth and power."[25] We don't usually think of politics and gardens in the same narrative, but gaining ground for more public gardens will require political will. A progressive social movement that can guide government support for green spaces will be necessary to wrest land from developers and to promote gardens in all neighborhoods.

This is not a new idea. Urban agriculture has already gained momentum in the eighty-eight cities that make up Los Angeles County. By 2013 a UCLA report tallied over 1,200 urban agricultural sites, including 761 school gardens, 382 commercial agricultural nurseries or farms, and 118 community gardens. School gardens in particular have received new infusions of support. But as this report by UCLA graduate students in urban and regional planning makes clear, the municipal codes vary widely and lag behind practice, with many rules and regulations restricting the sale of locally produced fruits and vegetables.[26]

Some advocates are working to change the local and municipal regulations that govern gardening and agricultural practices in the city (e.g., growing vegetables in the front yard, beekeeping, raising urban chickens, and making and selling home-prepared foods).[27] These are now seen as desirable authentic artisanal activities, but many immigrant communities have been performing them on their own for decades in Southern California (e.g., growing corn in the front yard, keeping a chicken coop in the back), sometimes in violation of municipal ordinances. Now activists are trying to change those regulations. Several organizations are also conducting systematic inventories of vacant, unused land in Los Angeles with an aim to transition those patches and plots to gardens of food cultivation.[28]

The high cost of property in metropolitan Southern California remains a constraint and explains why there are currently only about one hundred

Figure 36. The idea of guerrilla gardening is now commodified,
as seen in this "Seed Bomb" gum machine. Photo by author.

urban community gardens here. In depopulated urban centers where land
is cheaper and more plentiful (e.g., Detroit, Newark, Philadelphia), more
land is devoted to urban agriculture and community gardens, even when
the gardeners and farmers there face a far more inhospitable climate and
shorter growing season. In all of our metropolitan regions, more land and
better systems of democratic governance are needed. To some extent, the
problems with community garden governance parallel conflicts that arise
with NGOs elsewhere. Some "guerrilla gardener" activists feel too encum-
bered by all the rules of granting institutions, and they prefer gardening

without permission, throwing "seed bombs" in vacant lots and illicitly cultivating public land.[29]

Around the country, advocates have begun to weigh the produce from urban farms and community gardens to prove that these sites can address hunger and food insecurity among the urban poor. At the Dolores Huerta and Franklin community gardens, delicious tomatoes and squash, homeland medicinal and culinary herbs, as well as radishes, lettuce, beans, verdolaga, strawberries, cabbage, corn, and a variety of *chiles* were produced, but the quantity of food production here was not the main miracle. The community gardens were producing social value that was less quantifiable but no less essential to life: self-care and community care. Women, men, and children who gathered at these small community gardens claimed a new place of belonging and found regeneration in an otherwise bleak landscape. Sharing stories about their daily triumphs and troubles and engaging with homeland plant nature sustained them, momentarily restoring them and providing ballast for the next set of challenges.

Although the South Central Farm was bulldozed in 2006, many of the region's urban community gardens are no longer as vulnerable as they once were, with many now receiving institutional support from the Los Angeles Neighborhood Land Trust or the Los Angeles Community Garden Council or through contractual agreements with the City of Los Angeles Department of Recreation and Parks. Those are some of the main organizations serving as fiscal agents and governing bodies for urban community gardens here. Over time, different community gardeners cycle through the garden spaces, and the gardeners encounter different regimes of governance. As I discussed this issue with Yvonne Savio, now the program manager for the University of California Cooperative Extension in Los Angeles County, who for many years had overseen community garden spaces in Los Angeles, she surmised that one group might remain in a community garden for a dozen years or slightly more before a new group cycled through. I think a new question that scholar activists need to ask is the extent to which urban community gardens can enjoy self-governance and autonomy and the extent to which a paternalistic top-down model prevails.

In elite botanical gardens and museums, the question of whose culture can be represented looks less promising. Can only the culture of very wealthy elites be included in the pantheon? Are there ways that ethnic immigrant groups can display cultural heritage in public gardens even if they are not able to donate vast sums of money? There are now many efforts to remedy the paucity of parks in Los Angeles and in the region, but thus far, efforts to commemorate diverse ethnic and immigrant cultures in public gardens does not appear to have momentum.

METROPOLITAN GLOBAL GARDENS

Paradise Transplanted is about migration and the making of gardens in a specific place, Southern California, but there are global implications as well. We live in the age of global migration, with 212 million people living in nations other than where they were born. This is an era when the majority of us now live in metropolitan regions, and still more rural-urban migration is forthcoming. China, the most populous nation on earth, has announced plans to move 250 million peasant farmers from the countryside to the city during the next decade. On every continent, metropolitan regions and societies are becoming more globalized, reconfigured by transnational and rural-urban migration.

The late twentieth century and the early twenty-first century are also a time of heightened social inequalities and environmental peril. In many places, both cosmopolitan urbanites and working people feel disenchanted with hectic work schedules and packaged consumerism, and they crave foods, experiences, and settings that feel more natural and authentic. Only the very privileged will be able to move "back to the land" as lifestyle migrants in search of nature and idealized life—for example, as locavore gentry farmers and ranchers in places like Napa Valley or Montana. Most of us will stay in metropolitan regions, and that is where we will make our gardens. As people of diverse cultural and social class backgrounds fill the metropolitan regions, gardens can serve as sites that promote transcultural understanding and dialogue and address a range of social and environmental concerns.

Migration and dreams of fantasy mixed with natural beauty still define Southern California and lend the region dynamism and ingenuity, a feeling that anything is possible here. Gardens are finite places of plants rooted on the land, but as acts of migration on the land they hold the potential to simultaneously root us and transport us. From the microexperience of tending a tomato seedling, to the community mobilization of transforming vacant land into public green spaces, to the aesthetic representation of nation on the landscape, making, tending, and inhabiting diverse gardens requires active social engagement. The next challenge we face as a society is to reconcile gardening practices with practices of social, economic, and cultural sustainability. In the end, we are all migrants moving on the land, on earth for a finite span of time and working together to create our paradise.

Notes

1. GARDENS OF MIGRATION

1. Amir Dialameh died at age seventy-one in 2003, but "Amir's Garden" remains in Griffith Park, just behind the golf course and the Los Angeles Zoo, and is now tended by other volunteers. Summary information and quotes from Bailie (1989); Rourke (2003); and Ashtiani (2003).

2. Francis and Hester (1990a:2).

3. Historian Douglas Sackman (2005a:248) has referred to gardens as "anthropogenic landscapes," and anthropologist Devon Pena (2006) sees garden making by transnational migrants from Central America and southern Mexico as "autotopographical practices," ways that transnational migrants can express who they are and that allow them to shape the place where they live so they may connect their past to their future. Landscape architects Mark Francis and Randolph T. Hester (1990a:2) similarly stated that "gardens are mirrors of ourselves, reflections of sensual and personal experience. By making gardens . . . we create our own idealized order of nature and culture."

4. Sackman (2005b:24); Pena (2006); Graham (2011:xiii).

5. Plants are not passive. If you have ever planted a seed, you know that it can fail to sprout and that seedlings and plants may grow, wither, or even pop up in unexpected nearby places independently of your best gardening efforts. In *The Botany of Desire* (2002), Michael Pollan brilliantly develops this theme by viewing plants not as objects but as subjects. Just as human desires for sweetness,

beauty, intoxication, and sustenance have reshaped plants, resulting in sweeter apples and marijuana with higher levels of THC, Pollan suggests that it is possible to see cultivated plants as bossing us around, getting us to do the critical work of weeding, watering, and tending so they can flourish. As an extension of this idea, writer Jim Nollman (2005:9) champions the primacy of nature and the garden, suggesting that "the greatest gift of gardening is the control of humans by nature." Other ecologically oriented writers seek to upset the anthropocentric view that human societies and culture unidirectionally shape plants and gardens.

6. Klindienst (2006:xxi). See also Handlin ([1951] 2002) and Bodnar (1987).

7. Lesley Head and colleagues (Head, Muir, and Hampel 2005; Head and Muir 2007) chronicle this process among Vietnamese refugees and Macedonian and Greek immigrants in Australia, and Klindienst (2006) among various immigrant and refugee groups in the United States.

8. "The Global Garden" was an ongoing series in the *Los Angeles Times*, written by Jeff Spurrier, that began in 2011 and ran through December 2013. On *papalo*, see Spurrier (2012). For *Saveur*'s feature on *papalo* growing in urban community gardens, see Gold (2010).

9. Chang (2006); Levitt (1998).

10. Chang (2006:169).

11. Ruggieri (2007:109).

12. K. Mitchell (2004).

13. Vertovec (2007).

14. Menjivar (2006).

15. Espiritu (2003:2).

16. Leonard (1997:134).

17. Harrison (2008).

18. Clare Cooper Marcus, a professor emerita in University of California–Berkeley's landscape architecture program, is widely credited as the founder of the therapeutic healing gardens. Her book with landscape architect Marni Barnes, *Healing Gardens: Therapeutic Benefits and Design Recommendations* (1999), based in part on a study of hospital gardens, is considered the seminal text in the field. A key contributor to this field, Roger S. Ulrich (1984), conducted research showing that the heart rate of postsurgical hospital patients lowered when they experienced gardens. Being in a garden appears to reduce stress. Research reported by environmental psychologists Kaplan and Kaplan (1989, 1993) points to how mental fatigue is alleviated by nature, earth scientist Eric Lambin (2012) assembles studies showing that contact with nature promotes vitality and happiness, and conservation biologist Sarah Hayden Reichard (2011) cites evidence that some soil bacteria activate serotonin-releasing neurons. Today, therapeutic healing gardens have proliferated in convalescent homes and Alzheimer wings, hospitals, prisons, and recovery centers. The Therapeutic

Landscapes Network offers information and resources for making gardens that promote health and well-being. They use quantitative and qualitative data to design health-promoting garden environments. The website mission statement for the Therapeutic Landscapes Network explains what they do this way: "We are an international, multidisciplinary community of designers, health and human service providers, scholars, and gardeners. Though our focus is broad, our primary emphasis is on evidence-based design in healthcare settings" ("Mission: Who We Are and What We Do," n.d., www.healinglandscapes.org/about/mission.html, accessed August 20, 2013). See also Kaplan and Kaplan (1993) and Milligan, Gatrell, and Bingley (2004).

19. Helphand (2006:23).

20. Espiritu (forthcoming).

21. Mukerji (1997).

22. Hoyles (2005:22). See also Riley (1990).

23. D. Mitchell (1996).

24. Pulido (2000).

25. Veblen ([1899] 1912:38).

26. Deverell and Hise (2005:4); Wolch and Dear (1989:4).

27. In his 1924 essay "The Morphology of Landscape," Sauer pithily expressed his approach: "The cultural landscape is fashioned from the natural landscape by a cultural group. Culture is the agent, the natural area is the medium, the cultural landscape the result" (quoted in Groth and Wilson 2003:5). Beginning in the 1930s and continuing until the 1990s, John Brinckerhoff Jackson extended these ideas by emphasizing the cultural landscape as a force actively shaping society. In their excellent overview of J. B. Jackson, Groth and Wilson (2003:16) note that a subsequent generation of radical geographers, political economy theorists, and postmodernists unpacked the notion of culture as a homogeneous entity and brought attention to power and inequality. Most of them dropped the term *landscape* in favor of *space* or *social space* in order to "distance themselves from the rural and bourgeois overtones of traditional concepts of landscape." While acknowledgment of power and inequalities is essential to any social analysis, *space* and *social space* strike me as unproductive and abstract terms for the subject matter in this book, so I use basic terms such as *garden landscapes* or *gardens*.

28. Zukin (1991:220).

29. Deverell (2004).

30. Avila (2004).

31. Culver (2010:11).

32. Alfred W. Crosby ([1972] 2003) coined the term *Columbian exchange* in his eponymous book, drawing attention to the role of plant and animal circulation across the continents. On the trans-Pacific exchange, see Gerber and Guang (2006).

33. Farmer (2013a).

34. Ramirez and Hondagneu-Sotelo (2009).

35. Ramirez (2011).

36. For these exceptions, see Bhatti and Church (2000, 2001); Bhatti (2006); Cerwonka (2004); Francis and Hester (1990b); Head and Muir (2007).

37. Several books analyze the obsession with lawn in the United States, including Bormann, Balmori, and Gabelle (2001); Haeg (2008); Jenkins (1994); Robbins (2007); and Steinberg (2006). The only one of these firmly rooted in social science is *Lawn People: How Grasses, Weeds, and Chemicals Make Us Who We Are* (Robbins 2007). This National Science Foundation (NSF)-sponsored study focused on the history and political economy of North American lawns and relied on a survey of 594 respondents in different regions of the United States, eight semistructured household interviews conducted in one cul de sac, and quantitative data culled from tax assessor data to estimate the ratio of land dedicated to lawn. People and lawns, Robbins (2007) argues, are constituted mutually through constant interaction and are mediated through the corporate chemical manufacturers that facilitate lawn cultivation and veneration. In the process, people become turf grass subjects, and Robbins assesses the role of corporate manufacturers in promoting one of the biggest twentieth-century American cultural products, lawns.

38. See Lawson (2005); Hanson and Marty (2012).

39. Gandy (2003:7).

40. As Campbell, Bell, and Finney (2006:19) remark, "Many people think of nature as being spatially located somewhere 'out there' (looking out from the city) and point it the same direction they might point if they were asked where 'the rural' was located."

41. Pollan (1991:5).

42. Mabey (1996:12).

43. Sackman (2005a:248).

44. Approximately twelve million people live in the Los Angeles region, four million in the San Diego metropolitan area, and four million in the "Inland Empire" located in San Bernardino and Riverside counties.

45. W. Li (1999, 2011).

46. Tavernise and Gebeloff (2010).

47. The median value of owner-occupied house units in Los Angeles County for 2007–11 was $478,300, according to US Census Bureau, State and County Quick Facts for Los Angeles County, http://quickfacts.census.gov/qfd/states/06/06037.html (accessed January 24, 2013).

48. Banham ([1971] 2009:13).

49. Davis (1998); Davis and Monk (2007).

50. Hondagneu-Sotelo (2010).

2. ELLIS ISLAND ON THE LAND

1. Brook (1893).

2. Ibid.

3. McWilliams ([1946] 1979:96).

4. Sackman (2005b:28).

5. Donald H. Hodel, environmental horticulture adviser at the University of California Cooperative Extension, pers. comm., February 10, 2014.

6. This ambitious planting is said to have been a beautification project in preparation for the 1932 Olympic Games, but according to Nathan Masters (2011) it was also part of a huge Great Depression relief effort, putting four hundred unemployed men to work planting trees along 150 miles of Los Angeles boulevards and avenues. "Palm Drives" and "Palm Avenues" were created in Northern California too, such as the stately one leading up to the entrance of Stanford University in Palo Alto, but they proliferated more widely in Southern California. Palm trees were planted by the City of Los Angeles until 2006, when the city council passed a motion to limit the planting of palm trees in favor of native, shade-producing trees.

7. Starr (1985:141); Sackman (2005b).

8. Henrich (2011). Henrich is a botanist, a board member of the Southern California Horticultural Society, and the living plants collection curator at the Los Angeles County Arboretum and Botanical Garden.

9. Anderson (2005:2).

10. Anderson (2005:125–26). See also Cunningham (2010).

11. Anderson (2005). For a historical and philosophical analysis of the "recovery narrative" of Europeans recovering "wilderness" and transforming it into a garden of Eden, see Merchant (2004).

12. Cronon (1995:79). For a historical discussion of immigrant flora and fauna, invasive species, and American perceptions of these, see Coates (2006).

13. Silko (2000).

14. In his seminal discussion of this process in New England colonies, William Cronon (1983:5) comments on the European stance toward repopulating the land with non-native plants: "In this vision, the transformation of wilderness betokened the planting of a garden, not the fall from one; any change in the New England environment was divinely ordained and wholly positive."

15. For an alternative view that prioritizes Native Hawaiian genealogical connections to the land and sees Asian immigrants as unwanted purveyors of Asian settler colonialism in Hawaii, see Fujikane and Okamura (2008).

16. Wilson (1880:20).

17. The English navigator George Vancouver, writing in 1793, quoted in Padilla ([1961] 1991:21–22).

18. See Deverell (2004).

19. Wilson (1880:64). Wilson writes, "In 1841 when Mr. Benjamin D. Wilson came to the country, the vineyards were still in a flourishing condition, and so remained until the vandal Mexicans thereabout gradually dug them up and burned them for fire-wood."

20. Padilla ([1961] 1991:33).

21. Laura Pulido, pers. comm., July 11, 2013.

22. Laura Pulido, pers. comm., July 11, 2013.

23. Farmer (2013b) observes that many towns were the sites of lynchings and that others invented a local lore around "lynching trees." For example, Calabasas, an affluent residential city in the hills west of the San Fernando Valley, had a "hangman's tree" proudly displayed until 1995, when it fell in a storm.

24. Sackman (2005b).

25. M. Wild, *Street Meeting: Multiethnic Neighborhoods in Early Twentieth-Century Los Angeles* (Berkeley: University of California Press, 2005), 18–19, cited in Lewthwaite (2010:41).

26. Harvey Rice, *Letters from the Pacific Slope; or, First Impressions* (New York: D. Appleton, 1870), 95, quoted in Sackman (2005b:23); Southern Pacific Company, *The Inside Track* (n.d.), quoted in Garcia (2001:23).

27. McWilliams ([1946] 1979:101).

28. Sackman (2005a:247).

29. Banham ([1971] 2009:143).

30. Sackman (2005a:251).

31. Sackman (2005a: 253).

32. Here's what Governor Perkins said in his speech: "Look at the wonderful array of nature's gifts spread before us, amplified and enriched by the effort of your Association. A few short years ago and these valleys, now emparadised in fruits . . . raised their unturned faces in sullen, uninviting barrenness. . . . The whole world lies before us here. That fig speaks to us of Syria; that luscious peach recalls to us the fertile land of Persia" (Sackman 2005b:34–35).

33. Garcia (2001:35).

34. McWilliams ([1946] 1979:217). The term *instant townscape* is from Banham ([1971] 2009).

35. *Land of Sunshine, Fruit and Flowers* (1893).

36. Garcia (2001); Sackman (2005b); Gonzalez (1994).

37. Watters (2007, 1:22).

38. Norwood (1993).

39. Norwood (1993:119).

40. Watters (2012).

41. These images appeared in *Country Life in America* in 1904." (Watters 2012).

42. R. Johnson (2009:112).

43. R. Johnson (2009:112).

44. T. S. Van Dyke, *Millionaires of a Day: An Inside History of the Great Southern California "Boom"* (New York, 1890), quoted in Sackman (2005b:41).

45. Padilla ([1961] 1991:236).

46. Although I am not sure how to determine the veracity of this statement, Victoria Padilla confidently declared that "of the many varieties of trees and palms seen in southern California today, more than 80 per cent were introduced between 1850–1900" ([1961] 1991:234).

47. Padilla ([1961] 1991:72). The Rose Parade initially featured horse-drawn carriages covered in roses, and Charles Holder purportedly said: "In New York, people are buried in the snow. Here our flowers are blooming and our oranges are about to bear. Let's hold a festival to tell the world about our paradise.""

48. Walter Woehlke, "The Land of Sunny Homes," *Sunset*, March 1915, 470, quoted in Sackman (2005a:256).

49. Dr. Francesco Franceschi from Italy became a famed horticulturalist and nurseryman in Santa Barbara in 1894 and purportedly introduced more plant varieties to California than any other individual. Theodore Payne came to California from England in 1893 and became a native flowers enthusiast, collecting seeds, propagating, and preserving native plants. He ran a nursery in Los Angeles on Los Feliz Boulevard from 1922 to 1958 and is credited with making available for general use four hundred to five hundred California native plants. Additionally, he is credited with the out-migration of these California natives, as he sent California seeds and sold cuttings to nurseries and plant collectors in Australia, England, Argentina, and elsewhere. John S. Armstrong migrated to Ontario, California, from Ontario, Canada, and began a nursery business. One of the few women and California-born horticulturalists of the day was Kate O. Sessions, a University of California–Berkeley graduate who developed the nursery trade and did landscape design in San Diego from 1885 to 1940, disseminating acacia trees imported from Australia and many South African plants, as well as popularizing South American jacarandas and pepper trees, which she liberally blended with California natives (Padilla [1961] 1991). She is also credited with planting over one thousand trees in San Diego's Balboa Park.

50. The garden grew to include thirty acres of interconnecting grass terraces with planting beds, as well as a pond, a flock of grazing sheep, and whimsical elements that paid homage to German and Bavarian culture, tapping into the popularity of the "Gardenesque movement." According to landscape architectural historian Sam Watters (2007, 1:84), "The design elements of the Gardenesque movement in the Busch gardens—interconnecting serpentine pathways through manicured, grassy areas, brightly colored planting beds, and discrete specimen trees and shrubs—were found in other late 19th century public and private Los Angeles gardens."

51. William Hertrich, *The Huntington Botanical Gardens, 1905–1949: Personal Recollections of William Hertrich* (San Marino, CA: Huntington Library), quoted in Prentice (1990, 24).

52. Graham (2011:162).

53. Charles Francis Saunders, *Trees and Shrubs of California Gardens* (New York: Robert M. McBride, 1926), 198, quoted in Sackman (2005a:257).

54. Graham (2011:160).

55. Lancaster (1963).

56. Lancaster (1963).

57. Christ (2000:676).

58. Carey McWilliams ([1946] 1973:358) observed that "Southern California was Hispanicized in appearance as quickly as, at an earlier date, it had been Anglicized," but he was noting the change in the built environment.

59. Padilla ([1961] 1991:92); McWilliams ([1946] 1973:355).

60. Padilla ([1961] 1991:92).

61. Watters (2012:149).

62. Charles Spaulding, "The Development of Organization and Disorganization in the Social Life of a Rapidly Growing Working-Class Suburb within a Metropolitan District" (PhD diss., University of Southern California, 1939), 45–46, quoted in Nicolaides (2002:39).

63. Rachel A. Surls, sustainable food systems adviser, University of California Cooperative Extension of Los Angeles County, pers. comm., March 6, 2013; Wickson cited in Starr (1985:139).

64. Surls (2011).

65. Garcia (2001).

66. Garcia (2001:54).

67. Joseph Timmons, "Citrus Workers in Model Homes," *Los Angeles Examiner*, September 2, 1920, quoted in Garcia (2001:67).

68. Helen O'Brien, "The Mexican Colony: A Study of Cultural Change" (senior thesis, Pomona College, 1932), quoted in Garcia (2001:95).

69. Home Missions Council, *A Study of Social and Economic Factors Relating to Spanish-Speaking People in the United States* (n.p., [late 1920s?]), 23, quoted in Monroy (1999:37).

70. Monroy (1999:37–38). Monroy quotes from a sociology student of the era: "Many of the homes [were] garden spots, a wealth of flowers and vegetables providing an inspiring contrast to the hideous, jammed, foul-smelling courts of New High, Alameda, Olivera [*sic*], North Broadway, and other streets near the heart of the city."

71. Garcia (2001:69).

72. The Los Angeles Housing Commission Report of the Los Angeles Commission, July 1, 1910 to March 31, 1913, quoted in Monroy (1999:29).

73. Historian Douglas Monroy (1999:30) reports that fifty of the eighty-five Mexican families evicted from the house courts in this pre–World War I era were relocated and even brought their houses on wheels to new 25 × 100–foot lots, where they reestablished their flower and vegetable gardens.

74. Douglas Monroy (1999:33) comments, "Middle-class Mexicans aspired to refinement and culture. They valued individualistic family enterprise. . . . In other words, other social reforms besides the rough peasant communalism of the working classes in Mexican Los Angeles appeared on the landscape." But the historical record of the Mexican middle-class impact on Southern California gardens remains vague. Another garden and agricultural engagement with the land from 1914 to 1916 was fomented by the anarchist brothers Ricardo and Enrique Flores Magón, who established a commune on five acres, just north of downtown Los Angeles, "on which they lived and farmed communally with several others" (33).

75. Hayden (1997).

76. Helen O'Brien, "The Mexican Colony: A Study of Cultural Change" (senior thesis, Pomona College, 1932), written about the Arbol Verde *colonia*, which was located just east of the Claremont campus, quoted in Garcia (2001:71).

77. Quoted in Chan (1986:99–100).

78. This circumspect statement is my best hypothesis, and a firm conclusion on this matter will require primary research.

79. Tsuchida (1984); Tsukashima (1991, 1995–96, 1998).

80. The Metropolitan Water District of Southern California relies on three well-traveled sources of water: the California Aqueduct, which brings water from the Sacramento River and Delta in Northern California; the Los Angeles Aqueduct, transporting water from the Owens Valley and the precipitation on the eastern side of the Sierras; and the Colorado River Aqueduct, bringing water from out of state.

81. Maria Kaika, *City of Flows: Modernity, Nature, and the City* (New York: Routledge, 2005), quoted in Gottlieb (2007:104).

82. The Federal Housing Administration (FHA) formed in 1934, offered federally insured long-term, low-interest loans for home buyers, and the GI Bill in 1944 opened the possibility of home ownership to any veteran with a steady job. From 1945 to 1960, new home construction exploded in the United States, and both working-class and middle-class single-detached homes and gardens expanded over land that had previously held citrus orchards and agricultural crops in Southern California. Housing starts in the United States averaged 1.4 million per year between 1945 and 1960, buoyed by the FHA and the GI Bill (Grampp 2008:95). According to historian Becky Nicolaides (2002), development and sales of working-class homes were well represented in the Los Angeles area.

83. Avila (2004).

84. With these big plateglass windows, "the house and yard could appear that much more spacious," bringing the outdoor garden into the interior. According to Christopher Grampp (2008:155–57), the book *California Ranch Homes by Cliff May*, published by Sunset in 1946, inspired fifty years of suburban ranch-style home construction in California and elsewhere, also promoting the expansion of California-style gardens in the South, in the Midwest, and on the East Coast.

85. Grampp (2008:114); Padilla ([1961] 1991:112).

86. Robbins (2007:53, 59).

87. Henrich (2011). In Southern California, the Arboretum, the South Coast Gardens, the Descanso Gardens, and the Virginia Robinson Garden were the sites providing plant introduction, but plant patents and trademarks were held by private nurseries.

88. Grampp (2008:115).

89. Writing in the early 1960s, garden historian Victoria Padilla gushed about the new plants and products that mid-twentieth-century science and industry produced. "Never have there been more neighborhood nurseries to entice the home gardener with bright little annuals and flowering shrubs and never has the gardener's job been made easier with gadgets of all types and pest controls and fertilizers of every description" ([1961] 1991:134).

90. *Sunset*, August 1952:43.

91. Graham (2011:287–88).

92. In her dissertation "Representational Conquest: Tourism, Display, and Public Memory in 'America's Finest City,'" Margaret Salazar-Porzio analyzes the post–World War II development of tiki style at the Shelter Island resort area in San Diego and argues that this new built environment reordered race, gender, and class hierarchies.

93. Gottlieb (2007:117).

94. Paul Robinson (2010) notes that African American did work as janitors, house servants, and horsemen and later as chauffeurs in early twentieth-century Los Angeles.

95. W. E. B. DuBois, "Colored California," *Crisis* (August 1913:193), quoted in D. Hunt (2010:12). According to historian Douglas Flamming (2005:51), DuBois inserted photographs of lushly landscaped homes where black Angelenos lived, showing lawns, palm trees, and flowers.

96. D. Hunt (2010). Black home ownership rates cited in Sides (2003:16).

97. Sides (2003:38).

98. Cleeland (2006).

99. On Asian immigrants in Southern California suburbs, see Fong (1994); Saito (1998); and W. Li (1999). On the Mexican American middle class in Southern California, see Vallejo (2012).

100. Fong (1994); Saito (1998).

101. W. Li (1999); W. Cheng (2013).

102. Among Latinos in California, the home ownership rate rose from 43 percent in 2000 to 46 percent in 2003. Hans Johnson and Amanda Bailey, "California's Newest Homeowners: Affording the Unaffordable," *California Counts: Population Trends and Profiles* 7 (August 2005): 8, cited in Teaford (2008:67).

3. THE GARDENERS OF EDEN

1. Hondagneu-Sotelo ([2001] 2007).

2. On the polarization of jobs, see Kalleberg (2011). On income inequality in Los Angeles, see Milkman, Reese, and Roth (1998).

3. Grampp (2008) contends that residential yards have gone through three stages since the early 1800s, moving from agricultural spaces for growing food for the family, to utilitarian yards supporting the home and family, to outdoor garden rooms of leisure.

4. National Gardening Association, "Garden Market Research: Homeowners Spend a Record $45 Billion on Lawn and Landscape Services," March 20, 2012, www.gardenresearch.com/index.pp?q=show&id=2872 (no longer available online); 2010 National Gardening Survey (National Gardening Association 2010).

5. The median value of owner-occupied houses in LA County for 2006–10 was reported at $508,000. See "Los Angeles County Housing," USA.com, www.usa.com/los-angeles-county-ca-housing.htm#House-Value (accessed September 20, 2012).

6. Schor (1992); Arnold et al. (2012:72).

7. Kilkey, Perrons, and Plomien (2013). In New Zealand, masculine domestic labor is also outsourced and advertised as "hire a hubby," but there mostly New Zealanders, not immigrants, do the work (Cox 2013).

8. Lareau (2011:2); Messner (2009:12).

9. On the development of the Japanese gardening occupation, see Tsuchida (1984); Tsukashima (1991, 1995–96, 2000); Hirahara (2000); and Bonacich and Modell (1980). On the transition from Japanese to Mexican immigrant gardeners, see Ramirez and Hondagneu-Sotelo (2009) and Huerta (2011).

10. Tsukashima (2000:75) cites a UCLA survey of Issei, Nisei, and Sansei men in Los Angeles and Orange counties who reported gardening as their main occupation. It shows that 23 percent of these Japanese immigrant men were gardeners in 1946–52, and 35 percent in 1953–65. During the 1950s and 1960s, Japanese gardeners up and down the West Coast formed gardeners' associations, offering credit unions, health insurance, and social activities for their members (Hirahara 2000). The Southern California Gardeners' Federation offered several

thousand Japanese gardeners and their families health insurance, published a newsletter, sponsored picnics, and kept a little depot where the Japanese gardeners could purchase supplies. By 2012, full-time gardener members had dwindled to only one hundred—the rest were widows and retirees—and the co-op closed in March 2012. See Knoll (2012:A1, A10).

11. Shima (2000:119).

12. Tsuchida (1984).

13. Quoted in Hirahara (2000:117).

14. Ramirez and Hondagneu-Sotelo (2009). See also Huerta (2007, 2011).

15. Grampp (2008:45). Urban historian Dolores Hayden (2003:27) also attributes the convention of setting the suburban house back on the green lawn to Downing: "Downing's obsession with setting a suburban residence behind a wide swath of lawn and his insistence on exaggerated rooflines as proof of 'style' are still part of suburban house design today." And historian and landscape designer Wade Graham (2011:58) concurs, noting that Downing's *Treatise* "became the suburban homeowner's bible" and that even today "Downing is everywhere.... He in effect designed the first hundred years of American suburbia."

16. Downing ([1846] 2012:160–61).

17. Downing ([1846] 2012:156).

18. Quoted in Hayden (2003:32).

19. Hayden (2003:33). See also Jenkins (1994).

20. Norwood (1993).

21. Banham (1971, 2009:81–82).

22. Caitlin Flanagan, who writes brutally direct reflections on her experiences managing motherhood and household help in her home, located in the patrician Hancock Park neighborhood of Los Angeles, describes the depersonalized relations with her gardener: "He's been working here for two years, and I don't even know his last name" (2006: 109). The well-preserved historic residential neighborhood of Hancock Park includes some of the most beautiful, meticulously tended classic gardens in Southern California. It was developed in the 1920s, just five miles west of downtown LA. Most of the palatial homes, which feature Mediterranean, Tudor, and Spanish Colonial Revival styles popular here in the early part of the century, are set back fifty feet from the street, as required by the developer, and feature substantial sweeping lawns and side driveways leading to a detached rear garage. For photographs and more information, see "A Brief History of Hancock Park, Hancock Park Homeowners Association, established 1948," n.d., www.hancockparkhomeownersassociation.org/?page_id=20 (accessed September 7, 2012).

23. Flanagan underlines the contrast in the relationship she maintains with the nanny, Paloma, and the gardener (who remains totally nameless in the text). Of the gardener, she says: "We have never quarreled. We have never had a glass of

wine together. We have never discussed our marriages. I have never spoken sharply to him and made him cry. I have never felt paralyzed in his absence, or dreamed about him, or heard my children call out for him in the night" (Flanagan 2006:110).

24. Flanagan (2006:109).

25. I did come across two exceptions. Two upper-income home owners that I interviewed had changed gardeners, choosing more customized service, so they paid a higher rate for that work (e.g., the Kleins, going from $200 to $300 a month, and Hutchins, now paying $450 for a twice-a-week particularized garden service).

26. In the early 1900s, Frederick Winslow Taylor developed scientific management principles to encourage the most efficient expenditures of labor in manufacturing work, breaking down jobs into a series of discrete repetitive tasks. This logic is the basis of industrial engineering and management today.

27. Rodriguez (2011). Burton Sperber started the ValleyCrest Landscape Company in 1949 when he bought a North Hollywood nursery from Italian nurseryman Mossimo Giannulli. ValleyCrest now counts $1 billion in annual revenue from tree care, golf course maintenance, and landscape installations at well-known museums and resorts. ChemLawn, a national landscaping company now greenwashed with the name Tru Green, is in the business of residential gardening and lawn maintenance but maintains a scarce presence in Southern California, where the immigrant labor gardener system predominates.

28. Tobar (2012:10).

29. The Immigration Reform and Control Act, signed into law in November of 1986, allowed 3.1 million formerly undocumented immigrants to become legal permanent residents.

30. *Ranchero masculinity* is a term introduced by sociologist Robert C. Smith (2006) in his analysis of practices and ideologies that allow Mexican immigrant men from rural origins to dominate women, and it shares much with Gloria Gonzalez-Lopez's (2005) notion of "rural patriarchies." In this discussion I am focusing on ranchero masculinity as a particular type of preindustrial work practice and orientation that favors working independently and autonomously outdoors with plants and animals.

31. Farr (2006:168). See also Nugent and Alonso (1984).

32. For analyses of the leaf blower bans and the formation of the Association of Latin American Gardeners of Los Angeles (ALAGLA), see Cameron (1999–2000); Huerta (2007, 2011).

33. In Southern California, the liberal and affluent city of Santa Monica has perhaps been the most effective in pursuing green policies and banning leaf blowers. But even Santa Monica cannot effectively eradicate the blowers because there is still residential demand for tidy gardens maintained at a set price. For a list of the regulations, see City of Santa Monica Office of Sustainability and the

Environment, "Landscape Leaf Blower Ban," n.d., www.smgov.net/Departments/
OSE/Categories/Landscape/Leaf_Blower_Ban.aspx (accessed April 10, 2013). For
a report on the effectiveness of enforcement, see "After Residents Complain Ban Is
Too Soft, Santa Monica Gets Tough on Leaf Blowers," NBS Southern California,
November 12, 2012, www.nbclosangeles.com/news/local/Santa-Monica-Gets-
Tough-on-Leaf-Blowers-179037061.html,.

34. These are verbatim quotes posted to the online site under "Should
Mexican Gardeners Have Their Leaf Blowers Taken Away?" *Los Angeles Forum*,
www.topix.com/forum/city/los-angeles-ca/T8FA59IM9Q8LVGKOP, September
16 and October 1, 2008.

35. *A Better Life* is an American drama film, directed by Chris Weitz and
released in 2011.

4. "IT'S A LITTLE PIECE OF MY COUNTRY"

1. To protect anonymity, "Franklin" and "Dolores Huerta" are the pseudonyms
I am using for two community gardens, and I am also using pseudonyms for all
of the gardeners discussed in this chapter.

2. I describe the ethnographic and interview research methods in more detail
in chapter 1. This chapter is based on approximately three hundred hours of my
own participant observation that I recorded in typed field notes, twenty-five in-
depth, audio-recorded transcribed interviews with community gardeners, and
five informal interviews with community leaders.

3. The documentary *Fear and Learning at Hoover Elementary* (1997) was
made by former teacher Laura Simon. See the film's website at PBS, POV docu-
mentaries, www.pbs.org/pov/fearandlearning/.

4. Schmelzkopf (1995); Hassell (2002); Saldivar-Tanaka and Krasny (2004);
Lawson (2005).

5. Espiritu (2003).

6. Between 1997 and 2011, deportations and removals from the United States
increased ninefold. By 2011, the Department of Homeland Security had deported
392,000 migrants and returned an additional 324,000 to their home countries
without a removal order, and the vast majority were Latino working-class immigrant men (Golash-Boza and Hondagneu-Sotelo 2013). Persons from Mexico,
Guatemala, Honduras, and El Salvador accounted for 93 percent of deportations
in 2011. While Latino immigrant men have been the focus of these deportation
campaigns, these programs have caused widespread social suffering constituting a new form of legal violence in Latino communities (Menjivar and Abrego
2012), also causing fear, insecurity, and anxiety for immigrants with legal status
(Kanstroom 2007). For multiple analyses of how immigration law shapes immigrant illegality, and how this concept is deployed, resisted, and experienced, see

Menjivar and Kanstroom (2013). For analysis of the ways in which the urban community gardens served as palliative sanctuaries in the context of a climate of fear and hardship created by deportations and detentions, see Hondagneu-Sotelo and Ruiz (2013).

7. Perhaps the earliest formations were in Britain's allotment gardens, a response to the Industrial Revolution and the enclosure movement, which had deprived workers and peasants with places to grow food. The private enclosure of the commons in England in eighteenth-century England led to both philan-thropic and self-help movements of leased plots of land for laborers to develop community gardens, which according to Sam Bass Warner (1987:8) eventually shaped "a national policy for the municipal provision of land for community gardening." Then as now, not everyone was in favor of allowing the poor and the propertyless to have community gardens. The English philosopher and political economist John Stuart Mill (1806–73), for example, deplored community gardens. According to Warner (1987:9), "He thought the little village gardens would cause the shiftless to rest in their villages, to garden, and to have babies, and thereby so to multiply that in time they would impoverish all of England by their incontinence and their improvidence."

8. Lawson (2005:21)

9. Lawson (2005:52).

10. Lawson (2005:69).

11. Horatio Rust to James McLaughlin, November 20, 1900, Rust Papers, Huntington Library Manuscripts, San Marino, CA, quoted in Sackman (2005a:245). Horatio Nelson Rust, a contemporary of Abbot Kinney, Helen Hunt Jackson, and Alfred E. Kroeber, was born in Amherst, Massachusetts, and migrated to Southern California, where he settled in South Pasadena, California. He was enthralled with the West, and in his garden he posed for photo-graphs in front of a "gold of ophir rose bush" that was twenty-five feet in diame-ter and fifteen feet high. He is best known as a self-trained archaeologist-collector of Indian antiquities, but he also owned an important wholesale plant nursery, served as Southern California commissioner of immigration, was a founder of the Pasadena Public Library, and worked as an Indian agent to the Mission Indi-ans. As Donald Chaput (1982:1) notes, Horatio Rust "was involved in many other activities that would fill several normal lives."

12. Today, a new crop of school gardens has emerged. These have been spear-headed by the organic food movement and by concern for food security, urban social justice, childhood obesity, and land stewardship. To some extent they have been inspired by the school garden projects of Chez Panisse's Alice Waters and by Michelle Obama's White House garden. The school garden movement is, as of yet, not as institutionalized as it was the last turn of the century, but some critics believe these projects reinforce white paternalism. Racial discourses are promi-nent in them, and Guthman (2008) reports on the disappointment of white

college students at the University of California at Santa Cruz when they discover that black urban youth do not resonate with the activity of "putting their hands in the soil," which they tend to see as unpaid labor and perhaps continuous with the legacy of slavery and white appropriation. See also Slocom (2007). An alternative view sees public spaces such as urban community gardens as potential sites for "transcultural placemaking," a term introduced by Jeffrey Hou (2013:7) to refer to the "cultural trans-formation that takes place in urban places and through urban placemaking." This view finds potential in marginal sites and emphasizes "the instrumentality of placemaking as a vehicle for cross-cultural learning, individual agency, and collective actions" (7). Also on the importance of public space, see Low (2000).

13. Warner (1987:17).

14. Hynes (1996: xii).

15. Rachel Surls, the director of the Los Angeles County Cooperative Extension, claims that from 1910 to 1955 Los Angeles County was the biggest agricultural producer in the nation. She cites a report showing that ten thousand small farms still existed in the county as late as the 1950s. See "Rachel Surls—County Director at UC Cooperative Extension," n.d., www.kcet.org/socal/departures/richland-farms/the-present/rachel-surls---county-director-at-uc-cooperative-extension.html (accessed March 1, 2013).

16. Hassell (2002); Tracey (2007). Today the Green Guerillas continue as a nonprofit organization offering services to over three hundred community garden groups. See www.greenguerillas.org.

17. The New York City Department of Parks and Recreation started the Green-Thumb program in 1978. It currently offers supplies and support to over six hundred community gardens. The New York Restoration Project oversees fifty-two other community gardens. See Finn (2011).

18. In New York City, Sharon Zukin observes that these changes have come about with the gentrification of neighborhoods and the inclusion of gentrifiers in many community gardens (2010). In the Los Angeles urban community gardens that I studied, professionalization of the community garden administration is under way, but gardens in Pico Union and Westlake do not include gentrifiers— at least not yet.

19. African American farmers of the Detroit Black Community Food Security Network and advocates at the Detroit Food Policy Council champion community self-reliance, responding to widespread distrust of the government's capacity to provide a safe and clean food supply. In Detroit, the Progressive Era's focus on vocational training and cultural assimilation in the garden has been replaced by a focus on self-determination, resistance, black power, and self-sufficiency as an alternative to government dependency (White 2010, 2011a, 2011b).

20. See Detroit Food Justice Task Force, "Urban Agriculture," n.d., www.detroitfoodjustice.org/?page_id=28 (accessed October 20, 2012).

21. As Mark Bittman has described, the weekly Eastern Market draws fifty thousand shoppers who buy "grown in Detroit" veggies and flats of flowers, while a Capuchin monastery runs a community garden on twenty-four empty lots, and a church group started the "Peaches and Greens" vegetable market, which sells to the local liquor stores and takes out a mobile truck to sell to residents who don't have a car (see Bittman 2011). The D-Town Farm is now a seven-acre farm that includes organic vegetable cultivation, composting, beehives, and hoop houses that allow vegetables to grow in the cold winter months. See Detroit Black Community Food Security Network website, http://detroitblackfoodsecurity.org/ (accessed October 30, 2012).

22. Klindienst (2006:104).

23. Peter Biro, "Refugees Plant New Roots in Community Gardens," August 17, 2011, International Rescue Committee, www.rescue.org/news/refugees-plant-new-roots-community-gardens-11524.

24. Wilkinson (2012:25). See also website of GrowNYC, www.grownyc.org/openspace (accessed October 16, 2012).

25. Lynch and Brusi (2005).

26. The documentary *The Garden*, by Scott Hamilton Kennedy, is available for purchase or on Netflix. See their website at www.thegardenmovie.com/. See also Lawson (2007), and Irazabal and Punja (2009).

27. Initial funding for the South Central Farm came from the Los Angeles Regional Food Bank, the City of Los Angeles, the US Department of Agriculture, thirty private restaurants, and site preparation provided by the Los Angeles Conservation Corps (Lawson 2005:271).

28. Lawson (2005:271).

29. Peña (2006:2).

30. Peña (2006:2).

31. Flores (1998:263).

32. The community gardeners pay $15 a month here and sell their produce in a vibrant on-site market to taco truck and restaurant owners. Conversation with Al Renner, of the LA Community Garden Council, on-site at Stanford Avalon Community Garden on October 31, 2010.

33. See www.southcentralfarmers.com/, accessed October 16, 2012. As a cooperative, South Central Farmers have also branched out and developed new markets, developing community-supported agriculture and producing and selling trendy products such as kale chips and beet chips.

34. The official websites list seventy community gardens, but activist scholars Paula Sirola, Evelyn Blumenberg, and Edna Bonacich, who are currently involved in an enumeration and survey of all these gardens, place the figure closer to one hundred (Paula Sirola, pers. comm., March 13, 2013). A 2013 study produced by UCLA students in the urban and regional planning master's program counted over one thousand urban agricultural sites in Los Angeles County, with the

majority (761) being school gardens. They counted 118 community gardens in Los Angeles County and 382 commercial nurseries and farms (Jackson et al. 2013).

35. A survey conducted by Kaley Terwilliger for a 2006 UC Santa Cruz student thesis concluded that 97 percent of community gardens in Los Angeles include gardeners with incomes lower than $25,000 and that 65 percent support gardeners with incomes of $15,000 or less. The survey also reported that 91 percent of the urban community gardeners in Los Angeles are Spanish speakers (Terwilliger 2006:7). In Los Angeles, a combination of private, federal, and city funding has been used to build and maintain community gardens. Until the mid-1990s, the US Department of Agriculture funded the UC Cooperative Extension Program to administer the community gardens in Los Angeles and other metropolitan areas (Yvonne Savio, pers. comm., December 6, 2012). In 2011, the USDA awarded ten grants throughout the nation, totaling $725,000 to support community gardens. See the "People's Garden Grant Program," n.d., www.usda.gov/wps/portal/usda/usdahome?navid=GARDEN_RT5 (accessed July 25, 2013). Today, new funding sources for urban community gardens also come from public programs targeting the obesity epidemic.

36. With recent Mexican and Central American migration, the area immediately surrounding MacArthur Park has been deemed "denser than any urban area west of New York." This assessment comes from "An Oasis in L.A.'s Core," *Los Angeles Times*, June 19, 2004, http://articles.latimes.com/2004/jun/19/opinion/ed-park19. In 2010 it had a density of 38,214 people per square mile. Los Angeles Times Neighborhood Project, "Mapping L.A.: Westlake," n.d., http://projects.latimes.com/mapping-la/neighborhoods/neighborhood/westlake/ (accessed October 24, 2012).

37. This neighborhood, once well-to-do, then abandoned, is now being revitalized by Central American and Mexican immigrants. In the late nineteenth century, swampland was developed into Westlake Park, a public leisure park in the tradition of New York City's Central Park (it was renamed MacArthur Park after General MacArthur in the 1940s). Elegant homes were built in the area, and the Pacific Electric streetcar transported businessmen to downtown offices, earning the area the appellation of "Los Angeles' first suburb," a moniker that I saw emblazoned on the banner of the First District LA city council member Ed Reyes when he and his staff came to neighborhood events. From the 1890s through the early decades of the twentieth century, Westlake developed into a fancy, high-priced destination spot with luxury hotels and shops. When the exclusive department store Bullocks Wilshire opened in a luxurious 1929 art deco building, outfitted with travertine floors, murals, and brass elevators, customers arriving by automobile were greeted by valets dressed in livery uniforms at the porte cochere. Until the exclusive shops moved further west, this was the defining spot of high-end consumption in Los Angeles.

38. For a comprehensive overview of Guatemalan and Salvadoran settlement and transformation of Westlake during the 1980s and 1990s, see Hamilton and Chinchilla (2001). For general insights into how Latinos have invigorated US cities, see Davis (2000).

39. Everyone called this large shade structure *la casita*, but this collective gathering space should not be confused with the small rustic *casitas* in New York City's community gardens, directly inspired by vestiges of Puerto Rican rural dwellings. For an analysis of the *casita-batey*-garden complex in community gardens in New York City, see Lynch and Brusi (2005).

40. Linking objects are physical objects or places that comfortingly connect mourners to the deceased. The psychologist Ricardo Ainslie (1998) explains that as newcomer immigrants grieve their losses they seek out "linking objects" that lessen the pain of this loss. Ainslie analyzes the Austin *pulga* (flea market) as a place that serves this purpose in that it is reminiscent of social life in the plaza, and Clara Irazabal and Macarena Gomez-Barris (2007) similarly analyze Plaza Mexico, a commercial mall with replicas of Mexican architecture in Lynwood, a small city south of Los Angeles. Here shops and restaurants are enjoyed by Mexican clientele, but it was constructed by and remains owned and operated by Korean entrepreneurs. This recreational mall, they argue, gains new meaning during the current regime of illegality and militarization of the border. Little Italys and Chinatowns can also be seen as places where immigrants sought to recreate lost worlds, serving as extensions of immigration processes writ on the land.

41. As Chambers and Momsen (2007) note, gendered patterns of maize cultivation in Mexico have changed with US-bound labor migration, and I noted this also when I interviewed Mexican immigrant women who had stayed behind while their bracero husbands had migrated north (Hondagneu-Sotelo 1994). In the interviews with the community gardeners, I noted regional gender differences in agricultural work in Central America and Mexico. Some women, particularly indigenous women from Oaxaca and the Guatemalan highlands, reported that they had been farming and plowing since age six or seven, while other women, from Mexico and El Salvador and from Ladino (mestizo) backgrounds in Guatemala, said that in their homes and communities either farming was considered men's work or they had been involved in only one aspect, say the corn harvest, or bringing meals to their fathers and brothers working in the fields. Additionally, I found few Salvadorans at these community gardens. Many Salvadorans in the United States come from the city, and another reason that may explain their relative absence in the community gardens is that the civil wars of the 1980s violently destroyed the countryside, severely limiting possibilities for land cultivation (Professor Manuel Vasquez, pers. comm., October 14, 2011).

42. Mares (2012:335). On the use of food in producing cultural memories in urban community gardens, see also Lynch and Brusi (2005).

43. The book *Healing Gardens: Therapeutic Benefits and Design Recommendations*, by Clare Cooper Marcus and Marni Barnes (1999), is a classic in the field. See also the website for Therapeutic Landscapes Network, www.healing-landscapes.org/ (accessed October 22, 2012), which serves as a network and information source for landscape designers and health care providers on therapeutic gardens. It claims as its primary purpose "evidence-based design in healthcare settings." See also Kaplan (1973).

44. See Cornelius and Myhre (1998).

45. While some observers may insist that Latino immigrants feel a great emotional sense of place attachment to MacArthur Park, none of the women who gathered at the Franklin or Dolores Huerta gardens saw MacArthur Park as a safe, desirable place to go for recreation. MacArthur Park and especially Lafayette Park, located directly across the street, are public spaces where men congregate.

46. While the teens in this neighborhood were not drawn to the urban community gardens, teens are involved in many high school organic vegetable gardens in Southern California, including Venice High School's Learning Garden, which includes a seed bank, and the John Muir High School garden in Pasadena, where they cultivate entrepreneurial skills as they tend organic vegetables for sale. There is also a national organization, Rooted in Community, that sponsors a national gathering of young people (mostly of color) who are engaged in urban agriculture and food justice. In the summer of 2013, they held their annual summit in Los Angeles. See their website, www.rootedincommunity.org/.

47. Harrison (2008); Peña (2006).

48. "The Scotts Miracle-Gro Community Garden Academy," n.d., http://columbusfoundation.org/grants/columbus-foundation/scotts/ (accessed March 26, 2013). See also Spurrier (2011).

49. NGOs must now regularly supply numbers to their granting institutions, showing how many people they have served. As sociologist Nina Eliasoph (2011) has indicated, this dynamic now characterizes a good deal of community volunteerism and civic engagement in the United States. At the Franklin garden, this made community garden members *feel* like a number, and some of the gardeners resented this.

50. "Teresa Tobillo" is a pseudonym.

51. The money had been raised from the now defunct Community Redevelopment Agency (CRA) of Los Angeles. Green Spaces applied for the funds to purchase an adjacent property, and the women had been trotted before a CRA board to testify how important the Franklin garden was to the gardeners and their families. Several of them later told me they felt they had been used, but this was after they already felt bitter over the conflict with the parcel contracts. The owner of the adjacent property refused to sell his land, so the $350,000 was put toward infrastructural improvements on the Franklin Community Garden. But

funds were *never* spent on what the community gardeners wanted, namely, chickens, a toilet, and a basic barbecue and cooking area. Randolph Hester (2006:4), a professor of landscape architecture and an advocate of public spaces, has argued passionately in favor of community-based decision making. "Ecological democracy," he writes, "is government by the people emphasizing direct, hands-on involvement." While the leadership and staff at Green Spaces may have believed in these principles, they abnegated responsibility to implement these principles in their work with the community gardeners.

5. CULTIVATING ELITE INCLUSION

1. Levitt (2012).

2. Zhou (2009:80). On "flexible citizenship" and access to multiple passports, see Ong (1999).

3. Saito (2001).

4. W. Li (1999, 2011). While Monterey Park is generally recognized as the heart of the Chinese ethnoburb, by the late twentieth and early twenty-first centuries many cities in the San Gabriel Valley had multiracial populations with significant numbers of whites and Latinos and with a strong percentage of Asian Americans, especially those of Chinese origin. See also W. Cheng (2009, 2013).

5. Veblen ([1899], 1912:45).

6. The style of Suzhou scholar's gardens has come to represent Chinese gardens as a whole, even though imperial gardens and hunting parks have also been part of Chinese cultural tradition. For a discussion of these matters, see J. Hunt (2012:202) and Keswick (2003).

7. Bourdieu (1984).

8. Benzecry (2011).

9. Early botanic gardens developed as medicinal collections in what are today Italy, China, Egypt, Syria, and Mexico. Italy is widely credited for establishing some of the earliest botanic gardens. These were medicinal plant collections for teaching purposes in mid-sixteenth-century Pisa, Padua, and Florence. But in fact, the Aztecs also assembled garden collections, as did the Egyptians and Syrians, and scholars now believe that the earliest traces of botanic gardens were those planted in China 2,800 years ago. Feng Chin Tung and Cheng-Yih Wu, eds., *The Blossoming Botanical Gardens of the Chinese Academy of Sciences* (Beijing: Science Press, 1997), cited in B. Johnson (2007:64).

10. The premier exemplar, the Royal Botanic Gardens at Kew, began as "the Physic or Exotic Garden," a collection of medicinal plants in the 1700s, but it expanded significantly in the 1800s, during the age of the expanding British Empire. Botanic gardens such as Kew served as key sites for scientific research and for the economic development of empire. For a discussion rethinking the

dichotomy between disinterested scientific curiosity and colonial mercantilism and exploitation, see Miller and Reill (1996).

11. Joseph Banks to Henry Dundas, June 15, 1787, quoted in Desmond (1995:126).

12. Johnson (2007:73).

13. In *The Brother Gardeners*, Andrea Wulf tells the story of American plant hunter and farmer John Bartram selling and sending hundreds of boxes of seeds and plants to British merchant Peter Collinson. Plants from around the globe streamed into England, and as Andrea Wulf writes, "By the end of the century Banks had added thousands of plants from Africa, Australia and the Far East. . . . As the nineteenth century dawned, even the most humble garden could boast exotic flowers and shrubs" (2008:5).

14. Wulf (2008).

15. The Huntington Library is a place of serious scholarship and significant archival holdings and serves as a principal granting institution for research in the humanities, awarding $1.7 million in grants annually, second only to the National Endowment for the Humanities (Steven Koblik, "President's Message," July–August 2012, http://dev.huntington.org/huntingtonlibrary_02.aspx?id= 9578).

16. The Chinese did not passively accept these restrictions and often turned to the courts for judicial remedies, as the historian Lucy E. Salyer has shown. They also innovated a method to facilitate undocumented migration by documenting the birth of "paper sons" (Salyer 1995:44). For an analysis of the Asian exclusionary immigration laws that focuses on the role of eugenics and geopolitics, see Tyner (2006). See also the collection of essays edited by Chan (1991).

17. According to Chan (1991), the 1943 repeal opened US entry largely to Chinese brides, wives, and refugees seeking political asylum.

18. I am indebted to religious and American studies scholar Jane Iwamura for this insight.

19. By the 1960s, a Chinatown neighborhood thickly threaded with ethnic organizations and family ties had eroded. As Betty Lee Sung put it, "The new Chinatowns will be characterized more as loosely knit ethnic neighborhoods with an artificially contrived Oriental atmosphere mainly for the sake of the tourist trade" (1967:150). More recent sociological research in New York City by Min Zhou (1992) has called attention to the positive aspects and resources of Chinatown. Relying on ethnic enclave theory, Zhou has underlined how solidarity and trust among coethnic business owners, workers, and customers can facilitate economic mobility in Chinatown.

20. Fong (1994); Saito (1998).

21. As Saito (1998:47) puts it, "To frame the discourse without specifically rejecting Chinese influences, history was invoked that included the Mexican past of the region. Mexicans and Mexican Americans were momentarily elevated

from being a target of suspicion to being appreciated and used to counter the influence of the Chinese."

22. K. Mitchell (2004:168).

23. Chang (2006).

24. It is affiliated with a Taiwanese Buddhist organization, and it gained notoriety in national news during the 1996 presidential campaign when Gore attended a luncheon there and accepted Democratic National Committee donations that were later discovered to be illegal, as they had been reimbursed with (nonprofit) temple money provided by Buddhist monks and nuns (Suro 1998).

25. According to Irene Lin, opposition to the construction of the temple emerged from "many conservative, affluent, and retired European Americans" who feared not only that the temple buildings and statues would be "jarringly inappropriate" to the style of the neighborhood but that the new neighbors would hunt dogs for food and seduce the youth into a cult (Lin 1999:138). As a report in the *Washington Post* (Claiborne 1996:A36) summarized, the temple "was fought bitterly by local residents who claimed that it would overwhelm a neighborhood of single-family homes and disturb the quiet suburb with predawn gongs and raucous Chinese New Year's celebrations."

26. Lin (1999). The temple opened in 1988, and although temple members have worked hard to win over the Hacienda Heights community with American-style civic participation by offering language classes and by fighting a landfill and the opening of adult book stores (Claiborne 1996), coverage of the Gore controversy suggests that it is still identified as a site of suspicion and un-American foreignness.

27. In 2009 the national newspaper *USA Today* reported that Asian American students now make up 40 percent of UCLA's student body, 43 percent at UC Berkeley, 50% at UC San Diego, and 54 percent at UC Irvine, while constituting 12 percent of California's population (Chea 2009). Public pressure against this trend has resulted in new admissions policies intended to diminish the competitive Asian American presence at the most elite public universities in California (Chea 2009), and discussion has also focused on the extent to which quotas are used in the Ivy League to restrict the number of Asian American students, much as these were once used to limit Jewish student enrollment. Controversy focuses not only on the numbers but on a perception that highly competitive Chinese students specialize in fields that are antithetical to humanistic values. "American educational availability at the global scale has not necessarily produced a constituency of humanistic values," Ong suggests, "but it has produced highly trained calculative individuals capable of maneuvering effectively in the fields of corporate business, law, medicine, engineering, biotechnology, and architecture (favorite fields of specialization among overseas Chinese)" (2006:154). Excellence in science and engineering is seen as detracting from humanistic and cultural attributes.

28. Fishman (2005).

29. T. Li (2009).

30. One month after opening in March 2008, attendance at the Huntington doubled to twenty thousand. As the Huntington's communication director said, "I think it's safe to say that was primarily due to the Chinese garden" (Mason 2008).

31. Clunas (1996); Keswick (2003); Congzhou (2009); T. Li (2009).

32. Cotter (2012:C29) writes perceptively about the relation between garden design and social inequality: "A visit to the Suzhou gardens is a stimulating but disorienting experience. You get a firsthand sense of the complex stop-and-start movement and expansion and contraction of space that classical garden design creates. You also see how manipulative and coercive the designs can be, based on rigid rules of ritual protocol and hierarchy."

33. Levick and Brown (1999:8). See also Brown (2013).

34. T. Li (2009:63).

35. Watanabe (2008).

36. Cheng (1988).

37. Hardie (1988:9). Hardie clarifies that the manual is not a "how to" book on plants and cultivation but is more about architecture, the selection of rocks to display, and the creation of pavilions and moon gates for viewing the garden "recreations" of nature.

38. One year after the opening of the Chinese garden, the Huntington announced the For Generations to Come Campaign to raise money for the refurbishing of the Japanese garden's koi ponds, stream infrastructure, and house and for building a new teahouse. As Steve Koblik, the president of the Huntington, wrote in the July/August 2009 calendar, "Chinese traditions have come to the forefront at The Huntington. . . . Now we have an opportunity to celebrate the centennial of the Japanese Garden in a fitting way" (Huntington Library, Art Collections and Botanical Gardens Calendar, July/August 2009, 7).

39. Chan (1991).

40. Conversation with Jim Folsom, director of botanical gardens, and George Abdo, vice president for development at the Huntington.

41. That same year, Monterey Park had a Chinese population of similar proportion (44 percent) but a more modest median household income of $40,000 (Zhou 2009:85).

42. US Census Bureau, Quick Facts for San Marino (City), http://quickfacts. census.gov/qfd/states/06/0668224.html (accessed January 3, 2013).

43. Zhou (2009).

44. In the San Francisco Bay Area, the *New York Times* reports there are more than 385 private philanthropic foundations run by Chinese American families and that in New York City wealthy Asian Americans are donating to both dominant cultural institutions (e.g., the symphony, museums) and Asian American communities and homeland causes (Semple 2013).

45. Huntington Library, Art Collections and Botanical Gardens, "Honoring Chinese Garden Donors," 2014, www.huntington.org/WebAssets/Templates/content.aspx?id=1240.

46. Ong (1999); Zhou (2009).

47. Huntington Library, Art Collections and Botanical Gardens Calendar, January/February 2012, 8.

48. Watanabe (2008).

49. Mason (2008).

50. J. Hunt (2001:22).

51. Wada (2009:E8).

52. Wada (2009:E8).

53. For a series of critical essays on the limitations of multiculturalism, see Gordon and Newfield (1996).

54. In 2013, the Huntington Board of Trustees included five people, none with Chinese names. The Huntington Board of Overseers, composed of sixty individuals, had three people with Chinese names, although it is possible that others may have acquired other last names through marriage. The only Latino on these boards is a CEO of a Fortune 500 medical corporation. See Huntington Library, Art Collections and Botanical Gardens, "Huntington Leadership," 2014, www.huntington.org/WebAssets/Templates/content.aspx?id=298. The Huntington Board of Trustees and Board of Overseers are surely not unique in this lack of racial ethnic diversity, but given that Los Angeles and the San Gabriel Valley have a majority-minority population, and given the institution's expressed intent to better reflect the world, the disparity between the surrounding communities and the Huntington leadership is particularly striking.

6. PARADISE, FUTURE

1. Cassidy, Newell, and Wolch (2008).

2. The Los Angeles Food Policy Council is one example. It is a dynamic group, regularly bringing together over one hundred diverse advocates in the sub-basement of a downtown LA public works building, where they gather to discuss solutions for improving the regional food system. Urban agriculture, community gardens, school gardens, and changing municipal regulations to permit the growing of food in the parkways are part of the agenda. See their website at http://goodfoodla.org/ (accessed August 23, 2013).

3. In Spain, the hard-hitting global economic crisis has prompted new alternatives including time banks, bartering, consumption groups, and urban gardening. For a short summary, see Gaupp-Berghausen (2012). In Jamaica, Haiti, and the Bahamas, a move toward local farm-to-table food production seeks to replace island dependence on food imports. In Jamaica, the government

promotes the campaign with the slogan "Grow what we eat, eat what we grow," and four hundred schools in Jamaica now boast school gardens. Elsewhere in Antigua and Barbuda, students participate in fruit tree planting missions (see Cave 2013). There is also an organic food and urban gardening movement in Cuba.

4. The partners included the UCLA Labor Center, IDEPSCA (Instituto de Educacion Popular del Sur del California), the Department of Water and Power, Rio Hondo Community College, Green People, the commissioner of the Board of the Public Works Paula Daniels, and the Los Angeles and San Gabriel Watershed Council.

5. Native Green Gardening LLC Business Plan, September 28, 2009, prepared by IDEPSCA.

6. Victor Narro, immigrant labor lawyer, pers. comm., March 19, 2013. Serena Lin, an attorney who helped with the startup of the cooperative, and Marlom Portillo, the executive director of IDEPSCA, agreed that to thrive, Native Green must focus more on business professionalism and marketing for new clients (pers. comms., March 21 and March 26, 2013, respectively).

7. The first quote comes from the website of Grow Me Organics in Portland, Oregon (http://growmeorganics.com/?page_id=11, accessed August 3, 2012). The second comes from a business in North Carolina, Micro Farm Organics (http://microfarmgardens.com/, accessed August 3, 2012). There was a flush of entrepreneurial initiative in these organic vegetable gardening services in 2008, but some quickly went out of business. For example, 2008 spawned My Farm in San Francisco, which proposed to establish a "decentralized urban farm." For an installation fee of $600 to $2,000, My Farm would install vegetable beds and maintain these for a fee of $35 per week. In this model, which also featured permaculture techniques, the owners of the residence were given a box of food per week, and the remainder of the produce from their yards went to Community Supported Agriculture boxes. A customer on Yelp posted this experience of the demise: "I'm giving them two stars because although I never got any vegetables and the communication with them was really disorganized, they did come and weed my garden, cut some concrete and install drip irrigation. I paid for that, of course, but I like my yard a lot more now, so I can't be too mad. . . . We're busy people (which is why we thought it would be nice to let others farm the back fortieth) so we just had time to wonder in passing now and again what had become of them. So we just got a call from our farmer, and he gave us the news" (Yelp, MyFarm reviews, Karen H., September 15, 2009, www.yelp.com/biz/myfarm-san-francisco).

8. Alexander (2007).

9. Arnold et al. (2012).

10. Tsukashima (2000); Huerta (2011).

11. The city of Santa Monica is one of the few municipalities where the gas-powered leaf blower ban remains on the books and is enforced.

12. Lourdes Cordova Martinez, community relations manager, science and technology advancement, South Coast AQMD, pers. comm., March 5, 2013.

13. In *Green Illusions*, Ozzie Zehner argues that these new green technologies are not as clean and environmental as they seem and that we should be focusing on limiting consumption rather than creating new sources or energy. And in remarks that seem borne out by the fervor over developing solar-powered mowers and blowers, Zehner (2012:161) offers this analysis: "Unsurprisingly, profit motives likely induce much of the gravitational field surrounding productivist energy solutions. For the most part, knowledge elites can patent or otherwise control productivist technologies—manufacturing, marketing, and selling them for a profit (or at least federal handout)."

14. Michael Gould, interview by author, March 3, 2013; and website of Seabreeze Landscaping (www.seabreezelandscaping.com/eco.html, accessed March 3, 2013). See also the Greenstation's descriptions of its electric mowers at "The Greenstation: South Coast Air Quality Management District Lawn Mower Exchange 2014" (http://thegreenstationproducts.com/scaqmd.html.

15. Bormann, Balmori, and Geballe (2001).

16. In 2009, the Los Angeles Department of Power and Water, copying a more extensive and successful campaign in Las Vegas, Nevada, offered home owners rebates of up to $2,000 to replace thirsty lawn with drought-tolerant plants or permeable cover that requires no more than fifteen inches of water per square foot a year, as compared to the fifty to ninety inches of water that standard turf grass requires. Lawn still prevails as the most popular type of residential front and back yard landscaping in Southern California, but in a few municipalities, including Altadena (in the San Gabriel foothills) and Mar Vista (near Venice), more residents have switched out the lawn in favor of drought-tolerant native plants. The City of Santa Monica has sponsored workshops, has offered landscape grants and rebates to residents, and since 2004 has collected information on water, waste, and maintenance labor deployed at two side-by-side public demonstration gardens in the front yards of two houses. The construction costs were more expensive for the native garden, but it has required far less labor, water, and chemicals. More than two hundred Santa Monica residents have replaced their traditional, nonecological gardens with more sustainable native gardens. See City of Santa Monica, Office of Sustainability and the Environment, "Landscape," www.smgov.net/Departments/OSE/categories/landscape.aspx (accessed August 5, 2013).

17. Harris et al. (2013).

18. Data from the Mexican Migration Project show that most Mexican immigrants in the 1970s and 1980s came from backgrounds in rural communities, but by the 1990s many Mexican migrants were well educated, with experience in manufacturing jobs in urban metropolitan areas of Mexico (Garip 2012:417). As sociologist Ruben Hernandez-Leon (2008) has shown, this shift was due to economic restructuring in Mexico and globalization.

19. For more information on the land bank model at the International Rescue Committee, see "IRC Land Bank," www.rescue.org/us-program/us-san-diego-ca/irc-land-bank (accessed March 9, 2013).

20. For more information, photos, and a blog, see the Growing Home, "About the Home" (http://thegrowinghome.net/about/the-home/, accessed April 16, 2013).

21. Ron Finley, "A Guerilla Gardener in South Central L.A." TED Talk, February 2013, www.ted.com/talks/ron_finley_a_guerilla_gardener_in_south_central_la.html.

22. Food Forward is a Los Angeles volunteer organization that addresses hunger by harvesting locally grown food and fruit from private yards and public spaces and then donating the yield to food pantries and organizations. They began in 2009, and by March 12, 2013, according to their website, they had distributed 1,322,254 pounds of fresh produce. See www.foodforward.org/about/ (accessed March 12, 2013). Further north in San Jose, California, a "Garden to Table" project has spawned seven community gardens in a poor immigrant neighborhood where most of the households speak a language other than English at home. The organizers also innovated a "gleaning project," recruiting sociology students to walk around the neighborhood and record the location of public hanging fruit with hand-held GPS devices. Later, they picked the fruit for a food bank. They now provide nearly two thousand pounds of fruit for homeless and working poor families who cannot afford to purchase fresh fruit. The program began as the master's project for urban planning student Zach Lewis at San Jose State University. See Romney (2013).

23. Neelam Sharma, pers. comm., March 11, 2013.

24. Wolch, Wilson, and Fehrenbach (2005).

25. Molotch (1976:309).

26. See Jackson et al. (2013).

27. Backward Beekeepers and Urban Chickens have a regional presence, and in 2012 the California Homemade Food Act sponsored by Assemblyman Michael Gatto of Southern California passed, so as of January 2013 some foods made in private homes may be sold to the public. Sidewalk vending, a source of prepared consumer foods and economic livelihood in poor Latino neighborhoods here, remains illegal in Los Angeles, but advocates are working to legalize that too. Southern California is a vast amalgam of municipalities with a very decentralized system of governance, and the patchwork quilt of different cities with different regulations—there are eighty-eight cities in Los Angeles County alone—may provide an aperture for local residents to challenge city ordinances.

28. The Los Angeles Food Policy Council (LAFPC), a vibrant organization that formed in 2009–11, seeks to have a collective impact through a collaborative approach. LAFPC has asked people to take photographs of vacant lots and strips of land that might be converted to urban agriculture or community gardens, and

the Los Angéles Neighborhood Land Trust is conducting an inventory of all Los Angeles city-owned land for this purpose too.

29. See Tracey (2007) and Reynolds (2008). See also www.guerrillagardening. org/ (accessed August 3, 2013). In Los Angeles, there is a small group of young guerrilla gardeners who claim to have installed twenty small gardens in Inglewood, South Central, near metro spots and other parts of Los Angeles since 2008. See LA Guerrilla Gardening, "Past Missions," n.d., www.laguerrillagardening.org/index.php/past-missions-3/ (accessed August 4, 2013).

References

Ainslie, Ricardo C. 1998. "Cultural Mourning, Immigration, and Engagement: Vignettes from the Mexican Experience." In *Crossings: Mexican Immigration in Interdisciplinary Perspectives*, edited by Marcelo M. Suarez-Orozco, 285–305. Cambridge, MA: Harvard University Press and David Rockefeller Center for Latin American Studies.

Alexander, William. 2007. *The $64 Tomato: How One Man Nearly Lost His Sanity, Spent a Fortune, and Endured an Existential Crisis in the Quest for the Perfect Garden*. Chapel Hill, NC: Algonquin Press.

Anderson, M. Kat. 2005. *Tending the Wild: Native American Knowledge and the Management of California's Natural Resources*. Berkeley: University of California Press.

Arnold, Jeanne E., Anthony P. Graesch, Enzo Ragazzini, and Elinor Ochs. 2012. *Life at Home in the Twenty-First Century: 32 Families Open Their Doors*. Los Angeles: Cotsen Institute of Archeology Press.

Ashtiani, Farrokh A. 2003. "Amir's Garden." *Iranian.com*, December 9. http://iranian.com/Ashtiani/2003/December/Garden/index.html.

Avila, Eric. 2004. *Popular Culture in the Age of White Flight: Fear and Fantasy in Suburban Los Angeles*. Berkeley: University of California Press.

Bailie, Jane. 1989. "Immigrant's Hard Work Creates an Oasis of Trees, Plants: After 12 Years, Iran Native Plans Vacation, Seeks Volunteers to Tend Garden." *Los Angeles Times*, September 28. http://articles.latimes.com/1989-09-28/news/gl-239_1_immigrant-s-hard-work.

Banham, Reyner. (1971) 2009. *Los Angeles: The Architecture of Four Ecologies*. Berkeley: University of California Press.

Benzecry, Claudio E. 2011. *The Opera Fanatic: Ethnography of an Obsession*. Chicago: University of Chicago Press.

Bhatti, Mark. 2006. "'When I'm in the Garden I Can Create My Own Paradise': Homes and Gardens in Later Life." *Sociological Review* 54 (2): 318–41.

Bhatti, Mark, and Andrew Church. 2000. "'I Never Promised You a Rose Garden': Gender, Leisure and Home-Making." *Leisure Studies* 19:183–97.

———. 2001. "Cultivating Natures: Homes and Gardens in Late Modernity." *Sociology* 35 (2): 365–83.

Bittman, Mark. 2011. "Imagining Detroit." *New York Times*, May 17. http://opinionator.blogs.nytimes.com/2011/05/17/imagining-detroit/.

Bodnar, John. 1987. *The Transplanted: A History of Immigrants in Urban America*. Bloomington: Indiana University Press.

Bonacich, Edna, and J. Modell. 1980. *The Economic Basis of Ethnic Solidarity: Small Business in the Japanese American Community*. Berkeley: University of California Press.

Bormann, F. Herbert, Diana Balmori, and Gordon T. Geballe. 2001. *Redesigning the American Lawn: A Search for Environmental Harmony*. 2nd ed. New Haven, CT: Yale University Press.

Bourdieu, Pierre. 1984. *Distinction: A Social Critique of the Judgement of Taste*. Cambridge, MA: Harvard University Press.

Brook, Harry Ellington. 1893. *The Land of Sunshine, Southern California, an Authentic Description of Its Natural Features, Resources and Prospects "Containing Reliable Information for the Homeseeker, Tourist and Invalid."* Los Angeles: World's Fair Association and Bureau of Information Print, Henry E. Huntington Library.

Brown, Kendall H. 2013. *Quiet Beauty: The Japanese Gardens of North America*. Photographs by David M. Cobb. North Clarendon, VT: Tuttle.

Cameron, Christopher David Ruiz. 1999–2000. "The Rakes of Wrath: Urban Agricultural Workers and the Struggle against Los Angeles's Ban on Gas-Powered Leaf Blowers." *UC Davis Law Review* 33:1087–1103.

Campbell, Hugh, Michael Mayerfeld Bell, and Margaret Finney. 2006. "Masculinity and Rural Life: An Introduction." In *Country Boys: Masculinity and Rural Life*, edited by Hugh Campbell, Michael Mayerfeld Bell, and Margaret Finney, 1–22. Pittsburgh: Pennsylvania State University Press.

Cassidy, Arly, Josh Newell, and Jennifer Wolch. 2008. *Transforming Alleys into Green Infrastructure for Los Angeles*. Los Angeles: University of Southern California, Center for Sustainable Cities.

Cave, Damien. 2013. "As Cost of Importing Food Soars, Jamaica Turns to the Earth." *New York Times*, August 4. www.nytimes.com/2013/08/04/world/

americas/as-cost-of-importing-food-soars-jamaica-turns-to-the-earth.
html?pagewanted=all&_r=0.

Cerwonka, Allaine. 2004. *Native to the Nation: Disciplining Landscapes and Bodies in Australia*. Minneapolis: University of Minnesota Press.

Chambers, Kimberlee J., and Janet Henshall Momsen. 2007. "From the Kitchen and the Field: Gender and Maize Diversity in the Bajio Region of Mexico." *Singapore Journal of Tropical Geography* 28:39–56.

Chan, Sucheng. 1986. *This Bitter-Sweet Soil: The Chinese in California Agriculture, 1860–1910*. Berkeley: University of California Press.

———. 1991. *Entry Denied: Exclusion and the Chinese Community in America, 1881–1943*. Philadelphia: Temple University Press.

Chang, Shenglin. 2006. *The Global Silicon Valley Home: Lives and Landscapes within Taiwanese American Trans-Pacific Culture*. Stanford, CA: Stanford University Press.

Chaput, Donald. 1982. "Horatio N. Rust and the Agent-as-Collector Dilemma." *Southern California Quarterly* 64 (4): 281–95.

Chea, Terence. 2009. "University of California Admissions Rule Angers Asian Americans." *USA Today*, April 4.

Cheng, Ji. 1988. *The Craft of Gardens*. Translated by Alison Hardie. New Haven, CT: Yale University Press.

Cheng, Wendy Hsin. 2009. "Episodes in the Life of a Place: Regional Racial Formation in Los Angeles's San Gabriel Valley." PhD diss., University of Southern California.

———. 2013. *The Changs Next Door to the Diazes: Remapping Race in Suburban California*. Minneapolis: University of Minnesota Press.

Christ, Carol Ann. 2000. "'The Sole Guardians of the Art Inheritance of Asia': Japan and China at the 1904 St. Louis World's Fair." *positions* 8 (3): 675–709.

Claiborne, William. 1996. "Site of Tranquillity in Cash Controversy." *Washington Post*, October 18, A36.

Clecland, Nancy. 2006. "L.A. Going to Extremes as the Middle Class Shrinks." *Los Angeles Times*, July 23, B1. http://articles.latimes.com/2006/jul/23/local/me-extremes23.

Clunas, Craig. 1996. *Fruitful Sites: Garden Culture in Ming Dynasty China*. Durham, NC: Duke University Press.

Coates, Peter. 2006. *American Perceptions of Immigrant and Native Species: Strangers on the Land*. Berkeley: University of California Press.

Congzhou, Chen. 2009. *On Chinese Gardens*. New York: Better Link Press.

Cornelius, Wayne A., and David Myhre, eds. 1998. *The Transformation of Rural Mexico: Reforming the Ejido Sector*. Boulder, CO: Lynne Rienner.

Cotter, Holland. 2012. "Ancient Havens of Reflection and Renewal." *New York Times*, August 17, C23, 29.

Cox, Rosie. 2013. "The Complications of 'Hiring a Hubby': Gender Relations and the Commoditisation of Home Maintenance in New Zealand." *Social and Cultural Geography* 14 (5): 575–90.

Cronon, William. 1983. *Changes in the Land: Indians, Colonists, and the Ecology of New England.* New York: Hill and Wang.

———. 1995. "The Trouble with Wilderness; or Getting Back to the Wrong Nature." In *Uncommon Ground: Toward Reinventing Nature*, edited by William Cronon, 69–90. New York: Norton.

Crosby, Alfred W. (1972) 2003. *The Columbian Exchange: Biological and Cultural Consequences of 1492.* 30th anniversary ed. New York: Praeger.

Culver, Lawrence. 2010. *The Frontier of Leisure: Southern California and the Shaping of Modern America.* New York: Oxford University Press.

Cunningham, Laura. 2010. *State of Change: Forgotten Landscapes of California.* Berkeley, CA: Heyday.

Davis, Mike. 1998. *Ecology of Fear: Los Angeles and the Imagination of Disaster.* New York: Vintage Books.

———. 2000. *Magical Urbanism: Latinos Reinvent the U.S. City.* London: Verso.

Davis, Mike, and Daniel Bertrand Monk, eds. 2007. *Evil Paradises: Dreamworlds of Neoliberalism.* New York: New Press.

Desmond, Ray. 1995. *The History of the Royal Botanic Gardens Kew.* London: Harvill Press.

Deverell, William. 2004. *Whitewashed Adobe: The Rise of Los Angeles and the Remaking of Its Mexican Past.* Berkeley: University of California Press.

Deverell, William, and Greg Hise. 2005. "Introduction: The Metropolitan Nature of Los Angeles." In *Land of Sunshine: An Environmental History of Metropolitan Los Angeles*, edited by William Deverell and Greg Hise, 1–12. Pittsburgh, PA: University of Pittsburgh Press.

Downing, Andrew Jackson. (1846) 2012. "A Chapter on Lawns." In *Andrew Jackson Downing: Essential Texts*, edited by Robert Twombly, 145–62. New York: Norton.

Eliasoph, Nina. 2011. *Making Volunteers: Civic Life at Welfare's End.* Princeton, NJ: University of Princeton Press.

Espiritu, Yen Le. 2003. *Homebound: Filipino American Lives across Cultures, Communities, and Countries.* Berkeley: University of California Press.

———. Forthcoming. *Body Counts: The Vietnam War and Militarized Refuge(es).* Berkeley: University of California Press.

Farmer, Jared. 2013a. *Trees in Paradise: A California History.* New York: Norton.

————. 2013b. "Witness to a Hanging." *Boom*, Spring, 71–79.

Farr, Marcia. 2006. *Rancheros in Chicagoacan: Language and Identity in a Transnational Community*. Austin: University of Texas Press.

Finn, Robin. 2011. "Pilfered Peppers in City Gardens; Tomatoes, Too." *New York Times*, August 7. www.nytimes.com/2011/08/07/nyregion/community-gardens-find-theft-is-a-fact-of-life.html?pagewanted=all.

Fishman, Ted C. 2005. *China, Inc.: How the Rise of the Next Superpower Challenges America and the World*. New York: Scribner.

Flamming, Douglas. 2005. *Bound for Freedom: Black Los Angeles in Jim Crow America*. Berkeley: University of California Press.

Flanagan, Caitlin. 2006. *To Hell with All That and Loathing Our Inner Housewife*. New York: Little, Brown.

Flores, William V. 1998. "Citizens vs. Citizenry: Undocumented Immigrants and Latino Cultural Citizenship." In *Latino Cultural Citizenship: Claiming Identity, Space and Rights*, edited by William V. Benmayor and Rita Benmayor, 255–78. Boston: Beacon Press.

Fong, Timothy P. 1994. *The First Suburban Chinatown: The Remaking of Monterey Park, California*. Philadelphia: Temple University Press.

Foucault, Michel. 1986. "Of Other Spaces: Utopias and Heterotopias." Translated by Jay Miskowiec. *Diacritics* 16 October 1984): 22–27. Originally published as "Des espaces autres," *Architecture/Mouvement/Continuité* 5 (March 1967): 46–49.

Francis, Mark, and Randolph T. Hester Jr. 1990a. "The Garden as Idea, Place, and Action." In *The Meaning of Gardens: Idea, Place, and Action*, edited by Mark Francis and Randolph T. Hester Jr., 2–20. Cambridge, MA: MIT Press.

————, eds. 1990b. *The Meaning of Gardens: Idea, Place, and Action*. Cambridge, MA: MIT Press.

Fujikane, Candace, and Jonathan Y. Okamura, eds. 2008. *Asian Settler Colonialism: From Local Governance to Habits of Everyday Life in Hawai'i*. Honolulu: University of Hawai'i Press.

Gandy, Matthew. 2003. *Concrete and Clay: Reworking Nature in New York City*. Cambridge, MA: MIT Press.

Garcia, Matt. 2001. *A World of Its Own: Race, Labor, and Citrus in the Making of Greater Los Angeles, 1900–1970*. Chapel Hill: University of North Carolina Press.

Garip, Filiz. 2012. "Discovering Diverse Mechanisms of Migration: The Mexico-U.S. Stream, 1970–2000." *Population and Development Review* 38 (3): 393–433.

Gaupp-Berghausen, Jorge. 2012. "Spanish Revolution 2.0: Yes, There Are Alternatives." *Volunteer*, September 9. www.albavolunteer.org/2012/09/spanish-revolution-2-0-yes-there-are-alternatives/.

Gerber, James, and Lei Guang, eds. 2006. *Agriculture and Rural Connections in the Pacific, 1500–1900.* Aldershot: Ashgate.

Golash-Boza, Tanya, and Pierrette Hondagneu-Sotelo. 2013. "Latino Immigrant Men and the Deportation Crisis: A Gendered Racial Removal Program." *Latino Studies* 11 (3): 271–92.

Gold, Jonathan. 2010. "A Farm to Table Revolution," *Saveur*, February 9. www.saveur.com/article/Travels/A-Farm-To-Table-Revolution.

Gonzalez, Gilbert. 1994. *Labor and Community: Mexican Citrus Worker Villages in a Southern California County, 1900–1950.* Urbana: University of Illinois Press.

Gonzalez-Lopez, Gloria. 2005. *Erotic Journeys: Mexican Immigrants and Their Sex Lives.* Berkeley: University of California Press.

Gordon, Avery F., and Christopher Newfield, eds. 1996. *Mapping Multiculturalism.* Minneapolis: University of Minnesota Press.

Gottlieb, Robert. 2007. *Reinventing Los Angeles: Nature and Community in the Global City.* Cambridge, MA: MIT Press.

Graham, Wade. 2011. *American Eden: From Monticello to Central Park to Our Backyards: What Our Gardens Tell Us about Who We Are.* New York: HarperCollins.

Grampp, Christopher. 2008. *From Yard to Garden: The Domestication of America's Home Grounds.* Chicago: Center for American Places, Columbia College Chicago.

Groth, Paul, and Chris Wilson. 2005. "The Polyphony of Cultural Landscape Study: An Introduction." In *Everyday America: Cultural Landscape Studies after J.B. Jackson,* edited by Chris Wilson and Paul Groth, 1–22. Berkeley: University of California Press.

Guthman, Julie. 2008. "Bringing Good Food to Others: Investigating the Subjects of Alternative Food Practice." *Cultural Geographies* 15:431–47.

Haeg, Fritz. 2008. *Edible Estates: Attack on the Front Lawn.* New York: Metropolis Books.

Hamilton, Nora, and Norma Chinchilla. 2001. *Seeking Community in a Global City: Guatemalans and Salvadorans in Los Angeles.* Philadelphia: Temple University Press.

Handlin, Oscar. (1951) 2002. *The Uprooted: The Epic Story of the Great Migrations That Made the American People.* Philadelphia: University of Pennsylvania Press.

Hanson, David, and Edwin Marty. 2012. *Breaking through Concrete: Building an Urban Farm Revival.* Berkeley: University of California Press.

Hardie, Alison. 1988. Introduction to *The Craft of Gardens,* by Ji Cheng, translated by Alison Hardie. New Haven, CT: Yale University Press.

Harris, Edmund M., Deborah G. Martin, Colin Polsky, Lillian Denhardt, and Abigail Nehring. 2013. "Beyond 'Lawn People': The Role of Emotions in

Suburban Yard Management Practices." *Professional Geographer* 65 (2): 345–61.

Harrison, Robert Pogue. 2008. *Gardens: An Essay on the Human Condition.* Chicago: University of Chicago Press.

Hassell, Malve von. 2002. *The Struggle for Eden: Community Gardens in New York City.* Westport, CT: Bergin and Garvey.

Hayden, Dolores. 1997. *The Power of Place: Urban Landscapes as Public History.* Cambridge, MA: MIT Press.

———. 2003. *Building Suburbia: Green Fields and Urban Growth, 1820–2000.* New York: Vintage Books.

Head, Lesley, and Pat Muir. 2007. *Backyard: Nature and Culture in Suburban Australia.* Wollongong: University of Wollongong.

Head, Lesley, Pat Muir, and Eva Hampel. 2005. "Australian Backyard Gardens and the Journey of Migration." *Geographical Review* 94 (3): 326–47.

Helphand, Kenneth I. 2006. *Defiant Gardens: Making Gardens in Wartime.* San Antonio, TX: Trinity University Press.

Henrich, James E. 2011. "Arboretum Plant Introduction Program: A Retrospective with Jim Henrich." Speech delivered at the Los Angeles County Arboretum and Botanical Garden, February 24.

Hernandez-Leon, Ruben. 2008. *Metropolitan Migrants: The Migration of Urban Mexicans to the United States.* Berkeley: University of California Press.

Hester, Randolph. 2006. *Design for Ecological Democracy.* Cambridge, MA: MIT Press.

Hirahara, Naomi. 2000. *Greenmakers: Japanese American Gardeners in Southern California.* Los Angeles: Southern California Gardeners' Federation.

Hondagneu-Sotelo, Pierrette. 1994. *Gendered Transitions: Mexican Experiences of Immigration.* Berkeley: University of California Press.

———. (2001) 2007. *Domestica: Immigrant Workers Cleaning and Caring in the Shadows of Affluence.* Berkeley: University of California Press.

———. 2010. "Cultivating Questions for a Sociology of Gardens." *Journal of Contemporary Ethnography,* 39:102–31.

Hondagneu-Sotelo, Pierrette, and Jose Miguel Ruiz. 2013. "Illegality and Spaces of Sanctuary: Belonging and Homeland-Making in Urban Community Gardens." In *Producing Immigrant Illegality,* edited by Cecilia Menjivar and Daniel Kanstroom, 246–71. Cambridge: Cambridge University Press.

Hou, Jeffrey. 2013. "Your Place and/or My Place?" In *Transcultural Cities: Border-Crossing and Placemaking,* edited by Jeffrey Hou, 1–16. New York: Routledge.

Hoyles, Martin. 2005. "The Garden and the Division of Labour." In *Vista: The Culture and Politics of Gardens,* edited by Tim Richardson and Noel Kingsbury, 21–38. London: Frances Lincoln.

Huerta, Alvaro. 2007. "Looking beyond 'Mow, Blow and Go': A Case Study of Mexican Immigrant Gardeners in Los Angeles." *Berkeley Planning Journal* 20:1–23.

———. 2011. "Examining the Perils and Promises of an Informal Niche in a Global City: A Case Study of Mexican Immigrant Gardeners in Los Angeles." PhD diss., University of California, Berkeley.

Hunt, Darnell. 2010. Introduction to *Black Los Angeles: American Dreams and Racial Realities*, edited by Darnell Hunt and Ana-Cristina Ramon, 1–17. New York: New York University Press.

Hunt, John Dixon. 2001. "'Come into the Garden, Maud': Garden Art as a Privileged Mode of Commemoration and Identity." In *Places of Commemoration: Search for Identity and Landscape Design*, edited by Joachim Wolschke-Bulmahn, 9–24. Washington, DC: Dumbarton Oaks Research Library and Collection.

———. 2012. *A World of Gardens*. London: Reaktion Books.

Hynes, Patricia H. 1996. *A Patch of Eden: America's Inner-City Gardeners*. White River Junction, VT: Chelsea Green.

Irazabal, Calra, and Macarena Gomez-Barris. 2007. "Bounded Tourism: Immigrant Politics, Consumption, and Traditions at Plaza Mexico." *Journal of Tourism and Cultural Change* 5 (3): 186–213.

Irazabal, Clara, and Anita Punja. 2009. "Cultivating Just Planning and Legal Institutions: A Critical Assessment of the South Central Farm Struggle in Los Angeles." *Journal of Urban Affairs* 31 (1): 1–23.

Jackson, Jaemi, et al. 2013. "Cultivate L.A.: An Assessment of Urban Agriculture in Los Angeles County, June 2013." July. http://cultivatelosangeles.org/2013/07/16/download-entire-report/.

Jenkins, Virginia Scott. 1994. *The Lawn: A History of an American Obsession*. Washington, DC: Smithsonian Institution.

Johnson, Brian. 2007. "The Changing Face of the Botanic Garden." In *Botanic Gardens: A Living History*, edited by Nadine Kathe Monem, 62–81. London: Black Dog.

Johnson, Rochelle. L. 2009. *Passion for Nature: Nineteenth Century America's Aesthetics of Alienation*. Athens: University of Georgia Press.

Kalleberg, Arne L. 2011. *Good Jobs, Bad Jobs: The Rise of Polarized and Precarious Employment Systems in the United States, 1970s to 2000s*. New York: Russell Sage Foundation.

Kanstroom, Daniel. 2007. *Deportation Nation: Outsiders in American History*. Cambridge, MA: Harvard University Press.

Kaplan, Rachel. 1973. "Some Psychological Benefits of Gardening." *Environment and Behavior* 5 (2): 145–62.

Kaplan, Rachel, and Stephen Kaplan. 1989. *The Experience of Nature: A Psychological Perspective*. Cambridge: Cambridge University Press.

———. 1993. "The Role of Nature in the Context of the Workplace." *Landscape and Urban Planning* 26 (1–4): 193–201.

Keswick, Maggie. 2003. *The Chinese Garden*. Cambridge, MA: Harvard University Press.

Kilkey, Majella, Diane Perrons, and Ania Plomien, with Pierrette Hondagneu-Sotelo and Hernan Ramirez. 2013. *Gender, Migration and Domestic Work: Masculinities, Male Labour and Fathering in the UK and USA*. London: Palgrave Macmillan.

Klindienst, Patricia. 2006. *The Earth Knows My Name: Food, Culture, and Sustainability in the Gardens of Ethnic Americans*. Boston: Beacon Press.

Knoll, Corina. 2012. "A Way of Life Withers." *Los Angeles Times*, September 26, A1, A10.

Lambin, Eric. 2012. *An Ecology of Happiness*. Translated by Teresa Lavendar Fagan. Chicago: University of Chicago Press.

Lancaster, Clay. 1963. *The Japanese Influence in America*. New York: W. H. Rawls.

The Land of Sunshine, Fruits and Flowers. 1898. Columbus: Ward Brothers. Henry E. Huntington Library, Los Angeles.

Lareau, Annette. 2011. *Unequal Childhoods: Class, Race, and Family Life*. 2nd ed. Berkeley: University of California Press.

Lawson, Laura J. 2005. *City Bountiful: A Century of Community Gardening in America*. Berkeley: University of California Press.

———. 2007. "Cultural Geographies in Practice: The South Central Farm: Dilemmas in Practicing the Public." *Cultural Geographies* 14:611–16.

Leonard, Karen. 1997. "Finding One's Own Place: Asian Landscapes Revisioned in Rural California." In *Culture, Power, Place: Explorations in Critical Anthropology*, edited by Akhil Gupta and James Ferguson, 118–36. Durham, NC: Duke University Press.

Levick, Melba (photographer), and Kendall Brown. 1999. *Japanese-Style Gardens of the Pacific West Coast*. New York: Rizolli.

Levitt, Peggy. 1998. "Social Remittances: Migration Driven Local-Level Forms of Cultural Diffusion." *International Migration Review* 32 (4): 926–48.

———. 2012. "The Bog and the Beast: Museums, the Nation and the World." *Ethnologia Scandinavica* 22:29–49.

Lewthwaite, Stephanie. 2010. "Race, Place, and Ethnicity in the Progressive Era." In *A Companion to Los Angeles*, edited by William Deverell and Greg Hise, 40–55. West Sussex: Wiley-Blackwell.

Li, T. June. 2009. *Another World Lies Beyond: Creating Liu Fang Yuan, the Huntington's Chinese Garden*. San Marino, CA: Huntington Library.

Li, Wei. 1999. "Building Ethnoburbia: The Emergence and Manifestation of the Chinese Ethnoburb in Los Angeles' San Gabriel Valley." *Journal of Asian American Studies* 2 (1): 1–28.

————. 2011. *Ethnoburb: Ethnic Community in Urban America*. Honolulu: University of Hawaii Press.

Lin, Irene. 1999. "Journey to the Far West: Chinese Buddhism in America." In *New Spiritual Homes*, edited by David K. Yoo, 134–68. Honolulu: University of Hawai'i Press and UCLA Asian American Studies Center.

Low, Setha. 2000. *On the Plaza: The Politics of Public Space and Culture*. Austin: University of Texas Press.

Lynch, Barbara Deutsch, and Rima Brusi. 2005. "Nature, Memory, and Nation: New York's Latino Gardens and *Casitas*." In *Urban Place: Reconnecting with the Natural World*, edited by Peggy F. Barlett, 191–211. Cambridge, MA: MIT Press.

Mabey, Richard. 1996. *Flora Britannica*. London: Chatto and Windus.

Mandela, Nelson. 1994. *Long Walk to Freedom: The Autobiography of Nelson Mandela*. Boston: Little, Brown.

Marcus, Clare Cooper, and Marni Barnes, eds. 1999. *Healing Gardens: Therapeutic Benefits and Design Recommendations*. New York: John Wiley and Sons.

Mares, Teresa M. 2012. "Tracing Immigrant Identity through the Plate and the Palate." *Latino Studies* 10 (3): 334–54.

Mason, Chelsea. 2008. "Growing to New Proportions: Chinese Gardens in the U.S." *US-China Today*, June 20. www.uschina.usc.edu/w_usci/showarticle.asp x?articleID=11917&AspxAutoDetectCookieSupport=1.

Masters, Nathan. 2011. "A Brief History of Palm Trees in Southern California." December 7. www.laassubject.org/index.php/articles/detail/article_a_brief_ history_of_palm_trees_in_southern_california.

McWilliams, Carey. (1946) 1979. *Southern California: An Island on the Land*. Santa Barbara, CA: Peregrine Smith.

Menjivar, Cecilia. 2002. "The Ties That Heal: Guatemalan Immigrant Women's Networks and Medical Treatment." *International Migration Review* 36 (2): 437–66.

————. 2006. "Liminal Legality: Salvadoran and Guatemalan Immigrants' Lives in the United States." *American Journal of Sociology* 111 (4): 999–1037.

Menjivar, Cecilia, and Leisy J. Abrego. 2012. "Legal Violence: Immigration Law and the Lives of Central American Immigrants." *American Journal of Sociology* 117 (5): 1380–1421.

Menjivar, Cecilia, and Daniel Kanstroom, eds. 2013. *Constructing Immigrant "Illegality": Critiques, Experiences, and Responses*. Cambridge: Cambridge University Press.

Merchant, Carolyn. 2004. *Reinventing Eden: The Fate of Nature in Western Culture*. New York: Routledge.

Messner, Michael. 2009. *It's All for the Kids: Gender, Families, and Youth Sports*. Berkeley: University of California Press.

Milkman, Ruth, Ellen Reese, and Benita Roth. 1998. "The Macrosociology of Paid Domestic Labor." *Work and Occupations* 25:483–510.

Miller, David Philip, and Peter Hanns Reill, eds. 1996. *Visions of Empire: Voyages, Botany, and Representations of Nature*. New York: Cambridge University Press.

Milligan, Christine, Anthony Gatrell, and Amanda Bingley. 2004. "'Cultivating Health': Therapeutic Landscapes and Older People in Northern England." *Social Science and Medicine* 58:1781–93.

Mitchell, Don. 1996. *The Lie of the Land: Migrant Workers and the California Landscape*. Minneapolis: University of Minnesota Press.

Mitchell, Katharyne. 2004. *Crossing the Neoliberal Line: Pacific Rim Migration and the Metropolis*. Philadelphia: Temple University Press.

Molotch, Harvey. 1976. "The City as a Growth Machine: Toward a Political Economy of Place." *American Journal of Sociology* 82 (2): 309–32.

Monroy, Douglas. 1999. *Rebirth: Mexican Los Angeles from the Great Migration to the Great Depression*. Berkeley: University of California Press.

Mukerji, Chandra. 1997. *Territorial Ambitions and the Gardens of Versailles*. Cambridge: Cambridge University Press.

National Gardening Association. 2010. *National Gardening Survey: The National Gardening Association's Comprehensive Study of Consumer Gardening Practices, Trends and Product Sales*. Burlington, VT: National Gardening Association.

Nicolaides, Becky M. 2002. *My Blue Heaven: Life and Politics in the Working-Class Suburbs of Los Angeles, 1920–1955*. Chicago: University of Chicago Press.

Nollman, Jim. 2005. *Why We Garden: Cultivating a Sense of Place*. Boulder, CO: Sentient Publications.

Norwood, Vera. 1993. *Made from This Earth: American Women and Nature*. Chapel Hill: University of North Carolina Press.

Nugent, Daniel, and Ana Maria Alonso. 1994. "Multiple Selective Traditions in Agrarian Reform and Agrarian Struggle: Popular Culture and State Formation in the *Ejido* of Namiquipa, Chihuahua." In *Everyday Forms of State Formation: Revolution and the Negotiation of Rule in Modern Mexico*, edited by Gilbert M. Joseph and Daniel Nugent, 209–46. Durham, NC: Duke University Press.

Ong, Aihwa. 1999. *Flexible Citizenship: The Cultural Logics of Transnationality*. Durham, NC: Duke University Press.

———. 2006. *Neoliberalism as Exception: Mutations in Citizenship and Sovereignty*. Durham, NC: Duke University Press.

Padilla, Victoria. (1961) 1991. *Southern California Gardens: An Illustrated History*. Santa Barbara, CA: Allen A. Knoll.

Park, Lisa Sun-Hee. 2005. *Consuming Citizenship: Children of Asian Immigrant Entrepreneurs*. Stanford, CA: Stanford University Press.

Peña, Devon. 2006. "Farmers Feeding Families: Agroecology in South Central Los Angeles." Keynote Address to the National Association for Chicana and Chicano Studies, Washington State University, Pullman, WA, March 6.

Pollan, Michael. 1991. *Second Nature: A Gardener's Education*. New York: Atlantic Monthly Press.

———. 2002. *The Botany of Desire: A Plant's Eye View of the World*. New York: Random House.

Prentice, Helaine Kaplan. 1990. *The Gardens of Southern California*. Photographs by Melba Levick. San Francisco: Chronicle Books.

Pulido, Laura. 2000. "Rethinking Environmental Racism: White Privilege and Urban Development in Southern California." *Annals of the American Geographers* 90 (1): 12–40.

Ramirez, Hernan. 2010. "Masculinity in the Workplace: The Case of Mexican Immigrant Gardeners." *Men and Masculinities* 14 (1): 97–116.

———. 2011. "Los Jardineros de Los Angeles: Suburban Maintenance Gardening as a Pathway to First and Second Generation Mexican Immigrant Mobility." PhD diss., University of Southern California.

Ramirez, Hernan, and Pierrette Hondagneu-Sotelo. 2009. "Mexican Immigrant Gardeners: Entrepreneurs or Exploited Workers?" *Social Problems* 56 (1): 70–88.

———. 2013. "Mexican Gardeners in the U.S." In *Gender, Migration and Domestic Work: Masculinities, Male Labour and Fathering in the UK and USA*, edited by Majella Kilkey, Diane Perrons, and Ania Plomien, with Pierrette Hondagneu-Sotelo and Hernan Ramirez, 122–48. London: Palgrave Macmillan.

Reichard, Sarah Hayden. 2011. *The Conscientious Gardener: Cultivating a Garden Ethic*. Berkeley: University of California Press.

Reynolds, Richard. 2008. *On Guerilla Gardening: A Handbook for Gardening without Boundaries*. New York: Bloomsbury.

Riley, Robert G. 1990. "Flowers, Power and Sex." In *The Meaning of Gardens: Idea, Place, and Action*, edited by Mark Francis and Randolph T. Hester Jr., 60–75. Cambridge, MA: MIT Press.

Robbins, Paul. 2007. *Lawn People: How Grasses, Weeds, and Chemicals Make Us Who We Are*. Philadelphia: Temple University Press.

Robinson, Paul. 2010. "Race, Space, and the Evolution of Black Los Angeles." In *Black Los Angeles: American Dreams and Racial Realities*, edited by Darnell Hunt and Ana-Cristina Ramon, 21–59. New York: New York University Press.

Rodriguez, Salvador. 2011. "How I Made It: Burton S. Sperber." *Los Angeles Times*, January 16, B2:2.

Romney, Lee. 2013. "Garden to Table Effort Bearing Fruit in San Jose." *Los Angeles Times*, August 14, A27-A31.

Rourke, Mary. 2003. "Obituary, Amir Dialameh, 71: After a Brush Fire He Turned Part of Griffith Park into a Garden." *Los Angeles Times,* December 7. http://articles.latimes.com/2003/dec/07/local/me-dialameh7.

Ruggeri, Laura. 2007. "'Palm Springs': Imagineering California in Hong Kong." In *Evil Paradises: Dreamworlds of Neoliberalism,* edited by Mike Davis and Daniel Bertrand Monk, 102–13. New York: New Press.

Sackman, Douglas C. 2005a. "A Garden of Worldly Delights." In *Land of Sunshine: An Environmental History of Metropolitan Los Angeles,* edited by William Deverell and Greg Hise, 245–66. Pittsburgh, PA: University of Pittsburgh Press.

———. 2005b. *Orange Empire: California and the Fruits of Eden.* Berkeley: University of California Press.

Saito, Leland T. 1998. *Race and Politics: Asian Americans, Latinos, and Whites in a Los Angeles Suburb.* Urbana: University of Illinois Press.

———. 2001. "The Politics of Adaptation and the 'Good Immigrant': Japanese Americans and the New Chinese Immigrants." In *Asian and Latino Immigrants in a Restructuring Economy,* edited by Marta Lopez-Garza and David R. Diaz, 332–49. Stanford, CA: Stanford University Press.

Salazar-Porzio, Margaret. 2010. "Representational Conquest: Tourism, Display, and Public Memory in 'America's Finest City.'" PhD diss., University of Southern California.

Saldivar-Tanaka, Laura, and Marianne E. Krasny. 2004. "Culturing Community Development, Neighborhood Open Space, and Civic Agriculture: The Case of Latino Community Gardens in New York City." *Agriculture and Human Values* 21:399–412.

Salyer, Lucy E. 1995. *Laws Harsh as Tigers: Chinese Immigrants and the Shaping of Modern Immigration Law.* Chapel Hill: University of North Carolina Press.

Schmelzkopf, Karen. 1995. "Urban Community Gardens as Contested Space." *Geographical Review* 85 (3): 364–81.

Schor, Juliet B. 1992. *The Overworked American: The Unexpected Decline of Leisure.* New York: Basic Books.

Semple, Kirk. 2013. "Asian-Americans Gain Influence in Philanthropy." *New York Times,* January 8. www.nytimes.com/2013/01/09/nyregion/as-asian-americans-numbers-grow-so-does-their-philanthropy.html?_r=0.

Shima, Tom. 2000. "My Father's Gardens." In *Greenmakers: Japanese American Gardeners in Southern California,* edited by Naomi Hirahara, 119–29. Los Angeles: Southern California Gardeners' Federation.

Sides, Josh. 2003. *L.A. City Limits: African American Los Angeles from the Great Depression to the Present.* Berkeley: University of California Press.

Silko, Leslie Marmon. 2000. *Gardens in the Dunes.* New York: Simon and Schuster.

Slocum, Rachel. 2007. "Whiteness, Space, and Alternative Food Practice." *Geoforum* 38 (3): 520–33.

Smith, Robert C. 2006. *Mexican New York: Transnational Lives of New Immigrants*. Berkeley: University of California Press.

Spurrier, Jeff. 2011. "Corporate Sponsorship at a Community Garden? At Proyecto Pastoral It's Not a Question." *Los Angeles Times*, June 8. http://latimesblogs.latimes.com/home_blog/2011/06/proyecto-pastoral. html.

———. 2012. "Papalo in the Garden: A Wild 'Summer Cilantro.'" *Los Angeles Times*, July 28. http://latimesblogs.latimes.com/home_blog/2012/07/papalo. html.

Starr, Kenneth. 1985. *Inventing the Dream: California through the Progressive Era*. New York: Oxford University Press.

Steinberg, Ted. 2006. *American Green: The Obsessive Quest for the Perfect Lawn*. New York: Norton.

Sung, Betty Lee. 1967. *The Story of the Chinese in America*. New York: Collier Books.

Surls, Rachel A. 2011. "Urban Homesteading™: An L.A. Story." *Los Angeles Agriculture*, February 21. http://ucanr.edu/blogs/blogcore/postdetail. cfm?postnum=4268.

Suro, Roberto. 1998. "Gore's Ties to Hsia Cast Shadow in 2000 Race." *Washington Post*, February 23, A01.

Tavernise, Sabrina, and Robert Gebeloff. 2010. "Immigrants Make Paths to Suburbia, Not Cities." *New York Times*, December 14. www.nytimes. com/2010/12/15/us/15census.html?_r=0.

Teaford, Jon C. 2008. *The American Suburb: The Basics*. London: Routledge.

Terwilliger, Kaley. 2006. "Sowing the Seeds of Self-Determination: Why People are Community Gardening in Los Angeles County." Undergraduate thesis, University of California–Santa Cruz.

Tobar, Hector. 2012. *The Barbarian Nurseries*. New York: Farrar, Straus, and Giroux.

Tracey, David. 2007. *Guerrilla Gardening: A Manualfesto*. Gabriola Island, BC: New Society.

Tsuchida, Nobuya. 1984. "Japanese Gardeners in Southern California, 1900–1941." In *Labor Immigration under Capitalism: Asian Workers in the United States before World War II*, edited by Lucie Cheng and Edna Bonacich, 435–69. Berkeley: University of California Press.

Tsukashima, Ronald Tadao. 1991. "Cultural Endowment, Disadvantaged Status, and Economic Niche: The Development of an 'Ethnic Trade.'" *International Migration Review* 25:333–54.

———. 1995–96. "Continuity of Ethnic Participation in the Economy: Immigrants in Contract Gardening." *Amerasia Journal* 21:53–76.

———. 1998. "Notes on Emerging Collective Action: Ethnic Trade Guilds among Japanese Americans in the Gardening Industry." *International Migration Review* 32:374–400.

———. 2000. "SCGF (Southern California Gardeners' Federation)." In *Greenmakers: Japanese American Gardeners in Southern California.*, edited by Naomi Hirahara, 74–93. Los Angeles: Southern California Gardeners' Federation.

Tyner, James A. 2006. *Oriental Bodies: Discourse and Discipline in U.S. Immigration Policy, 1875–1942.* Lanham, MD: Lexington Books.

Ulrich, R. S. 1984. "View through a Window May Influence Recovery from Surgery." *Science*, April 27, 420–21.

Vallejo, Jody Agius. 2012. *Barrios to Burbs: The Making of the Mexican American Middle Class.* Stanford, CA: Stanford University Press.

Veblen, Thorstein. (1899) 1912. *The Theory of the Leisure Class: An Economic Study of Institutions.* New York: Macmillan.

Vertovec, Steven. 2007. "Super-diversity and Its Implications." *Ethnic and Racial Studies* 30 (6): 1024–54.

Wada, Karen. 2009. "Where the Synergy Grows." *Los Angeles Times*, April 5, E8.

Warner, Sam Bass. 1987. *To Dwell Is to Garden: Histories and Portraits of Boston's Community Gardens.* Boston: Northeastern University Press.

Watanabe, Teresa. 2008. "Huntington Library's New Garden Celebrates Chinese Culture." *Los Angeles Times*, February 17.

Watters, Sam. 2007. *Houses of Los Angeles, 1885–1919.* Vol. 1. New York: Acanthus Press.

———. 2012. *Gardens for a Beautiful America, 1895–1935.* Preface by C. Ford Peatross. New York: Acanthus Press and Library of Congress.

White, Monica. 2010. "Shouldering Responsibility for the Delivery of Human Rights: A Case Study of the D-Town Farmers of Detroit." *Race/Ethnicity* 3 (2): 189–211.

———. 2011a. "D-Town Farm: African American Resistance to Food Insecurity and the Transformation of Detroit." *Environmental Practice* 13:406–17.

———. 2011b. "Sisters of the Soil: Urban Gardening as Resistance in Detroit." *Race/Ethnicity: Multicultural Global Contexts* 5 (1): 13–28.

Wilkinson, Alec. 2012. "Department of Agriculture: Indigenous." *New Yorker*, October 1, 25.

Wilson, Albert J. 1880. *Los Angeles County, California, with Illustrations Descriptive of Its Scenery.* Oakland, CA: Thompson and West.

Wolch, Jennifer, and Michael Dear. 1989. *The Power of Geography: How Territory Shapes Social Life.* Boston: Unwin Hyman.

Wolch, Jennifer, John P. Wilson, and Jed Fehrenbach. 2005. "Parks and Park Funding in Los Angeles: An Equity-Mapping Analysis." *Urban Geography* 26 (1): 4–35.

Wulf, Andrea. *The Brother Gardeners: Botany, Empire, and the Birth of an Obsession*. New York: Knopf.

Zehner, Ozzie. 2012. *Green Illusions: The Dirty Secrets of Clean Energy and the Secrets of Environmentalism*. Lincoln: University of Nebraska Press.

Zhou, Min. 1992. *Chinatown: The Socioeconomic Potential of an Urban Enclave*. Philadelphia: Temple University Press.

———. 2009. *Contemporary Chinese America*. Philadelphia: Temple University Press.

Zukin, Sharon. 1991. *Landscapes of Power*. Berkeley: University of California Press.

———. 2010. *The Naked City: The Death and Life of Authentic Urban Places*. Oxford: Oxford University Press.

Index